BEAUTIFUL
OLYMPIC PENINSULA
TRAVEL GUIDE

BEAUTIFUL OLYMPIC PENINSULA TRAVEL GUIDE

Best Attractions – Hidden Treasures
Easy Travel Planning Tools

Karen Patry

Columbus, Ohio

Contents

Welcome to the Beautiful Olympic Peninsula!

The Olympic Peninsula spans 3,600 square miles (9,324 square km); the Olympic National Park in the center of the peninsula occupies fully forty percent of that. The beauty of the region is so superlative that it is hard to describe with words; even photos do it only partial justice. This may be why the park consistently ranks as the fifth- or sixth-most visited national park in the United States. In 2016, 3.39 million people are estimated to have visited here[1].

When traveling, sometimes insider information is just what you need. After living, traveling, and photographing here for more than a decade, I created the website www.beautifulpacificnorthwest.com, and then prepared this book to give visitors a hold-in-the-hand travel guide, whether a paperback, or a Kindle version. Here you will find all the information and links needed for planning, creating, and enjoying an Olympic Peninsula vacation that is perfect for you.

When you get home, let us know how it went! You can share photos and join in the conversation at Beautiful Pacific Northwest or at https://www.facebook.com/BeautifulPacificNorthwest/.

Enjoy your journey!

---

1   http://outdoor-society.com/2016-was-olympic-national-parks-6th-busiest-year-in-history/

PART 1

Create Your Own Itinerary

It's YOUR vacation, and a glorious one it will be if you get to see and do ALL the things that are particularly meaningful to you.

So, here are itinerary suggestions, time frames, and a list of Top Twenty Attractions. Additionally, Part 1 provides an overview of where you may find various preferred terrain features in the Olympic Peninsula. It's all intended to help you make vacation choices that match your needs and preferences.

This map is not perfectly exact, but it will give you a good idea where points of interest are in relation to the rest of the Olympic Peninsula.

Visits to the Olympic Peninsula typically take three forms, or more likely, a combination of these approaches:

A. Some people focus almost exclusively on visiting the Olympic National Park.

B. An interest of some visitors is to "do the 101 Loop," that is, to circle the entire Olympic Peninsula on Highway 101.

C. Others choose to focus their travels in one region of the Olympic Peninsula, minimizing drive times, and seeing as many of the attractions as possible in that area.

Any of these approaches is satisfying. What is equally likely, however, is that the Olympic Peninsula visitor will see a whole lot of the Olympic National Park, will travel large chunks of the "101 Loop" simply as a matter of getting to the next day's destinations, and will tend to gravitate to a certain region or regions out of personal fascination with the area.

Olympic Peninsula Map: The letter labels correspond with the segments in Part 4. For example, find the information about Port Townsend in Part 4A, the info on Lake Quinault in Part 4P, etc.

1A) Focus on the Olympic National Park

The single most popular destination on the Olympic Peninsula is the enormous Olympic National Park. Twelve of the 22 segments in the main Guide (Part 4) take you into the Olympic National Park. Park rangers suggest that you select two or three of the Park's destinations that most fascinate you, and then fully immerse yourself in these environments for as long as your schedule allows.

What kind of terrain draws you?

Mountains:

- **Hurricane Ridge** (Part 4D): The center of the Olympic National Park is one massive mountain range. There are no roads into the interior of the mountains. The easiest way to experience the beauty of the Olympic Mountain Range is from the top of Hurricane Ridge, which is a 40 minute drive from Port Angeles. The views are breathtaking, and there are several options for easy to moderate hiking.

- **If it is mountain hiking you want,** then take a look at these attractions: **Elwha Valley** (Part 4H), **Lake Crescent** (Part 4I), **Sol Duc Valley** (Part 4J), **Hoh Rain Forest** (Part 4M), **Quinault Rain Forest** (Part 4P), and **Staircase Ranger Station** (Part 4V). All of these Olympic National

Park destinations provide trails leading high into the mountains. The views will be stellar once you get there.

Lakes:

- **Lake Crescent** (Part 4I): Highway 101 travels along the south shore of the lake. (Any closer and you'd be swimming.) The forested mountains plunge into the lake at precipitous angles, creating ridiculously aqua-blue water and scenes worthy of famous photographers. Lakeside hikes, waterfalls and mountain peaks with terrific views are within hiking distance of the lake.

- **Lake Quinault** (Part 4P) is ringed by rain forest. Options are: kayaking, taking easy treks along the shore or to gigantic trees, driving around the lake, or moderate to strenuous hikes rewarded by excellent lake views at the top.

Rain Forest:

- **Hoh Rain Forest** (Part 4M): As far as temperate rain forests go, this is my favorite, no doubt due to the beauty of the loop trails that wind through the gigantic mossy trees and Roosevelt elk habitat.

- **Quinault Rain Forest** (Part 4P) is another very popular rainy spot to visit with the added attraction of record-setting giant trees and more.

- **Queets Rain Forest** (Part 4O) is wild, mossy, even prehistoric.

Rivers:

- **Elwha Valley** (Part 4H): Madison Falls, natural hot springs, and miles of hiking along the Elwha River to places named "Goblin's Gate" and "Throat of a Monster."

- **Sol Duc Valley** (Part 4J): The Sol Duc River supports the spawn of five species of salmon. See spawning events at the Salmon Cascade, take a walk through the Ancient Grove, and do an easy hike to the Sol Duc Falls. If you have time you could also visit the hot springs and soak in the naturally mineralized water.

- **Hoh River** (Part 4M): Take a boating or rafting tour of the Hoh!

Beaches:

- **The Kalaloch Beaches, including Ruby Beach** (Part 4N): Ruby Beach is incredibly scenic, with beautiful sea stacks sitting in the surf. Beach 4 offers fascinating tide pools. Beach 3 and Beach 2 require short hikes in order to drop down to the sand. Kalaloch Beach is expansive and beautiful, with the added bonus of the "tree of life."

- **Rialto Beach, Second, and Third Beach** (Part 4L): Rialto Beach near La Push, WA, is another spectacular beach, with large offshore sea stacks and tide pools just a two-mile hike away. In fact, all the nearby beaches are photogenic. Dozens of needle-like sea stacks like shark teeth guard the surf at Third Beach.

- **Shi Shi Beach, Ozette Beach** (Part 4G): These rugged and remote beaches require some hiking to find.

1B) Circle the Olympic Peninsula on the Highway 101 Loop

How fun would it be to see the *entire* Olympic Peninsula? And you can certainly see most of it by circling the Peninsula on Highway 101. Seven or eight hours of driving the 330 miles of the 101 Loop will bring you back to where you started, whether your starting point is Olympia, Seattle, or Port Angeles.

Ruby Beach

Hwy 101 passes through forests, along beaches, lakes, the Hood Canal, and nearly all the towns and villages. It is a beautiful drive. We recommend including the following Park attractions in your itinerary because they are very close to the highway:

- Madison Falls, two miles from Highway 101 in the Elwha Valley (Part 4H)

- Lake Crescent, and a short hike to Marymere Falls (Part 4I)

- The Kalaloch Beaches, including Ruby Beach (Part 4N)

- The Quinault Rain Forest (Part 4P)

1C) Visit the Olympic Peninsula by Region

The Olympic Peninsula is easily divided into four regions:

North Olympic Peninsula: There are many vacation destinations and attractions in the North (and West) Olympic Peninsula! Port Angeles is the central choice as a home base for a North Peninsula vacation. Hurricane Ridge, Elwha Valley, Sol Duc Valley, and Lake Crescent are all here. Salt Creek County Park near Joyce offers some of the best camping and activities on the entire Peninsula. Both Neah Bay and the Hoh Rain Forest are less than two hours away from Port Angeles.

West Olympic Peninsula: Forks is the hub of action in "the west end," as this region is called locally. From Forks, one can reach Neah Bay in 1.5 hours, Quinault Rain Forest in one hour, seventeen minutes, Lake

Crescent in thirty-nine minutes, and the beaches near La Push in just twenty-two minutes. The Hoh and Queets Rain Forests are here.

South Olympic Peninsula: The South is where you'll find the wonderful Quinault Rain Forest, Wynoochee Lake, and the hike to Maidenhair Falls. Ocean Shores provides loads of seaside recreation and activities. Your hub in the south might be either Quinault or Ocean Shores, as lodging choices in the working towns of Aberdeen and Hoquiam are limited.

East Olympic Peninsula: The incredibly scenic Hood Canal is the main feature in the eastern side of the Peninsula. From Hoodsport you can access Lake Cushman and the Staircase trails in the Olympic National Park. A hike or a drive to the top of Mount Walker just south of Quilcene will reward you with extravagant views. There is no clear-cut vacationing hub in the East, unless you can book lodging very early in advance in Hoodsport or Shelton. Otherwise, try Union or Olympia.

Favorite Day Trips Leaving From and Returning to Port Angeles:

Port Angeles is approximately 2.5 hours from Seattle, and is the population center easiest to get to on the Olympic Peninsula that is also nearest to many Peninsula attractions. Each of the following nearby forays can be completed in one day; for some of them you might appreciate having a second day to fully enjoy the area:

- Victoria, BC via the Black Ball Coho. Stay a second day to visit Butchart Gardens or Goldstream Provincial Park during a salmon spawn.
- Hoh Rain Forest, Forks, Ruby Beach or La Push beaches. If you feel rushed, take another day.
- Lake Crescent, Sol Duc Valley, Neah Bay and Cape Flattery. Or move the Sol Duc Valley to day 2.

- Excursion to Madison Falls and into the Elwha Valley
- Hurricane Ridge in summer or winter, hike to Hurricane Hill or to Lake Angeles
- Sequim attractions, such as the Olympic Game Farm, the Dungeness National Wildlife Refuge, Dungeness Spit and New Dungeness Lighthouse, the Dungeness River Bridge Park, Sequim Bay State Park, or Sequim Museum and Arts Center.
- Historic Port Townsend and attractions

1D) Sample One-Day and Multiple-Day Itineraries

The following sample itineraries draw heavily from the above attractions. Each of these itineraries assumes some travel time in the morning. Each also includes Hurricane Ridge, an accessible, majestic, and impressive destination that tops my Top-20 Olympic Peninsula attractions list. (If you're not sure about going to Hurricane Ridge, Part 1D and 1E provide you the additional means to consider other destination(s) you might prefer.)

1-Day Itineraries:

Focus on Hiking: Includes 3 short but iconic hikes.

- Hike Hurricane Ridge in the morning.
- Lunch in Port Angeles
- Drive to Lake Crescent and hike the Marymere Falls Trail to the Falls.
- Or: Drive to Sol Duc Valley and hike to Sol Duc Falls. (If time, do both hikes!)
- Dinner at Sol Duc Hot Springs Resort, or Lake Crescent Lodge, or in Port Angeles.

Focus on Fun:

- Spend the available morning time at Olympic Game Farm in Sequim.
- Lunch in Port Angeles.
- Visit Hurricane Ridge for an hour or two (no hiking).
- Visit Port Townsend for culture and shopping.
- Dinner in Port Townsend (foodie town with great places to eat).

Focus on Beauty:

- Visit Hurricane Ridge in the morning.
- Lunch in Port Angeles.
- For the afternoon, pick one of the following:
  - Beautiful Hoh Rain Forest.
  - Beautiful lake and ocean views: Stop by Lake Crescent and enjoy the views, then head to Rialto Beach for ocean vistas studded with sea stacks and waterfowl
- Dinner in Forks or Port Angeles, depending on your choices.
- Long drive to Seattle or stop overnight in Port Angeles or Forks.

2 Day Itinerary:

The 1-day trips may seem rushed in order for you to create as many memories as possible. For a two day trip I recommend the following:

First day

- Drive to the Olympic Peninsula and visit Hurricane Ridge in the morning. Take lunch in Port Angeles or drive to Crescent Lake and dine at The Lodge there.

- Drive to Crescent Lake (if you haven't already) and enjoy the view there (right off the Highway) for less than an hour.
- Drive to Sol Duc and hike to Sol Duc Falls and/or soak in the hot springs (costs extra) at Sol Duc Hot Springs Resort.
- Dinner in Port Angeles.
- Hotel in Port Angeles.

Second Day

- After breakfast pack a lunch and drive to Ruby Beach.
- Enjoy the views for a while; shoot some photographs, do some beachcombing.
- Eat lunch on the Beach.
- Visit the Hoh Rain Forest.
- Drive back to Port Angeles; dinner in Port Angeles.
- Drive to next destination

3 Day Trip:

- For a three day trip we recommend the 2 day trip plus the following:
- If you have passports visit Victoria for a day
- If you do not have a passport visit Cape Flattery

4 Day Trip:

- Visit the Olympic Game Farm after breakfast
- Lunch in Sequim
- Visit Port Townsend
- Dinner in Port Townsend

Create Your Own 5-or-More Day Vacation

Use the Destinations Chart (Part 1E) and the list of Top 20 Attractions to select additional destinations and attractions to visit on as many additional days as you have allotted.

1E) Destinations Chart

This Destinations Chart lists ALL the main Olympic Peninsula attractions and destinations. Olympic National Park attractions are shaded light green. I took my best guess at minimum and maximum times generally needed, but your particular interests in various areas might dictate allowing more (or less) time than is suggested.

Attraction/Point of Interest	Section	Minimum/Maximum Times Needed. Add even more hours if necessary
FYI: Time frames start when you arrive – use mileage chart (Part 5G) to calculate transit times.		
North Olympic Peninsula and Victoria, BC		
Port Townsend	**Part 4A**	**2 - 8 hours** or more. (How much culture are you craving?)
Explore downtown Natl. Historic District		**1.5 - 5 hours**
Art Gallery Walk		**1 – 4 hours**
Theater, music, cultural pursuits		Depends on availability
Northwest Maritime Center		Depends on availability
Whale Watching		**4 - 6 hours**
Blyn	**Part 4B**	**1 - 3 hours**
7 Cedars Casino		Depends on you!
NW Native Expressions Art Gallery		**30 min** or more

Attraction/Point of Interest	Section	Minimum/Maximum Times Needed. Add even more hours if necessary
Sequim	Part 4C	1.5 - 8 hours
Dungeness National Wildlife Refuge		1 - 4 hours or more.
Dungeness River Audubon Center and Railroad Bridge Park		1 - 3 hours
New Dungeness Lighthouse hike		All Day (How far out onto the Spit do you wish to venture?)
Olympic Game Farmk		1 - 3 hours or more
Lavender Farms		1 - 4 hours or more. (How many lavender farms would you like to tour?)
Hurricane Ridge (Olympic National Park)	Part 4D	2 – 8 hours. Add more time if you do a hardcore hike or wish to return for a second visit.
Port Angeles	Part 4E	1 - 5 hours or more.
Downtown Port Angeles Attractions		1 - 4 hours.
Olympic National Park Headquarters		30 min - 1 hour
Whale Watching from Port Angeles		3 - 6 hours

Attraction/Point of Interest	Section	Minimum/Maximum Times Needed. Add even more hours if necessary
Victoria, BC, Canada (via the Coho)	**Part 4F**	**4.5 hours** between 10:15am ferry arrival and 3:00pm departure (fall/winter/spring schedule). **8.5 hours**: Stay for the 7:30pm ferry departure (summer schedule). If you need more time (and you might), spend a night and catch a ferry back the next day.
Victoria, BC Inner Harbour		**3 - 8 hours**, or more (plan a second visit)
Butchart Gardens		**3 - 8 hours**, or more (plan a second visit)
Elwha Valley in Olympic National Park	**Part 4H**	**Up to all day**. (Entry beyond kiosk depends on road conditions.)
Madison Falls		**45 min - 2 hours**
Glines Canyon Spillway Overlook		**30 min** or more
Whiskey Bend Trail		**2 - 6 hours**
Olympic Hot Springs		**1 - 2 hours**
Lake Crescent in Olympic National Park	**Part 4I**	**30 min – 8 hours** or more
Storm King Ranger Station		**30 min – 1 hour**
Marymere Falls Trail		**1.5 – 3 hours**
Spruce Railroad Trail		**1.5 – 6 hours**
Pyramid Mountain Hike (strenuous)		**6 – 8 hours**
East Shore Beach		**30 min – 2 hours** or more

Attraction/Point of Interest	Section	Minimum/Maximum Times Needed. Add even more hours if necessary
West End		
Strait of Juan de Fuca (Highway 112)	**Part 4G**	**5 – 16 hours** or more
Salt Creek Recreation Area		**1 - 8 hours**
Joyce, Joyce Museum		**1 - 3 hours**
Clallam Bay and Sekiu		Depends on your scheduled recreational and boating/fishing activities.
Ozette Lake in Olympic National Park, and 3 mi or 9 mi hike		**4 hours – all day**
Neah Bay and Cape Flattery		**2 - 6 hours**
Makah Museum and Research Center		**1 – 3 hours**
Shi Shi Beach in Olympic National Park		**4 - 8 hours**
Sol Duc Valley	**Part 4J**	**4 - 10 hours**
Salmon Cascade		**30 min – 2 hours** (if salmon are running)
Ancient Grove		**45 min – 1.5 hours**
Hot Springs Resort (Hot Pools)		**1 - 2 hours**
Sol Duc Falls		**1.5 – 3 hours**
Forks	**Part 4K**	**1 - 8 hours**
Forks Attractions		**1 - 6 hours**
Twilight Saga Tour		**2.5 – 6 hours**
Quileute Indian Reservation at La Push and First Beach	**Part 4L**	**1 - 3 hours**

Attraction/Point of Interest	Section	Minimum/Maximum Times Needed. Add even more hours if necessary
Olympic National Park Beaches near La Push (Rialto, Second, Third Beaches)	Part 4L	
Rialto Beach		**1 - 5 hours** (if you hike 2 mi to Hole-in-the-Wall and back)
Second Beach		**1.5 - 4 hours**
Third Beach		**2 - 5 hours**
Hoh Rain Forest (Olympic National Park)	Part 4M	**2.5 - 6 hours** or more
Kalaloch Beaches (Olympic National Park)	Part 4N	**1 - 4 hours** or more
Ruby Beach		**30 min - 2 hours**
Kalaloch Beach 4		**1 - 2 hours**, or more, if tidepools are available
Kalaloch Beach 3		**1 - 2 hours**
Kalaloch Beach		**0.5 - 2 hours**
Kalaloch Beach 2		**1 - 2 hours**
Kalaloch Beach 1		**0.5 - 1.5 hours**
Yahoo Lake	Part 4O	**8 - 24 hours** (camping excursion)
Queets Rain Forest	Part 4O	**2 - 8 hours**
South Olympic Peninsula and Westport		
Quinault Rain Forest	Part 4P	**2 - 10 hours** or more
Wynoochee Lake	Part 4Q	**3 - 10 hours** or more
Grays Harbor	Part 4R	**2 – 8 hours**
Aberdeen		**1.5 - 4 hours**
Hoquiam		**1.5 - 4 hours**

Attraction/Point of Interest	Section	Minimum/Maximum Times Needed. Add even more hours if necessary
Ocean Shores and Highway 109		**4 - 8 hours**
Westport		**3 - 5 hours**
Montesano, Elma, McCleary	**Part 4S**	**1 - 2 hours**, possibly more
East Olympic Peninsula and Olympia		
Olympia, Capital of WA State	**Part 4T**	**3 - 8 hours** or more
Shelton	**Part 4U**	**1 - 2 hours**
Hood Canal	**Part 4V**	**2 - 6 hours** or more
Lucky Dog Casino (Skokomish Tribe)		Depends on you!
Hoodsport		**1 - 3 hours**
Staircase Ranger Station/ Hiking in Olympic National Park		**2 - 7 hours** or more, depending on how far you wish to hike
Mt. Walker Viewpoints		**2 - 3 hours**, more if you hike to the top rather than drive.

NOTE: City Festivals are not included in this chart. If you can be in the right place at the right time, including a festival in your vacation could be a lot of fun! See Part 2C: Olympic Peninsula Festivals.

ALSO NOTE: Recreational activities such as fishing, kayaking, or hardcore hiking are also not included on this chart. Check Part 2 (D, G, H) for tips and ideas for equipment rentals, tour companies, fishing guides, and the like.

1F) Top Twenty Attractions

Must-See Attractions:

1. **Hurricane Ridge** (Part 4D): Spectacular panoramic 360-degree views over many Olympic mountain peaks to the south and to the Strait (and Canada) to the north, plus winter skiing and summer hiking opportunities. (This is #1 because Hurricane Ridge is the only easy way to see into the beautiful Olympic Mountains and because it is a very easy trip from Port Angeles. If you come to the Olympic Peninsula you will likely pass through Port Angeles, so why not see one of the most magnificent sights in the region while you are there?)

2. **Hoh Rain Forest** (Part 4M): Multiple trails provide opportunity to immerse oneself in quintessential, ultra-green, temperate and moss-draped rain forest, with good chances for seeing the local herd of Roosevelt elk. This attraction is #2 because temperate rainforests are not found in the United States outside of the Pacific Northwest. The haunting beauty of the moss-draped trees and ancient forests tends to create unique and lasting memories.

3. **Cape Flattery** (Part 4G): Easy hike to soul-gripping views of the Pacific Ocean, dramatic sea stacks, Tatoosh Island and lighthouse, and possibly sea animal life, all viewed from a clifftop.

4. **Lake Crescent** (Part 4I): Beautiful lake vistas and activities, including an easy hike through rain forest ambience to an impressive 119-foot waterfall.

5. **Ruby Beach** (Part 4N): Highly photogenic Pacific beach with several accessible sea stacks. Catch the evening light just right, and the garnet-laden beach sands might even glint pinkish. (Otherwise, the sand is just . . . sandy.)

6. **Sol Duc Valley** (Part 4J): Complete taste of the Pacific Northwest in one valley. View salmon spawning, enjoy a half-mile loop walk through rain forest, hike to a dramatic ravine and waterfall, and then soak in thermal hot pools (commercialized – pay to enter the pools).

7. **Native American Museums, Art, and Culture**: Learn more about the First Nations peoples who have populated the Pacific Northwest for millennia, especially through the excellent Makah Museum in Neah Bay (Part 4G). Elwha S'Klallam Tribe also has informative displays at their Education Center in Port Angeles (Part 4E). Or, visit the Quileute Reservation in La Push (Part 4L, but there are no museums in La Push). Lastly, attend a tribal festival in either Neah Bay or La Push (Part 2C: List of Olympic Peninsula Festivals).

Awesome:

1. **Victoria, BC** (Part 4F): Delightfully Canadian-British and very beautiful downtown Inner Harbour area that can be browsed on foot. Add to that lovely harbor tours on cute little boats and the excellent and fascinating Royal BC Museum. If time allows, Butchart Gardens is a taxi or bus ride away and unforgettable. Victoria is not on the Olympic Peninsula but if you bring a passport we highly recommend the ferry trip from Port Angeles.

2. **Beaches near La Push** (Part 4L): Some require a short hike to see, and reward you with views of rugged sea stacks and fascinating tide pools.

3. **Elwha Valley** (Part 4H): Easy-to-reach Madison Falls, wonderful moderate hike to Humes Ranch and Goblin's Gates, natural Olympic Hot Springs (may or may not be hike-in only, depending on flooding or changing course of the Elwha River).

4. **Salt Creek Recreation Area** (Part 4G): Sandy warm water beach, plus scenic sea stacks and tide pools nearby, plus the best camping on the North Olympic Peninsula.

5. **Kalaloch Beaches** (Part 4N): Beach 4 has impressive tide pools at low tide. Kalaloch Beach hosts the "tree of life" and its tree cave.

6. **Dungeness Spit and Lighthouse** in Sequim (Part 4C): Hike some or all of the 5.5 miles (one way) to the lighthouse, or boat or kayak there.

7. **Hood Canal** (Part 4V): Highly scenic drive along the Hood Canal with views of Mt. Rainier on clear days. Availability of local fresh clams and oysters, plus stop and wander through downtown Hoodsport.

8. **Quinault Rain Forest** (Part 4P): The road loops around Lake Quinault; interpretive trails take you to specific points, such as huge cedars, Douglas fir or spruce trees. Plus, possible elk, eagle and salmon sightings.

Coolly Beautiful:

1. **Port Townsend** (Part 4A): The downtown area is on the National Register of Historic Places, and very scenic. Satisfy a craving for culture in many artistic ways.

2. **Queets Rain Forest** (Part 4O): Primordial, heavily mossy, untouched and scenic, this is the often overlooked wild little sibling of the Hoh and Quinault rain forests.

3. **Sequim Lavender Farms** (Part 4C): Beautiful rolling fields of purple, pink, and white blooms, plus farm stores filled with a plethora of lavender oil, lavender buds, and lavender-related products.

4. **Wynoochee Lake** (Part 4Q): Dramatic views, interpretive info on forestry and hydroelectric power, lots of beautiful hiking trails, nearby Maidenhair Falls.

5. **Ocean Shores or Westport** in Greater Grays Harbor (Part 4R): Drive onto the sand, explore the beaches and jetties, and museums/interpretive centers. Plus, the harbor and beaches are great places to go birding.

1G) Prepare in Advance

Assume that some rain will probably fall. Consider bringing proper rain gear, or even sturdy umbrellas to the rain forest certainly, but possibly throughout the Olympic Peninsula. Include rain protection for your camera.

Bring calf-high rubber boots, or even hip waders depending on your plans. You can cross little streams by rolling up your pant-legs and going barefoot (I've done this way more than once). You can even reach sea stacks the same way if the tide is out. But if you intend to hike boggy rain forest trails after a rain squall, calf-high rubber boots will help you tame the muck.

Bring mosquito protection if you plan to spend evenings outdoors, such as while camping or RVing. You'll also appreciate bug protection against biting flies at Hurricane Ridge on summer afternoons and evenings – either bug spray, essential oils, or long sleeves.

PART 2

Tips and Info for Planning Your Itinerary

2A) Best Times to Visit the Olympic Peninsula

Summertime has got to be the best time to visit, assuming, of course, that you're not so "into" rainy vacations. Just 8% of the year's rainfall comes during summertime. July is typically the least rainy month throughout the region. Blue skies and puffy white clouds make a terrific backdrop for your gorgeous ocean, mountain, forest, and river photos and memories.

Rain Forests: Spring is a great time to visit. With consistent rain, the rain forest is so green that "even the air is green." I've been there during dry snaps. A few dry days in a row result in stress for the ubiquitous moss, which begins to dry and turn brown. The moss bounces back after a few more wet days, of course. Rain in a rain forest is a GOOD thing – don't begrudge the moisture; prepare for it with warm weatherproof clothing and an umbrella.

Whale Watching: Spring, summer and autumn are whale-watching season, as the mammoth beasts migrate past the Pacific Northwest on the way to their summer feeding grounds in Alaska and then back again. Gray whales and humpbacks are best seen in spring and autumn, while several orca pods live in the Puget Sound and Salish Sea year round.

Salmon Spawn: Depending on species and weather, springtime and autumn are usually great times to visit. The timing of the salmon spawn is tied to the weather and the season. Each year may vary both in timing, duration, and quantity of returning salmon. It is not always possible to guarantee with precision when the salmon will return to their spawning beds. Check with a fishery or a fishing guide who is familiar with the spawning times in the rivers of the areas where you'd like to visit.

Winter Sports: Early December is reliably cold, meaning possibly snow at sea level for a few days to a few weeks. Snow may be falling at Hurricane Ridge as early as mid-October. In December, rain in Port Angeles means snow at Hurricane Ridge, and the ski lifts will be humming. While Whistler it is not, Hurricane Ridge still provides a lot of great spaces for snowshoeing and lifts for skiing and snowboarding. Check these links for Hurricane Ridge winter info: https://www.nps.gov/olym/planyourvisit/hurricane-ridge-in-winter.htm

Skiing and snowboarding at Hurricane Ridge http://hurricaneridge.com/

The Olympic National Park website gives a good overview of seasonal weather on the Olympic Peninsula which might help you clarify the best timing for your trip: https://www.nps.gov/olym/planyourvisit/weather.htm#CP_JUMP_827766

2B) Cuisine, Music, Theater, and the Arts as Main Attractions

I tend to assume that the unique rain forests and spectacular beauty of the peninsula are what draw visitors to our shores. And I may be mostly right. But, if an interest in culture, music, and the arts is also one of your passions, consider these three suggestions:

1. **A visit to Port Townsend** will not fail to thrill and charm you. This is because Port Townsend is full of fascinating art, music and theater, and culture and cuisine.

2. **Victoria, BC** is distinctly Pacific Northwestern and also infused with lovely Canadian culture: pleasant, refined, a pleasure to visit.

3. **Local festivals** also offer a taste of Pacific-Northwestern culture, cuisine, music, arts and crafts. The list of Olympic Peninsula festivals starts below.

2C) List of Olympic Peninsula Festivals

The towns of the Olympic Peninsula throw their festivals with panache! If your vacation dates allow, perhaps you can get in on one or more of the region's celebrations. This list gives the time frame for each festival – check the websites for the exact dates. **REMINDER:** Book your Olympic Peninsula trip the winter before, or as early as possible because lodging often sells out months in advance.

Port Townsend:

Strange Brewfest, late January, downtown Port Townsend

http://strangebrewfestpt.com/ - Thirty Northwest breweries serve up their brews, along with dozens of crazy, "strangely crafted concoctions" using ingredients not usually associated with beer or ciders. Music, dancing, food and "strange brews."

Shipwrights Regatta, end of February, Port Townsend Bay

http://nwmaritime.org/shipwrights/ - Sailboat racing in Port Townsend Bay. Open to boats of all construction, even those who don't have a boat. See website for details on participating in regatta and watching it.

Port Townsend PlayFest, in March. Key City Public Theatre Playhouse, Port Townsend

http://www.keycitypublictheatre.org/ptplayfest/ - Local, regional and national playwrights present ten plays over two weekends. Workshops, interactive events, performances and more. See website for current dates.

Rhody Festival, 3rd weekend in May, various locations around Port Townsend

http://www.rhodyfestival.org/events/2017-05/ - Celebrate the blooming of wild rhododendrons with a pancake breakfast, carnivals, several parades, golf tournament, 6 or 12k Rhody Run and the Running of the Balls golf ball race.

Wooden Boat Festival, the second week in September, downtown Port Townsend

http://nwmaritime.org/events2/wooden-boat-festival/ - Wooden sailboats, motor boats, yachts, and their owners all gather to display the beauty of wooden boats and to educate and inspire all who attend. Live music, food, beer, wine, exhibits for kids.

Boat race during the Wooden Boat Festival in Port Townsend

Sequim:

Irrigation Festival, 2 weeks in May in Sequim

http://www.irrigationfestival.com/ - Celebrates the initiation, development and support of Sequim's irrigation ditches. Features a carnival, Car Show, Farmer's Market street fair, a Juried Art Show, and Parade, Logging Show, and Strongman Showdown.

Lavender Festival, in mid-July

http://www.lavenderfestival.com/ - Fill your senses with the sights and smells of lavender, tour a dozen local lavender farms, peruse street fair booths filled with artisanal goods, enjoy open air music and entertainment, purchase lavender plants and a plethora of lavender products.

Port Angeles:

Juan de Fuca Festival of the Arts, Memorial Day Weekend

http://jffa.org/ - Focus is on arts. Attend multiple "Juan de Fuca After Hours in the Clubs" evening performances, with ample opportunity to experience arts, crafts, and a street fair, all at the foot of the Olympic Mountains.

Independence Day Parade and Fireworks, Fourth of July

http://www.portangeles.org/pages/4thofJulyCelebration - Day-long activities culminating in a festive parade down Lincoln Street and fireworks display after dark.

Crab Festival, early October in downtown Port Angeles

http://www.crabfestival.org/ - Three-day celebration of aquaculture, agriculture and maritime traditions on the Olympic Peninsula. Explore exhibits, a clambake and plenty of other food, art, music, Native American activities and children's events.

Victoria, BC, Canada:

Canada Day http://www.tourismvictoria.com/events/canada150/ - Canada Day is July 1, Canada's Independence Day. 2017 marks Canada's 150-year anniversary. This year, festivities will begin on Jun 21 and end on July 1, and will include over 100 free live performances in Victoria's Inner Harbor.

Victoria Day http://www.tourismvictoria.com/events/victoriaday/ - The last Monday before May 25, in celebration of Queen Victoria's birthday. Victoria Day is accompanied with parades and entertainment.   http://www.tourismvictoria.com/events/festivals/ - this link provides information about Victoria's "dozens of annual festivals." Perhaps your visit will coincide with one of them that fascinates you.

Joyce:

Joyce Daze, first Saturday in August

https://joycedaze.org/ - Celebrates everything about blackberries, including dozens and dozens of home-baked blackberry pies for sale. Enjoy a small-town parade, during which Highway 101 traffic is detoured around "downtown" Joyce, and check out the many street fair booths.

Neah Bay:

Makah Days, held on the Saturday nearest August 26

http://makah.com/activities/makah-days/ - Makah tribal members and members not living on the Reservation, with related First Nations members from Vancouver Island, convene in Neah Bay to commemorate the Makah ancient culture *and* the anniversary of becoming citizens of the United States. All are welcome to come and enjoy festivities, food, and games.

Forks:

Old-Fashioned Fourth of July, held in early July

http://forkswa.com/event/forks-old-fashioned-4th-of-july/ - Celebrates American pride with a Grand Parade down the middle of Forks, breakfast, salmon bake, demolition derby, music in the park, arts and crafts show, fireworks in the evening and many more family events.

Forever Twilight in Forks, mid-September including the 13th

http://forkswa.com/forevertwilightinforks/ - Commemorates the September 13 birthday of the fictional Bella of *The Twilight Saga* fame. Calling all VITs (Very Important Twilighters) for nearly a week of celebration, *Twilight Saga* cosplay, food, tours, photo ops, games, and much more.

La Push:

Quileute Days, held in mid-July

http://forkswa.com/event/3256/ - A celebration of Quileute Tribal Cultural Heritage and modern lifestyle, with delicious traditional salmon bake, dancing and songs, native arts and crafts. Watch canoe races and an impressive fireworks display.

Quinault:

Lake Quinault Lodge sponsors several events or workshops throughout the year. Check the website: https://www.quinaultrainforest.com/Lake-Quinault/festivals-special-events.html, or call: 1-800-562-6672, or 360-288-2900 for specific event or workshop information.

Grays Harbor County:

Chocolate on the Beach Festival, in late February, Pacific Beach, WA

http://www.visitgraysharbor.com/events/2017/chocolate-on-the-beach-festival - Because, why not?! Get in on local arts and crafts and sample any number of chocolate-saturated baked goods.

Grays Harbor Shorebird and Nature Festival, in early May in Hoquiam, WA

https://www.shorebirdfestival.com/ - Held to recognize and observe the hundreds of thousands of shorebirds that stop in Grays Harbor estuaries as they migrate northward to arctic regions. Keynote speaker, field trips with expert birders, lectures, a birding marketplace, and a Nature Fun Fair for kids and families.

McCleary:

McCleary Bear Festival, during the second weekend in July

http://mcclearybearfestival.org/#events 360-495-3667, ext. 8 option 1. bearfestival@gmail.com

Enjoy time-tested and delicious "bear stew," as well as parades, fun run, Bear Claw Derby, street fair, and musical entertainment.

Shelton:

Mason County Forest Festival, in early June

http://masoncountyforestfestival.org/ - Celebrating everything forest, timber and the people who care for them. Enjoy a carnival, parades of people and pets, races, Logging Show, Fireworks, and much more.

Oyster Fest, in early October, near Sanderson Field in Shelton, WA

http://www.oysterfest.org/ - Everything oyster at this Washington state official seafood festival. Vendors, local music and entertainment, Washington wines and beer, and the largest festival food menu anywhere.

Hood Canal:

Hama Hama Oyster Rama at the end of April in Liliwaup, WA

http://www.hamahamaoysters.com/pages/events - Learn all about oysters, farming, shucking, cooking, you-pick oysters and clams,

Shuckathon oyster competition, live music, wine and beer garden, oyster cookoff, and fun stuff for kids.

Brinnon:

Hood Canal Shrimpfest, Memorial Day Weekend

http://www.brinnonshrimpfest.org/ - Celebrates local Hood Canal Shrimp season and more, with crafts and food booths, fun for kids, live music and decorated belt sander races.

2D) Professional Tour Companies on the Olympic Peninsula

Three companies offer tours featuring ecotourism, biodiversity, wine-tasting, Makah culture and scenic tours. Depending on your needs, you may even be able to arrange custom or private tours.

Experience Olympic, Permittee of Olympic National Park, Port Angeles, WA 98362

360-808-9237. http://experienceolympic.com/;

Email: tours@experienceolympic.com

Experience Olympic will take you on the ecotour or biodiversity tour of your choice, in and around the Olympic National Park. They specialize in small groups; tours cost around $25 - $35 per hour per person, kids under 16 are free. In their words: *Participating in our brand of Washington State ecotourism ensures that you will have quality time with your naturalist guide to ask many questions and receive quality one-on-one attention.*[1]

Tour options are too many to list – peruse their website for details, or contact them as they may be able to tailor a tour to your interests. In

---

1   http://experienceolympic.com/why/ecotourism, accessed June 9, 2017.

any case, schedule as early as possible to ensure they can provide the naturalist guide you need!

<u>All Points Charters and Tours</u>**, 325 W. 14th St., Port Angeles, WA 98362**

360-460-7131. <u>www.goallpoints.com</u>; E-mail: <u>tours@goallpoints.com</u>

Willie Nelson (your tour guide) will take you on a tour to destinations on the Olympic Peninsula. For full-day tours see:

- Hoh Rain Forest and Rialto Beach
- Lake Crescent and Hurricane Ridge
- Makah Tribal Culture and Cape Flattery
- Olympic Peninsula Winery Tour of our 7 local wineries.

Or, for a half-day excursion:

- Tour the Elwha River and learn about the dam removal project and the return of the salmon to the Elwha. See the website for even more options.

<u>Olympic Peninsula Adventures</u>**, Sequim, WA 98382**
360-775-1102.
http://www.olympicpeninsulaadventures.com/
E-mail: info@olympicpeninsulaadventures.com

Take one of four local tours:

- **Talk of the Towns Tour** (6 hours): Port Angeles, Sequim, Port Townsend, with emphasis on shopping, history, cuisine, and perhaps a touch of wine-tasting if the season allows.

- **Wild Beaches and Rivers Tour** (8 hours): La Push and Rialto Beaches, lunch on the coast, and a quick visit to Forks, WA.

- **Port Townsend Cider and Winery Tour** (6 hours): Visit and tasting at three cideries and one-to-two wineries in and around Port Townsend, with a bit of exploring around town, of course. (21 or older; bring your ID!)

- **Best of the Olympic National Park Tour** (8 hours): See the views at Hurricane Ridge. Visit Lake Crescent Lodge and take the short hike to Marymere Falls. Explore the rain forest in the Sol Duc River Valley, including the Salmon Cascade, the Ancient Grove Trail, and the Sol Duc Falls Trail.

2E) Recreational Activities on DNR-Managed Land

http://www.dnr.wa.gov/go - For the price of a Discover Card Pass (required – see Part 3F), a plethora of recreational activities on Washington Department of Natural Resources (DNR) lands opens up. The Olympic National Park doesn't permit many activities which *can* be enjoyed on DNR land. Pets are allowed. Follow the link above for descriptions and locations of DNR campgrounds on the Olympic Peninsula. Plus, find links to info on these activities: boating, camping, fishing, hang gliding, hiking, horseback riding, hunting, mountain biking, off-road vehicles, rock climbing, and target shooting,

2F) Campgrounds

Olympic National Park Campgrounds:

https://www.nps.gov/olym/planyourvisit/camping.htm - Lists and links to campgrounds within the Olympic National Park. The camp-grounds closest to Highway 101 are listed below. All have RV sites for twenty-one feet and a few for thirty-five feet, except where noted. All are handicap accessible, except where noted. Cost per night varies.

- **Fairholme Campground:** at the west tip of Lake Crescent. Open May through October, first-come, first-served. RV sites for 21 feet only. 88 sites. Flush toilets and potable water.

- **Heart O' the Hills Campground:** In Port Angeles. Year round, walk-in only during heavy snowfall. First-come, first-served. 105 sites. Flush toilets and potable water

- **Kalaloch Campground:** On the Pacific coast at Kalaloch. Open year round; online reservations accepted for dates June through September. Otherwise, first-come, first-served. 170 sites. Flush toilets and potable water.

- **South Beach Campground:** On the Pacific coast south of Kalaloch. Perched on a bluff very near the Pacific Ocean beach. Open May through September, first-come, first-served. Fifty-five sites. Flush toilets but no potable water. No handicap-accessible beach access trails.

Washington State Park Campgrounds:

http://parks.state.wa.us/281/Parks - This link gives you a list of *all* Washington State Parks. **Discovery Pass** needed for WA State Parks (Part 3F). **Campsite Reservations**: 888-226-7688. **Day Use Hours**: 8a-dusk. You may be interested in staying in one of these state parks.

- Bogachiel State Park, 185983 US-101, Forks, WA 98331

  360-374-6356. http://parks.state.wa.us/478/Bogachiel

- Dosewallips State Park, 306996 Highway 101, Brinnon, WA 98320

  360-796-4415. http://parks.state.wa.us/499/Dosewallips

- Fort Flagler Historical State Park, 10541 Flagler Rd., Nordland, WA 98359

  360-385-1259. http://parks.state.wa.us/508/Fort-Flagler

- Fort Worden Historical State Park, 200 Battery Way, Port Townsend, WA 98368

  800-233-0321. http://parks.state.wa.us/511/Fort-Worden

- Grayland Beach State Park, 3120 WA-105, Grayland, WA 98547

  360-267-4301.

  http://parks.state.wa.us/426/Grayland-Beach-State-Park

- Harstine Island State Park: administered by Jarrell Cove State Park

- Jarrell Cove State Park, 391 E. Wingert Rd., Shelton, WA 98584.

  360-426-9226.

  http://parks.state.wa.us/523/Jarrell-Cove

- Lake Sylvia State Park, 1812 N. Lake Sylvia Rd., Montesano, WA 98563

  360-249-3621.

  http://parks.state.wa.us/534/Lake-Sylvia

- Ocean City State Park, 148 SR 115, Hoquiam, WA 98550

  360-289-3553.

  http://parks.state.wa.us/554/Ocean-City

- Potlatch State Park, 21020 N. US-101, Shelton, WA 98584

  360-796-4415.

  http://parks.state.wa.us/569/Potlatch

- Sequim Bay State Park, 269035 Highway 101, Sequim, WA 98382

  360-683-4235.

  http://www.parks.wa.gov/582/Sequim-Bay

- Twin Harbors State Park, 3120 WA 105, Westport, WA 98595

  360-268-9717.

  http://parks.state.wa.us/431/Twin-Harbors-State-Park

- Westport Light State Park, 1595 Ocean Avenue, Westport, WA 98595

  360-268-9717.

  http://parks.state.wa.us/284/Westport-Light

US Forest Service Campgrounds:

https://www.fs.usda.gov/activity/olympic/recreation/camping-cabins/?recid=47687&actid=29

Seventeen USFS campgrounds, nearly all of them within reach of Highway 101.

- **Klahowya Campground (US Forest Service)**

  https://www.fs.usda.gov/recarea/olympic/recarea/?recid=47709

  Hours: Open May through October. First-come, first-served. The campground is situated along the south shore of the Sol Duc River. Fishing, float-tubing, hiking, interpretive trails. Trailers/RVs up to 30', potable water, flush and vault toilets. **Getting there:** Located on Highway 101 about 7.3 miles (11.75 km) west of Sol Duc Hot Springs Road, and about twenty miles (32.1 km) northeast of Forks, on the north side of Highway 101 at milepost 212.

- **Coho Campground (US Forest Service)**

  https://www.fs.usda.gov/recarea/olympic/recreation/camping-cabins/recarea/?recid=47807

  Hours: Open from mid-May to early October. Located at southern end of Wynoochee Lake. RVs, tents, yurt rentals.

Washington State Department of Natural Resources (DNR) Campgrounds:

Eight campgrounds in the north and western areas of the Olympic Peninsula. Open year round. Discover Pass required (Part 3F). See the DNR website for details on all these campgrounds: http://www.dnr.wa.gov/OlympicPeninsula

Salt Creek Recreation Area includes the Salt Creek Campground. This campground is considered the very best in the areas surrounding Port Angeles and the North Olympic Peninsula. See the full listing in Part 4G.

> **NOTE**: Camping near any bodies of water will mean swarms of mosquitoes in the summertime. **Exception**: Ocean shoreline camping, such as Salt Creek, Kalaloch, or South Beach Campgrounds.

2G) Where to Rent Kayaks, Canoes, Bicycles, Surf Gear

Since the Olympic Peninsula is bordered by water on three sides, the options for kayaking and canoeing are wonderful. The Strait of Juan de Fuca and the Hood Canal offer quieter seas, bays and coves in which to quietly glide along and enjoy nature. Prices vary and some areas are seasonal. Check with the individual companies for current rates and schedules. Some companies offer both kayaks, canoes, paddle-boarding and hiking tours.

Port Angeles:

Adventures Through Kayaking, 2358 Highway 101 West, Port Angeles, WA 98363

360-417-3015;   800-900-3015.   http://www.atkayaking.com/kayak-rentals/

Hours: Every day 9:30a-6p. Kayaking, biking, tours.

Olympic Raft and Kayak, 123 Lake Aldwell Rd., Port Angeles, WA 98363

360-526-8031; 888-452-1443.

http://www.raftandkayak.com/sea-kayak-tours/

Hours: Wed-Sun 8a-4p, Mon-Tue closed. Kayaking, kayak instruction, whitewater rafting.

Sound Bikes and Kayaks, 120 E. Front St., Port Angeles, WA 98362

360-457-1240. https://www.facebook.com/soundbikeskayaks/

Hours: Mon-Sat 10a-6p, Sun 11a-4p. Kayak and bicycle sales and rentals.

Olympic National Park:

Kayak and canoe rentals on Lake Quinault and Lake Crescent.

888-896-3818. http://www.olympicnationalparks.com/things-to-do/boat-paddleboard-rentals-olympic-peninsula/

Grays Harbor County:

North Coast Surf Shop, 773 Point Brown Avenue NW, Ocean Shores, WA 98569

360-289-0651. http://www.northcoastsurfshopwa.com/rentals.php

Surfing gear rentals, surf lessons.

Hood Canal:

Kayak Brinnon, 251 Hjelvicks Rd., Brinnon, WA 98320

360-796-4116. http://kayakbrinnon.com/blog/

Hours: Every day 10a-6p. Kayaking rentals, tours, kayaking, crabbing and camping trips, used kayak sales.

Hood Canal Adventures, 7211 North Lake Cushman Rd., Hoodsport, WA 98548

360-898-2628. http://hoodcanaladventures.com/

Kayaking, paddleboarding, biking. Rentals and tours.

2H) Fishing, Shellfishing, and Fishing Guides

If you wish to catch a fish, and take it home to make a dish, then read below to find out how, where and when; what they'll allow (Leah Patry).

The Olympic Peninsula is surrounded with great fishing and shellfishing opportunities. The Pacific Ocean on the west side offers excellent ocean fishing at Neah Bay, La Push, and the Grays Harbor region. The large rivers draining the Olympic Mountains offer excellent river fishing and fly fishing. Ozette Lake, Lake Sutherland, and Lake Pleasant are not only beautiful for an afternoon of boating but you can also bring home dinner, within regulation parameters. (Catch and release only in Lake Crescent.) The Hood Canal is prime habitat for shellfish like geoduck, clams, shrimp and oysters. Dungeness crab can be found throughout the region, including near the Dungeness Spit in Sequim.

Fishing regulations on the Olympic Peninsula are extensive, complicated, and subject to change. Check the following websites for current information regarding boundaries, seasons and required licensing before setting off.

WA State Fishing Regulations:

- National Park Service:

  https://www.nps.gov/olym/planyourvisit/fishing.htm

- Olympic National Park Fishing Brochure (subject to change after May 1 of the current year): https://www.nps.gov/

olym/planyourvisit/upload/fish_brochure_2014-2015_
final_11-30-16-2.pdf

- Olympic National Forest:

  https://www.fs.usda.gov/activity/olympic/recreation/
  fishing

- Washington Department of Fish & Wildlife: http://wdfw.
  wa.gov/publications/01818/wdfw01818.pdf

- Purchase a fishing license online: http://wdfw.wa.gov/
  about/regions/region6/

- WA Department of Fish and Wildlife Frequently Asked
  Questions: https://fishhunt.dfw.wa.gov/#/application/
  help?tab=2&subTab=1

Fishing on or near an Indian Reservation:

Additionally, local Indian tribes may or may not permit non-tribal
members to fish on tribal land. Or, they may require an additional
license and an accompanying tribal member. Depending on where
you intend to fish, please check with the appropriate tribal entities
regarding their regulations and requirements:

- Makah Nation (Neah Bay): http://www.makah.com/
- Quileute Nation (La Push):

  http://www.quinaultindiannation.com/fishingregs.htm

- Quinault Indian Nation (Quinault):

  http://quinaultindiannation.com/

- Skokomish Indian Tribe (Shelton):

  http://www.skokomish.org/

Hiring a fishing guide is a valid way to shed the worry. There are
a TON of fishing guides on the Olympic Peninsula. They typically
provide all the gear and are knowledgeable about the rules, regulations,
and best fishing or shellfishing areas.

A Few Fishing Guide Companies:

- **Westside Guide Service**, Port Angeles, 360-640-0546 http://westsideguide.com/
- **Waters West Fly Fishing Outfitters**, Port Angeles, 360-417-0937 http://waterswest.com
- **Three Rivers Resort**, Forks, 360-374-5300 http://www.threeriversresortandguideservice.com
- **Westport Marina** (Grays Harbor), Westport 425-736-8920

Westport Fishing Charters - Fishing or deep sea fishing

- **Advantage Charters**: 360-648-2277; http://advantagecharters.com/ Westhaven Drive Float 12, Westport WA 98595
- **Tommycod Charters**: 360-640-1824; http://tommycodcharters.com/ Westhaven Drive, Float 6, Westport WA 98595
- **Ocean Sportfishing**, 360-268-1000; http://www.oceansportfishing.com/ 2549 Westhaven Drive, Westport, WA 98595
- **Westport Charter**: 360-268-0900; http://www.westportcharters.com/ 2411 Westhaven Drive, Westport, WA 98595
- **Deep Sea Charters**: 360-268-9300; http://www.deepseacharters.biz/ 2319 North Westhaven Drive, PO Box 1115, Westport, WA

Links to many more Olympic Peninsula Fishing Guides, Charter Boats, Outfitters:

- Fishing guides from Port Townsend to Westport and beyond:

  http://www.olympicpeninsula.org/things-to-do/fishing-guides-and-charters

- Fishing guides mainly in the Forks area:

  http://forkswa.com/business-directory/fishing-guides-and-charters-2/

- Freshwater fishing guides for the southern reaches of the Olympic Peninsula such as the Wynoochee, Humptulips, and Chehalis Rivers (and more, of course).

  http://www.fishwaterswest.com/Humptulips.html

2I) Hiking on the Olympic Peninsula

Hiking is one of the best ways to get in touch with and feel the flavor of the Pacific Northwest. Hike through rain forest, along ocean beaches or one of the many trails through the mountains. Easy or difficult, there are trails and opportunities for everybody.

Ocean Hiking:

From the Makah Indian Reservation to the Quinault Reservation, 73 miles (117.5 km) of Pacific Ocean shoreline of Washington State has been protected within the boundaries of the Olympic National Park. It is possible to hike along the shore from, for example, Cape Alava near the Ozette Indian Reservation, all the way to Rialto Beach, just north of La Push, WA. To do this safely requires a tide table (Part 5E) so you don't get stranded (or worse, swamped) by the tides, a knowledge of where to use overland trails to bypass unpassable headlands, and also a wilderness camping permit (Part 3F) if you camp on the beach.

Mountain Hiking:

The back-country of the Olympic Mountains is crisscrossed with trails and dotted with primitive campgrounds. But you don't need to be a dedicated backpacker and camper to enjoy mountain hiking in the Olympic Peninsula. Nearly every attraction, especially within the Olympic National Park, has a variety of nearby trails, from ADA-accessible and very easy, to a couple miles round trip, to several miles one way leading to a worthy viewpoint. Here is a quick list of favorite hikes, and where to find them:

- Hurricane Hill (Part 4D)
- Multiple trail heads at Hurricane Ridge (Part 4D)
- Hikes around Lake Crescent (Part 4I)
- Hoh Rain Forest trails (Part 4M)
- North shore and south shore hikes around Lake Quinault (Part 4P)
- Enchanted Valley via the trailhead at Graves Creek near Lake Quinault (Part 4P)
- Wynoochee Lake (Part 4Q)
- Lake Cushman and Staircase Trails (Part 4V)

The Olympic National Park helps you plan your wilderness forays, including trail maps, camping permits, and safety—especially bear safety and food storage requirements—here:

https://www.nps.gov/olym/planyourvisit/wilderness-trip-planner.htm. Plus, see other bear safety links under Olympic Black Bears (Part 6D).

This web page lists several hardcore hikes into the back country of the Olympic National Park:

http://www.thekalalochlodge.com/olympic-national-park-hiking.aspx

Walking Trails:

The Olympic Discovery Trail: http://www.olympicdiscoverytrail. com/

"The Olympic Discovery Trail is a designated non-motorized, multi-use trail spanning the north end of the Olympic Peninsula in Washington State. The route spans around 126 miles between Port Townsend, WA and La Push, WA" (Wikipedia[2]). This trail is incomplete, but sixty-nine miles ARE complete, various areas are currently under construction, and fifty-seven miles still require proper grading and ADA-accessibility. Huge intact stretches can easily tucker you out, all for free. Equestrians are welcome on some portions of the trail.

Port Angeles East to Sequim: Beginning in downtown Port Angeles at the pier, a good four miles of trail tracks to the east directly along the Strait of Juan de Fuca. (Look for eagles and otters.) The trail turns inland, traveling along Morse Creek to Morse Creek trailhead. Continuing east, the trail brings you through over twenty miles of ADA-compliant trail weaving its way through the Dungeness Plain and into downtown Sequim. The trail continues east to the Sequim Bay Campground.

Port Angeles and West: From downtown Port Angeles, the trail travels west along Milwaukee Drive, Kacee Way and Stratton Road, eventually turning to the south and wending its way to the Elwha River Road bridge. The developed trail terminates after crossing the bridge, but you can pick it up again at the Spruce Railroad Trail on the north shore of Lake Crescent. The trail then continues 11.8 miles to the west of Lake Crescent, tracking near Highway 101 and using logging roads.

---

2   https://en.wikipedia.org/wiki/Olympic_Discovery_Trail. Accessed June 9, 2017

The Olympic Discovery Trail website (above) identifies temporary routes all the way to the Pacific Ocean. Locate the trail segments and trailheads that most interest you.

Walk to the New Dungeness Lighthouse in Sequim

The Dungeness Recreation Area provides several short stretches of trail. One takes you along the bluffs of the Strait of Juan de Fuca, and another goes through local forest. For a real challenge, you can hike the 5.5 mile (9 km) length of the Dungeness Spit out to the Lighthouse. The thing is: once you hike out, you have to hike back, unless you can make private arrangements for a boat to pick you up.

Please do be aware of the tides as very high tides are capable of washing over the entire spit. Additionally, according to www.newdungenesslighthouse.com, *"Attempt only at low tide; high tides require climbing over driftwood logs."*[3] See Part 5E for tide tables and smart phone apps.

A Few Other Popular Easy Walks and Hikes

There are many more walking and hiking opportunities than those mentioned below, and I'll point them out in the 101 Loop Guide. The following attractions provide very popular and easy-to-do hikes that are likely to be memorable:

- **Hurricane Ridge** (accessed via Port Angeles) provides some lovely strolls and hikes through a truly spectacular high mountain environment with incredible views both to the Olympic Mountains to the south and over the Strait of Juan de Fuca to the north

---

3   http://newdungenesslighthouse.com/hiking-to-the-lighthouse/   Accessed June 9, 2017.

- **In the Elwha Valley** (near Port Angeles), a view of the impressive Madison Falls requires a very short and easy walk from the parking area.

- **At Lake Crescent**, hike three miles round trip to Marymere Falls and enjoy rain forest, streams, and a stunning waterfall.

- **The Hoh Rain Forest** has three easy trails laid out near the Visitor Center. The shortest is a 0.25 mile (0.40 km) loop, and the longest is a 1.5 mile (2.41 km) loop through unforgettable temperate rain forest.

- **Ocean Shores** and nearby beaches offer walking along the beach and also along Grays Harbor for some terrific birding opportunities.

- **In the Lake Quinault Rain Forest** one can take a very short walk to the World's Largest Sitka Spruce and a short hike to the World's Largest Red Cedar, plus multiple other easy-to-moderate hiking loops through the Quinault Rain Forest.

PART 3

General Travel Info for the Olympic Peninsula

3A) Getting Here, and then Getting Around

- **Use incognito mode** to explore flight options.
- **Include Southwest Airlines and Alaska Airlines in your flight searches** (they don't put their flights on aggregator websites): https://www.southwest.com/; https://www.alaskaair.com/
- **Fly into the Seattle-Tacoma International Airport (SeaTac or SEA)**
- **Rent a car at the airport.** A car is absolutely the ideal way to get around because of the huge distances one will need to cover if you wish to see the Olympic Peninsula in its entirety. Having your own wheels, whether owned or rented, is just about the only way to simplify all the logistics. See Car Rental info below, provided for your convenience.
- **Motorcycling on the Olympic Peninsula is a great option**, if this is your thing. The Pacific Northwest air is incredibly fresh and smells glorious, no matter where you travel on the Peninsula.

- **Rent an RV.** See the RV Rental information below on picking up a rental in the Seattle area.

- **Drive your own RV to the Peninsula.** You can get to just about everywhere on the Olympic Peninsula in an RV, and you'll save a bundle on hotels. Some older or smaller campgrounds may not have spots long enough for a larger RV. See below for links to various campgrounds and their amenities and capabilities.

- **There is no train service** on, or to, the Olympic Peninsula.

- **There is no continuity of public transportation** on, or to, the Olympic Peninsula. There is public transportation between Forks, Port Angeles, and Sequim. Then there is the Rocket Shuttle Service and the Dungeness Bus Line (Part 4E: Port Angeles) which will take you off the Olympic Peninsula to Seattle and back. But there are no workable or convenient ways to pursue a complete Olympic Peninsula vacation using only public transportation.

- **The Washington State Ferry** system (WSF) can transport you and your vehicle (bicycle, motorcycle, car or RV) across the several bodies of water that dominate our lives in Northwest Washington. The sail saves wear and tear on both you and your vehicle, and is typically very enjoyable. See the WSF info in Part 3D.

3B) SeaTac Airport Car Rentals

If flying to the Pacific Northwest, I assume you're likely to arrive at Seattle or vicinity, where a dozen or more car rental companies will be happy to rent you a vehicle. Here are links to several companies with offices in downtown Seattle or Seattle-Tacoma International Airport:

- **Alamo:**
  https://www.alamo.com/en_US/car-rental/locations/destinations/us/seattle-washington.html

- **Avis:**
  https://www.avis.com/car-rental/html/landing/sea-rental.html
- **Budget:**
  http://www.budget.com/budgetWeb/html/rentals/sea-rental.html
- **Economy:**
  http://www.economycarrentals.com/go/car-rental/usa/seattle/
- **Enterprise:**
  https://www.enterprise.com/en/car-rental/locations/us/wa/seattle.html
- **E-Z Rent-A-Car:**
  http://www.e-zrentacar.com/Locations/Seattle-Airport
- **National:**
  https://www.nationalcar.com/en_US/location-details/us/seat01-sea-tac-intl-arpt.html
- **Payless:**
  https://www.paylesscar.com/
- **Thrifty:**
  https://www.thrifty.com/local_sites_index/LocalPages/Seattle-Car-Rental.aspx?PickupLocationCode=SEA

3C) Consider Renting an RV

With so many campgrounds on the Olympic Peninsula in national, state, county and city Parks, renting an RV is a fun option. Although there are no RV rental companies on the Peninsula itself, there are a number of options in and around Seattle:

- **CruiseAmerica** - Seattle, WA. 800-671-8042.

  http://www.cruiseamerica.com/rv-rental-locations/rv-rentals-seattle-everett/

- **RV Share** - Seattle, WA - Rent an RV from its owner. Check website for information:

  https://rvshare.com/rv-rental/seattle/wa

- **USA RV Rentals** - Seattle, WA. 877-778-9569.

  http://www.usarvrentals.com/seattle-RV-rentals.php

- **NW Adventure Rentals** - just north of Seattle in Lynnwood, WA. 425-220-6901. http://nwadventurerentals.com/

Most rental companies equip their RVs with the essentials like dishes, linens, camping chairs, and some have options for add-ons like generators or bike racks. You will need to provide your personal items like toiletries and clothing.

FYI: Most of the national and state park campgrounds can accommodate RVs up to 21 feet (6.4 m) in length, with a few camping spots for larger rigs. It will be much easier to find RV accommodations with a 21-foot or shorter RV.

3D) Washington State Ferries

The Washington State Ferry (WSF) system is an amazing and fun way to traverse the watery reaches of the Puget Sound area. Every ferry comes equipped with restrooms, snack bars, and places inside and out to relax and enjoy the view. You can take your car - and even your dog - with you.

Main information page for the WSF: http://www.wsdot.wa.gov/ferries/

Current Ferry Schedule: http://www.wsdot.com/ferries/schedule/

Tips for Using the Washington ferries:

- WSF Schedule flyers are everywhere: on ferries, in hotels, and at info desks.

- Route times change with the seasons. Ferries sail more frequently during busy long summer days, and make fewer crossings during short winter days.

- Reservations are recommended for the routes between Port Townsend and Coupeville (Whidbey Island), and between Anacortes and the San Juan Islands.

- Your pet can sail with you on the ferry, within limits. Leashes or kennels are always required. Go to this link for more details: http://www.wsdot.wa.gov/Ferries/infodesk/faq/pets/.

- Fares vary according to how many people are traveling, their ages, vehicle particulars, route and direction. See http://www.wsdot.wa.gov/ferries/pdf/CurrentFares.pdf. This is the Current Fares list available in paper copy in every ferry terminal.

WSF Transit Times

Ferry transit times are 30–40 minutes between points in and around Seattle. Add to that any wait time before boarding the ferry. Walk-on passengers can board the very next ferry, whereas vehicles travel on a first-come, first-served basis. Summer and weekends are highly traveled, especially if it's summer AND a weekend. Wait times can vary from, "it's your lucky day," to "come back tomorrow – early."

You can always "drive around," as we say. That is, from the Peninsula, head south on Highway 3 to Highway 16 to Interstate 5 North at Tacoma, heading back to Seattle area, or the reverse if you've been caught without a ferry in Seattle. Plan about 2.5 hours for this drive.

DO experience a Pacific Northwest ferry ride, if possible! Washington ferries are a typical Northwest mode of transportation throughout the Puget Sound and the Olympic Peninsula. Ferry rides are many times a necessity, and they can be very enjoyable. The perspective of the surrounding land as viewed from the water is special, and it's a fairly cheap way to snag a boat ride through some of the best boating waters in the U.S.

3E) Black Ball Ferry (The Coho)

The Coho Ferry has just one route: from Port Angeles to Victoria, BC, and back again. The sail takes about 90 minutes. Expect about 15–30 minutes to clear customs at each end.

- Website Home: https://www.cohoferry.com
- Ferry Schedule: https://www.cohoferry.com/Schedule
- Fares: https://www.cohoferry.com/Fares
- Reservations: https://www.cohoferry.com/
- ID Requirements and Restrictions:
  https://www.cohoferry.com/ID-Requirements

Port Angeles Terminal:

Black Ball Ferry, 101 E. Railroad Avenue, Port Angeles WA 98362
1-360-457-4491

Victoria, BC Terminal:

Black Ball Ferry, 430 Belleville St., Victoria, BC V8V 1W9
1-250-386-2202

3F) National Park and Recreational Pass Information

America the Beautiful Pass Series

The National Park service offers passes in various categories that are valid in Parks throughout the USA: https://www.nps.gov/olym/planyourvisit/national-parks-and-federal-recreational-lands-pass.htm - See website for full information.

- Annual Pass - $80 (includes entry to all national parks, including Olympic National Park)
- Annual Pass for Military – Free
- Seniors 62 years old and older - $80 for lifetime (includes entry to all national parks, including Olympic National Park).
- Access Pass for the Permanently Disabled – Free

Olympic National Park Passes

https://www.nps.gov/olym/planyourvisit/fees.htm - Entry fee for private vehicles is US$25 for vehicle and all passengers, and is good for 7 days.

- Entry for motorcycle and passenger is $15; entry for bicycle and rider is $10. Both are valid for 7 days.
- Persons walking in pay US$10 for 7 days; children 15 and younger are free.

An annual pass for the ONP is $50. If you already have a valid America the Beautiful Pass, you do NOT need an additional ONP entry fee. There is info on America the Beautiful Passes, annual Olympic National Park Pass, and various other entry fees and use fees such as backcountry use or dump stations at the same link. **Obtain an Olympic National Park Annual Pass** at any ONP Visitor Center or Park entry station.

Olympic National Park Wilderness Camping Permits

Permit fees are $8 per person per night, with 15-years-old and under free.

- **Wilderness Information Centers, wilderness permits:**

  https://www.nps.gov/olym/planyourvisit/wilderness-permits.htm

- **Some areas require reservations:**

  https://www.nps.gov/olym/planyourvisit/wilderness-reservations.htm

- **Planning Your Wilderness Trip:**

  https://www.nps.gov/olym/planyourvisit/wilderness-trip-planner.htm

Discover Pass

The Discover Pass provides motor vehicle access to 160-plus Department of Natural Resources (DNR) recreation lands, 100-plus Washington State Parks (www.parks.wa.gov/), 700 water access points, and hundreds of natural and wildlife areas managed by the Washington Department of Fish and Wildlife (www.wdfw.wa.gov/). Plus, check the Discover Pass website for the dates of 12 "free" days during which a pass is not required for day use. More details: http://parks.state.wa.us/167/Discover-Pass-Fees

Purchase your Discover Pass:

- Online at www.DiscoverPass.wa.gov/
- At automated pay stations in select state parks
- In person at more than 600 vendor locations

Makah Recreation Pass

A Makah Recreation Pass is required for recreation and sometimes parking on the Makah Reservation (Neah Bay). Cost is $10 per year, and can be purchased at one of 6 locations on the reservation. See the website for those locations and for more info: http://makah.com/activities/. In their words: *"Please respect the culture of the Makah Tribe and limit your activities to designated visitor facilities."*[4]

---

4   http://makah.com/activities/ Accessed June 9, 2017.

Several Interagency Passes, including the Forest Service Day Pass, provide access to recreational fee areas: Can be purchased online and printed at home for placement in the vehicle. Details here: https://www.fs.usda.gov/main/olympic/passes-permits/recreation

3G) Information Centers

- **Olympic Peninsula Gateway Visitor's Center, 93 Beaver Valley Rd., Port Ludlow, WA,**

  98365. 360-437-0120. http://www.enjoyolympicpeninsula.org/

- **Port Townsend Visitor Info Center, 2409 Jefferson St., Port Townsend, WA 98368.**

  360-385-7869. www.enjoypt.com/; https://visitjeffersoncountywa.com/visit/activities/adventures/

- **Sequim Welcome Center, 1192 E. Washington St., Sequim, WA 98382.**

  360-737-8462. www.visitsunnysequim.com/

- **Port Angeles Information Center, 121 E. Railroad Avenue, Port Angeles, WA 98362.** (just east of the ferry terminal). 360-452-2363. https://visitportangeles.com/

- **Olympic National Park Headquarters, Ranger Station, Wilderness Information Center:**

  3002 Mount Angeles Rd., Port Angeles WA 98362. 360-565-3130. https://www.nps.gov/olym/planyourvisit/visitorcenters.htm

- **Greater Victoria Visitors Bureau, 812 Wharf St., Victoria, BC V8W 1T3, Canada**

  +1-250-953-2033. http://www.tourismvictoria.com/. Hours: Every day 9a-5p.

- **Clallam Bay Visitor Center, Highway 112, Clallam Bay, WA 98326**

  360-963-2339. http://www.clallambay.com/tourism/visitors-center/. Hours: Apr-Oct 9a-5p

- **Forks Chamber of Commerce and Info Center, 1411 S. Forks Avenue, Forks, WA 98331.** 360-374-2531. www.forkswa.com/

- **Greater Grays Harbor Visitor Information Center, 506 Duffy St., Aberdeen WA 98520.** 360-532-1924. http://www.graysharbor.org/

- **Ocean Shores Tourist Info Center, 120 W. Chance a La Mer NW, Ocean Shores, WA 98569.** 360-289-9586. http://www.tourismoceanshores.com/

  City of Ocean Shores: http://osgov.com/Tourism.html

- **Shelton Info Station, 230 W. Railroad Avenue, Shelton, WA 98584** (in train in front of Post Office). 360-427-8168. http://www.sheltonchamber.org/information/vic/

- **Olympia, Lacey, Tumwater Tourist Information Center, 103 Sid Snyder Avenue SW, Olympia WA 98501.** 360-704-7544. http://www.visitolympia.com/attractions/olympia-lacey-tumwater-visitor-information-center

- **Hoodsport Information Center, 150 N. Lake Cushman Rd., Hoodsport, WA 98548.**

  360-877-2021. http://www.sheltonchamber.org/information/vic/

3H) Maps

Main Olympic National Park brochure map, and links to various other Park maps:

https://www.nps.gov/olym/planyourvisit/maps.htm

This is the same map you'll receive upon presenting yourself at any Park entrance kiosk. The advantage to viewing it online is that the map offers a zoom-in feature. The above link also connects you to 15 downloadable Destination Brochure PDFs.

Downloadable PDF maps:

- Olympic National Park brochure map:

  https://www.nps.gov/olym/planyourvisit/upload/olym_map.pdf

- Olympic National Park Wilderness Campsite Information:

  https://www.nps.gov/olym/planyourvisit/upload/wildernessmap-10-25-16.pdf

- Download Washington State Highway maps from the WA State Department of Transportation:

  http://www.wsdot.wa.gov/publications/highwaymap/view.htm

Topographical and WA Street Atlas:

Get good maps to take with you! Smart phones, tablets and laptops are excellent for researching your upcoming journey. However, signals can be spotty in the many out-of-the-way locations on the Olympic Peninsula. Having a real, hold-in-the-hands map for those areas you are most interested in visiting, whether topographical or a street map, will relieve most of your route questions.

Links to some excellent street, park, and topographical maps can be found here: http://www.beautifulpacificnorthwest.com/washington-state-map.html

PART 4

Beautiful Olympic Peninsula Travel Guide

This travel guide is very easy to use. Port Townsend is the first population center you are likely to encounter after crossing the Hood Canal Bridge, making it a logical starting point for this book. The book then moves in a counterclockwise fashion around the Peninsula via Highway 101, presenting and describing 22 destinations.

You, however, don't need to feel any sort of pressure to be as linear as that if you don't want to. There is no real starting or stopping point because the information is modular. No matter which way you get here, and which way you care to travel, you can get started and explore any of the destinations that interest you. Enjoy your journeys!

Next – Segment A: Port Townsend!

Getting to Port Townsend from east or west: Find the junction of Highway 101 and Highway 20 in Discovery Bay. Take Highway 20 north into Port Townsend.

Getting to Port Townsend from the east: Westbound travelers can also take Highway 19 (Beaver Valley Road) northbound, 5 miles

(8 km) after crossing the Hood Canal Bridge. When Highway 19 intersects Highway 20; turn right and follow Highway 20 into Port Townsend and to the downtown National Historic District.

4A) Port Townsend

The city of Port Townsend, WA, is the Jefferson County seat and is situated within the Olympic rain shadow at the northeast tip of Jefferson County about 40 miles northwest of Seattle. It looks across the Puget Sound toward Whidbey Island, Mount Baker and the Cascade Mountains, and on a clear day, even as far as the Canadian Cascades north of Vancouver, BC.

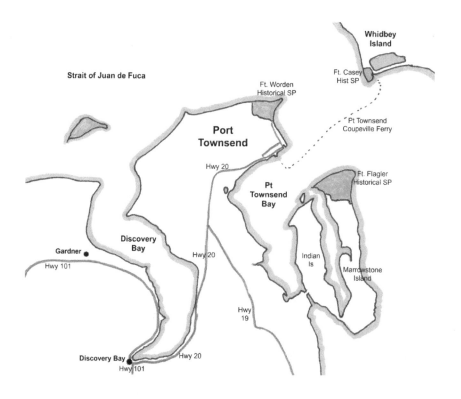

History of Port Townsend

Port Townsend bore its original name, "Port Townshend," from 1792 to 1851, thanks to Captain George Vancouver and his friend, the Marquis of Port Townshend. In addition to newly arrived Europeans, numerous Native American tribes lived in the area: the Chimakum, Hoh (a group of the Quileute), Klallam, Quinault and the Kwilcid band known as the Twana, or Quilcene.

Downtown Port Townsend along Water Street, one block from the water, and a few blocks from the ferry terminal.

The town grew into a booming shipping port and a major city by the time it was incorporated in 1851. However, by the late 1890s, when plans for the northwest extension of the Northern Pacific Railroad failed to materialize, Port Townsend experienced a rapid decline in population and the boom was over. Decades passed while Port Townsend managed to maintain economic stability, buoyed by the development of artillery fortifications at Fort Worden.

When the Port Townsend Paper Corporation built the mill south of town in the 1920s, Port Townsend's fortunes began to look up.

One of many beautiful Victorian buildings in Port Townsend.

Because the area's economy had declined so rapidly, the lack of industry preserved Port Townsend's now-iconic Victorian buildings for nearly 100 years. In 1976, its downtown area became the Port Townsend Historic District and was listed on the National Register of Historic Places. In 1977, downtown Port Townsend, WA was designated a National Historic Landmark District. Today, Port Townsend is one of only two preserved Victorian ports in the USA. Its population as of the 2010 census was 9,113, and is undergoing moderate growth.

Port Townsend Festivals

Port Townsend celebrates several annual festivals (Part 2C): Strange Brewfest in January, Shipwright's Regatta in February, Port Townsend Playfest in March, Rhody Festival in May, Wooden Boat Festival in September.

Port Townsend Points of Interest

Opportunities abound for beachcombing, boating, sailing, bicycling, whale watching, hiking, fishing, shellfishing, kayaking and more.

The Olympic National Park, Hood Canal and the Olympic Coast National Marine Sanctuary are all located nearby.

With two marinas, it is the perfect location for the Northwest Maritime Center, which offers various maritime educational programs for adults and youth.

Point Hudson Marina in Port Townsend, WA

Spend a day or two along Water Street browsing quaint bookstores, antique stores, clothing boutiques, and galleries featuring works by local and Native American artists. Relax in waterfront restaurants while you savor delicious dishes made from locally grown produce, and then obtain sweet creations from local bakeries or the old-fashioned ice cream parlor.

For sips, you'll find heavenly coffee shops and local wineries, cideries and breweries. Catch a film at the historic Rose Theatre while the night is young (or at least still kicking), then retire to your comfy hotel or B&B. For whatever piques your interest, floats your boat or gets your creative instincts flowing, Port Townsend will satisfy a yearning for culture, nature and art.

Port Townsend Ferry

The Washington State ferry terminal is located near the ports on Water Street. The ferry runs between Port Townsend and Coupeville on Whidbey Island. Ferry reservations are strongly recommended, and required a day in advance for RVs or if hauling a trailer.

Port Townsend Ferry Terminal, 1301 Water St., Port Townsend, WA 98368

WSF Ferry Schedule: http://www.wsdot.com/ferries/schedule/. Select the Port Townsend/Coupeville route. Then click on "Buy Ferry Tickets" or "Reservations."

Reservations can also be made by phone: 206-464-6400. Toll-Free: 1-888-808-7977.

Call Center Hours: Mon-Fri 7a-5p.

Additionally, depending where you'd like to travel next, visitors to Port Townsend, WA might instead catch a ferry at Kingston (to Edmonds), Bainbridge Island or Bremerton (both to downtown Seattle Washington). Schedules for these routes are also at the above link. Walk-on passengers to Seattle pay only for the return trip (the fare *to* Seattle is free). Traveling on the ferry by car will cost you both ways.

Port Townsend Attractions

Jefferson County Chamber of Commerce Info Centers in Port Townsend,

2409 Jefferson St., Port Townsend, WA 98368.

360-385-2722. https://visitjeffersoncountywa.com/
https://www.facebook.com/PortTownsendVIC/

Stop by the Jefferson County Information Center if you have any questions or wish additional direction.

Downtown Port Townsend:

Virtually the entire downtown area is a **National Historic District**, with many of the buildings built in the late 1800s or very early 1900s. Stroll many blocks along Water Street and nearby side streets; shop, browse art galleries, enjoy the architecture.

Port Townsend Parks:

Port Townsend's parks, scenic downtown historic area, and various landmarks, retired military forts, and lighthouses are all free to visit, or nearly free. Fort Worden requires a Discovery Pass.

- **Chetzemoka Park, Jackson St., Port Townsend, WA 98368**

  http://www.city-data.com/articles/Chetzemoka-Park-Port-Townsend-Washington.html

  10-acre park, lovely views, beach access, park setting, children's playground. Very close to downtown area and Point Hudson Marina. *(Pictured.)*

- **Fort Worden State Park, 200 Battery Way, Port Townsend, WA 98368**

  800-233-0321. http://parks.state.wa.us/511/Fort-Worden.

  Museums and music, beach walks and Pt. Wilson Lighthouse, kite-flying and incredible views. No wonder it tops TripAdvisor's list of Port Townsend attractions.

Port Townsend Marine Science Center, 532 Battery Way, Port Townsend, WA 98368

360-385-5582. Hours: Fri - Sun 12n-5p. Located within Fort Worden State Park. Educational, entertaining, active.

Jefferson County Historical Society Museum, 540 Water St., Port Townsend, WA 98368

360-385-1003. http://www.jchsmuseum.org/

Entry fee is $3.00. This is a great place to stop and learn more of the history of Port Townsend. They will also provide you with a street map and direct you to the scenic Victorian-era homes and buildings throughout Port Townsend.

Northwest Maritime Center, 431 Water St., Port Townsend, WA 98368

360-385-3628. http://nwmaritime.org/

The Northwest Maritime Center in Port Townsend sponsors educational programs for adults and children: life as a mariner on the water, boat-building, learning to sail, more.

Northwest Maritime Center in Port Townsend, WA

Whale Watching

Puget Sound Express, 227 Jackson St., Port Townsend, WA 98368

360-385-5288. https://www.pugetsoundexpress.com/

A whale-watching tour could easily become a highlight of your visit to the Pacific Northwest and Port Townsend. They operate several high-powered boats with inside cabins for your comfort. Whale sightings guaranteed; see the website for specifics. (Whale watching is also possible from Port Angeles or Victoria, BC.)

Art and Culture

Depending on your visit dates, you might get in on some wonderful art and culture in Port Townsend.

- **Art:** Gallery Walks every first Saturday of the month. "Stroll the town" as a group and view the art galleries.

- **Theatre:** Key City Public Theatre – Port Townsend's premier theatre has been in operation for over fifty years. www.keycitypublictheatre.org/

- **Music:** Olympic Music Festival conducts "Concerts in the Barn" on Saturdays and Sundays throughout the summer. www.olympicmusicfestival.org/

- **Blues and jazz:** Centrum sponsors summer performance festivals in both music and literature that draw visitors from across the nation. Centrum is based at Fort Worden State Park. http://centrum.org/

- **Dance:** Several dance groups hold frequent dances which are open to all, with live music. Salsa, Tango, Contra, square dancing, and more.

   www.ptguide.com/arts-music-theatre/dance

For more info about Port Townsend culture and attractions, explore these websites:

- "City Guide to Port Townsend, WA" www.ptguide.com/

- "One of the coolest small towns in America" www.enjoypt.com/

Port Townsend Recreational Activities:

The Pacific Northwest Trail is a collection of foot trails spanning 1,200 miles (1,900 km) and stretching from the Continental Divide in Montana, to the beaches of the Olympic National Park on Washington's Pacific coast. One of those sections travels through Port

Townsend and around the Port Townsend peninsula. For more info: http://www.pnt.org/

The Olympic Discovery Trail has its beginning in Port Townsend. The trailhead is located one mile south of the ferry terminal near the corner of Boat Street and Washington Street, in the boatyard. The first 6-mile ADA-accessible section is complete, and tracks along the Pacific Northwest Trail. It is great for biking, running/walking, and horseback riding. http://www.olympicdiscoverytrail.com/

Other various recreational opportunities include Bicycling, kayaking, boating, motor-boating, sailing, birding, horseback riding, fishing, and clam-digging. Recreation activities and any guidelines or permit requirements are listed here: www.ptguide.com/recreation-activities/

Go fishing, clamming, or shrimping with a tour guide: http://peninsulasportsman.com/fishing/.

Fly fishing, clam digging, and Dungeness crab-fishing are authentic Pacific Northwest activities. Your tour guide will have all the equipment you will need.

Port Townsend Hotels

Ann Starrett Mansion Boutique Hotel,

744 Clay St., Port Townsend, WA 98368

360-385-3205. http://www.starrettmansion.com/

Eight hotel suites in this 1889 Victorian hotel are decorated true to the period.

Bishop Victorian Hotel, 714 Washington St., Port Townsend, WA 98368

800-824-4738. http://www.bishopvictorian.com

The Bishop is located in the heart of historic downtown Port Townsend, and offers sixteen elegant fireplace suites including one or more bedrooms, private baths, sitting rooms, mini-kitchenette, rooms graced with period furniture. Complimentary in-room breakfast service.

Harborside Inn, 330 Benedict St., Port Townsend, WA 98368

360-385-7909; 800-942-5960. http://harborside-inn.com

On the waterfront with views of Boat Haven Marina and Admiralty Inlet, about 1 mile from downtown Port Townsend.

Manresa Castle, 651 Cleveland St., Port Townsend, WA 98368

360-385-5750. http://www.manresacastle.com/

Manresa Castle is a very old "castle" which is now repurposed as a hotel, restaurant and lounge.

Manresa Castle

Old Consulate Inn, 313 Walker St., Port Townsend, WA 98368.
360-385-6753. www.oldconsulateinn.com

This historically restored Queen Ann B&B is situated on a bluff overlooking Puget Sound. Enjoy spectacular views of the Olympic Mountains, and three-course gourmet breakfasts.

Palace Hotel, 1004 Water St., Port Townsend, WA 98368

360-385-0773; 800-962-0741. http://www.palacehotelpt.com/

Highly ranked, restored Victorian hotel in the heart of downtown Port Townsend not far from the ferry dock. Call for available "Special Packages" and "Romance Packages."

Ravenscroft Inn Bed & Breakfast, 533 Quincy St., Port Townsend, WA 98368

360-205-2147; 855-290-8840. www.ravenscroftinn.com

Located in a quiet neighborhood in Uptown but still just a short walk to downtown restaurants, bakery, and shops. Sweeping views of Townsend Bay.

Swan Hotel, 222 Monroe St., Port Townsend, WA 98368

800-776-1718. www.theswanhotel.com

On the waterfront in the heart of Port Townsend. Suites, studios, hotel-style accommodations, cottages. Swan Hotel is adjacent to Hudson Point Marina and NW Maritime Center.

The Tides Inn, 1807 Water St, Port Townsend, WA 98368

360-385-0595; 800-822-8696.

www.tides-inn.com

Conveniently located beachfront motel in downtown Port Townsend with views of the Cascades and Olympic Mountains.

Port Townsend Restaurants

Alchemy Bistro and Wine Bar, 842 Washington St., Port Townsend, WA 98368

360-385-5225. www.alchemybistroandwinebar.com/index.html

Hours: Every day - Lunch 11a; Dinner 5p; Bar & Bites 4p–closing; Sunday brunch 9a-3p. Mediterranean cuisine.

Owl Sprit Café, 218 Polk St., Port Townsend, WA 98368

360-385-5275. http://www.owlsprit.com/;

https://www.facebook.com/owlsprit

Hours: Wed-Sat 11:30a-7:30p. Highly regarded Northwest Cuisine with grass-fed and local organic ingredients.

Blue Moose Café, 311 Haines Place, #B, Port Townsend, WA 98368

360-385-7339.

https://www.facebook.com/Blue-Moose-198393041370/

Hours: Sat-Sun: 7a-2p, Mon-Fri: 6:30a-2p. The dining space is moose-themed, and the food brings visitors back for multiple visits.

Doc's Marina Grill, 141 Hudson St., Port Townsend, WA 98368

360-344-3627. www.docsgrill.com/

Hours: 11a-11p every day; Bar closes at 11p. Northwest cuisine on the water.

The Fountain Café, 920 Washington St., Port Townsend, WA 98368

360-385 1364. http://fountaincafept.blogspot.com/

Hours: Sun-Thu: Lunch 11:30a-3p; Dinner 5p-9p; Fri-Sat: Lunch 11:30a-3p; Dinner 5p-9:30p

Eclectic menu of consistently great meals.

Hillbottom Pie, 215 Tyler St., Port Townsend, WA 98368

360-385-1306.

https://www.facebook.com/pages/Hillbottom-Pie/1458946927694256

Hours: 11a-9p. Excellent pizza, best pies ever, and specialty coffees.

Lanza's Ristorante, 1020 Lawrence St., Port Townsend, WA 98368

(360) 379-1900. http://www.lanzaspt.com/Home_Page.html

Hours: Tues-Sat 5p-close; Sun-Mon closed. Call after 3p for reservations.

Serving traditional, authentic Italian cuisine 30 years.

Point Hudson Café, 130 Hudson St., Port Townsend, WA 98368.

360-379-0592.

https://www.facebook.com/pages/ Hudson-Point-Cafe/111918065505876

Hours: Sun 8a–2p, Mon-Sat 8a–3p. The place is usually busy, probably because of the very good food. (*Pictured*)

Waterfront Pizza, 951 Water St., Port Townsend, WA 98368.

(360) 385-6629.

https://www.facebook.com/Waterfront-Pizza-61382185589/.

Hours: Sun-Thurs: 11a-8p, Fri-Sat: 11a-10p

Excellent pizza, hand-tossed sourdough crust made with 150 year old starter dough topped with traditional toppings.

Mexican Cuisine

El Sarape, 628 Water St., Port Townsend, WA 98368

(360) 379-9343. http://www.elsarapept.com/

Hours: 11a-9p. Family restaurant offering traditional Mexican cuisine and atmosphere, good food and service.

Thai, Chinese Cuisine

123 Thai, 2219 E. Sims Way, Port Townsend, WA 98368

360-344-3103. http://www.123thaifood.net/#123-thai.

Hours: Mon-Sat 11a–8:30p. Thai fast food, authentic and excellent. Not much room for eating; get it to go and take it to the beach or back to the hotel.

Banana Leaf Thai Bistro, 609 Washington St., Port Townsend, WA 98368

360-379-6993. www.bananaleafthaibistro.com/

Hours: Mon-Tue, Thur-Sat 11a-3p, 5-9p; Sun 12p-3p; 5-9p. Closed Wed.

Port Townsend Coffee Houses

Better Living Through Coffee, 100 Tyler St., Port Townsend, WA

360-385-3388. www.bltcoffee.com/

Hours: 7a-6p; closed Tues. Organic local foods and fair trade, locally roasted, organic coffee. Ingredients are locally sourced, grass-fed, and organic. Included are gluten-free items. Great place to sit, sip, and chill.

Port Townsend Old-Fashioned Ice Cream Parlor

Elevated Ice Cream Co, 627 & 831 Water St., Port Townsend, WA 98368

360-385-1156. www.elevatedicecream.com/

Hours: Fri-Sat, 10a - 10p; Sun-Thur, 10a - 9p. You'd certainly expect a "refreshingly modern old-fashioned Ice Cream Parlor" in an old Victorian town. The ice creams, sherbets, and Italian ices (non-dairy) are all homemade on the premises. Also get espresso coffees and home-baked desserts.

Next – Segment B: Discovery Bay and Blyn, WA!

Getting there from Port Townsend: Return to Highway 101 via Highway 20.

Getting there from the west: Blyn is 7.2 miles (11.6 km) east of Sequim. Both destinations are on Highway 101.

4B) Discovery Bay and Blyn

Discovery Bay

At the tip of Discovery Bay at the junction of Highway 101 and Highway 20 is an unincorporated location in Jefferson County aptly called Discovery Bay. There are several points of interest here, all of them right on Highway 101.

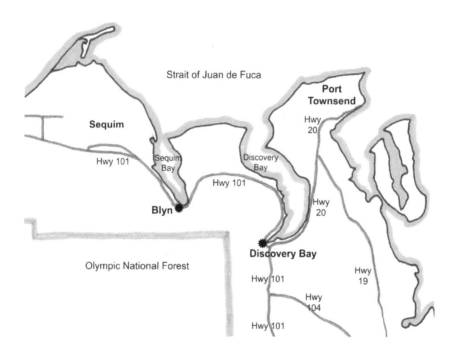

Native American Gifts in Discovery Bay

Lucky Deer Trading, 282343 US-101, Discovery Bay, WA 98368

360-379-2772. **Hours:** Wed-Sun 10a-5p; closed Mon-Tue. Lucky Deer is a Native American-themed gift shop featuring Native American designs in blankets, rugs, clothing, hats, moccasins, drums, books, and much more.

Food in Discovery Bay

Fat Smitty's, 282624 US-101, Port Townsend, WA 98368

360-385-4099.

https://www.facebook.com/pages/Fat-Smittys/111433978890681

Hours: Lunch/Dinner. You can't miss the big carved burger sitting next to the big carved man, nor the money-covered walls and ceiling inside. And indeed, they leave markers at every table in case you'd like to leave your own personalized $1. Yes, they offer terrific burgers, served old-Americana style in baskets on checkered paper.

Snug Harbor Café, 281732 US-101, Port Townsend, WA 98368

360-379-9131. http://www.snugharborcafedb.com/

Hours: Daily 11:30a-9p. Serves lunch and dinner. Steaks, seafood, great fish and chips in a cozy little shingled cabin at the tip of Discovery Bay.

Blyn

The Jamestown S'Klallam Indian Reservation is situated in Blyn at the end of the Bay, roughly centered on the mouth of Jimmycomelately Creek.

Jamestown S'Klallam Reservation, 1033 Old Blyn Highway, Sequim, WA 98382

360-683-1109. E-mail: info@jamestowntribe.org.

http://jamestowntribe.org/

"S'Klallam" means Strong People. In 1874, the various communities of S'Klallam Indians living along the Strait of Juan de Fuca joined together and purchased 210 acres in the Dungeness Valley. They named the community "Jamestown" in a nod to their leader, James Balch. Over the years, and with brilliant foresight, the Jamestown S'Klallam people continued to purchase land, currently owning over 1,000 acres in the area. Sequim's upscale Cedars at Dungeness Golf Course is owned and managed by the tribe. Also, the Railroad Bridge Park is on S'Klallam-owned land.

After petitioning the federal government for several years, they received official recognition as the Jamestown S'Klallam Tribe of Native Americans. The tribal reservation is comprised of just 13.5 acres in Blyn. The Seven Cedars Casino is there, as is the Longhouse Market, deli and gas station. Because of their foresight and excellent management, they have the means to be self-sufficient and provide various programs and services for their people, all while "*preserving, restoring and sustaining our Indian heritage and community continuity*"[5] (from the tribal mission statement). The Jamestown Tribe website provides excellent insights into Klallam life in a past generation.

Blyn Attractions:

Tribal Rest Stop in Blyn: Sequim Bay Scenic Pullout on Highway 101

This easily accessible turn-out rest stop with restrooms on the right (north) side of the highway is much, *much* more than just a "rest stop." This fascinating scenic pullout is owned and managed by the Jamestown S'Klallam native tribe, which offers information about the area, the native peoples, a museum, and more, including a Tribal Welcome Center and a gallery of native art (below). If you're passing through during the day, feel free to stop and stretch your legs on the nearby Olympic Discovery Trail which follows near or along the neighboring Old Blyn Highway.

---

5   http://www.jamestowntribe.org/main/main_mission.htm, Accessed June 10, 2017.

Northwest Native Expressions Art Gallery, 1033 Old Blyn Highway, Sequim, WA 98382

360-681-4640.

http://www.jamestowntribe.org/enterprise/enter_artgallery.htm

Hours: Mon-Sat, 9a - 5p.

Shop online here: http://stores.northwestnativeexpressions.com/

The Native Art Gallery and gift shop is located on Highway 101 at the Sequim Bay Scenic Pullout. Learn about the various native artists and purchase some truly impressive native artwork at genuinely reasonable prices. Also available are various souvenirs, for example, mugs, tee shirts, sweatshirts and more, featuring native designs.

7 Cedars Casino, 270756 Highway 101, Sequim, WA 98382

360-683-7777. http://www.7cedarsresort.com/casino.html

The casino offers "*some of the hottest games around.*" Visitors have differing opinions about how "loose" the slots are. The casino also features a calendar full of live entertainment, gaming tournaments, and special offers. The facilities are new and upscale, even if not huge.

Blyn Restaurants

7 Cedars Dining:

Several bars and restaurants at the casino, along with live entertainment. You won't lack for alcohol. Details on the 7 Cedars Resort website.

- **Totem Bar & Grille**
- **Napoli's: Stone-Fired Cuisine**
- **Salish Room Buffet**
- **Rain Forest Bar**
- **Club SEVEN Bar**

Longhouse Market and Deli, 271020 US-101, Sequim, WA 98382
360-681-7777. https://www.7cedarsresort.com/

The tribe operates a Chevron gas station with its Longhouse Market and Deli under the umbrella of 7 Cedars Casino. The place is open 24 hours a day. This is more than your typical gas station mini-mart. It is more like a deli attached to a small supermarket. They'll even offer you wine and cigars.

> **Next – Segment C: Sequim and Carlsborg!**

Getting to Sequim and Carlsborg from the east: Sequim is just 7.2 miles (11.6 km) west of Blyn along Highway 101. Exit the highway at either the **Washington Street** off ramp or the **Sequim Avenue** off ramp.

OR, if you'd like to do a scenic detour along Sequim Bay: Take West Sequim Bay Road which intersects Highway 101 directly across from Sequim Bay Lodge. The intersection is not controlled – turn right (north), and follow the road through country farms and fields, along the shore of Sequim Bay, and past the John Wayne Marina through continuing residential areas until the road intersects with East Washington Street. Turn right (west) on East Washington Street to enter downtown Sequim.

Getting to Sequim and Carlsborg from the west: Carlsborg is fourteen miles (22.5 km) east of Port Angeles. Sequim is seventeen miles (27.3 km) east of Port Angeles. Both destinations are on Highway 101.

4C) Sequim and Carlsborg

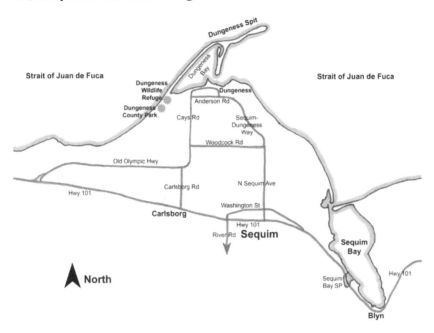

Sequim, population 6,606+, is located in the middle of the semi-arid Dungeness Valley. You can almost (but not quite) count on a Sequim visit to be a dry one. The area is considered semi-arid, thanks to the **Olympic Mountain rain shadow**.

This greeting spans Washington Street, Sequim's main drag.

Just so you know, Sequim is pronounced SKWIM. I know, weird. But you're SURE to be corrected if you call it *SEE-kwim*. Oh what the heck! Try it out on an unsuspecting cashier, just for kicks.

The Meaning of the word "Sequim": According to the Sequim Bay State Park website, *"the word 'Sequim' was believed by many to mean 'quiet waters.' In 2010, a tribal linguist who is an expert in the study of dying languages determined ... the correct translation of '**Sequim**' is a '**place for going to shoot**, 'a reference to the Sequim-Dungeness Valley's once great elk and waterfowl hunting."*[6]

Getting only **sixteen inches** of rain a year is quite remarkable in the midst of the generally rainy Pacific Northwest. Yes, the weather is dry and mild, but it's not like you'll find prickly pear cactus or Gila monsters here. The area is green because it doesn't get scorched by 110+F (43.3C) heat, and most of the sixteen inches per year fall during late autumn, winter, and early spring.

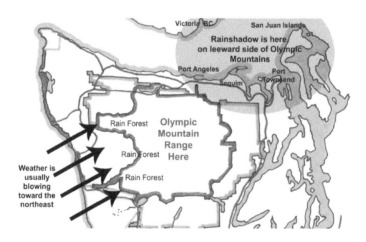

Rain Shadow Effect on the Olympic Peninsula

Despite the fact that the mountains are less than 8,000 feet tall, they still affect most of the weather in the region. They are tall enough to

---

6   http://parks.state.wa.us/582/Sequim-Bay, accessed June 10, 2017.

create a reliable rain shadow on the north and northeast sides of the Olympic Mountains. The North Olympic Peninsula towns of Sequim, Port Townsend, and, to a lesser extent, Port Angeles, sit in the midst of the Olympic Rain Shadow. While it's raining buckets in Neah Bay, Forks, or Aberdeen, there may indeed be blue sky over Sequim. In fact, this condition is so consistent they call it the **Blue Hole**.

The Olympic rain shadow can be reliably found within the shaded area, although prevailing weather conditions may alter the shape and size of the shadow from time to time.

Depending on the prevailing weather system, the blue hole may cover Sequim, Port Angeles, or Port Townsend; or it might be open enough to brighten all three towns, the southern parts of the San Juan Islands, *and* Victoria, BC.

The Blue Hole

This photo was taken on an early spring evening in Sequim-Dungeness. The horizon was literally ringed with angry storm clouds to the north, south, east, and west, but on this early evening the Blue Hole over Sequim prevailed.

The Blue Hole is why you can almost (but not quite) count on a dry Sequim visit, and why the northeastern Olympic Peninsula is sometimes called the "Banana Belt of Washington State."

Looking to the west from the Dungeness Plain toward Port Angeles.

Sequim, Washington Festivals

The town of Sequim indulges in two yearly festivals, both running approximately one week long.

Sequim Irrigation Festival: Two Weekends in Mid-May

http://www.irrigationfestival.com/

In Sequim, WA, the fields need to be irrigated. On May 1, 1895, the first irrigation channel filled with water in Sequim with great fanfare. Folks came from as far afield as Port Angeles (on horses and in buggies) and Port Townsend (on a tug boat and then bicycles) to see the water flow. The following year, everyone was invited to "Crazy" Callen's farm to celebrate the success of their irrigation plans. And the people of Sequim have celebrated every year since then. It is the oldest continuing festival in Washington State. May, 2017, marked the 121st year of recognizing the necessity of irrigation throughout the Sequim Dungeness Valley.

The Irrigation Festival features an Arts and Crafts fair, Driftwood Art Show, Truck and Tractor Pull Competitions, Loggers and Strongmen competition, a High School Operetta, a carnival for the kids, and a Farmer's Market, among many other activities. It's a LOT of fun.

Sequim Lavender Festival: Third Week in July

Check these websites for all the details:

- Lavender Festival http://www.lavenderfestival.com/
- Sequim Lavender Farms: http://www.sequimlavender.org/
- Sequim's Festival page: http://www.visitsunnysequim.com/index.aspx?NID=166

The cool, dry climate is very kind to lavender, which is no doubt why the Sequim-Dungeness Valley and surrounding areas host over 30 lavender farms, and why Sequim bears the title of Lavender Capital of North America. The growers team together to feature their wares in the middle of summer as the lavender fields reach their peak.

Tour many of the lavender farms, satiate your curiosity and appetite for all things lavender. (Lavender ice cream, anyone? It's remarkably good!) The week is interspersed with events such as a street fair where local artisans will offer you a plethora of one-of-a-kind handmade goods, live entertainment, fun for kids, farm tours, and more.

Sequim, Washington Tourism

You'll find unique shopping opportunities, art galleries, gifts, books and clothing in and around downtown Sequim. Sequim's Farmer's Market is active every Saturday (May through October), where you can find local fresh produce plus hand-crafted artisanal goods.

Sequim Attractions

A summertime view of the Dungeness Spit.

Dungeness National Wildlife Refuge, 554 Voice of America Rd West, Sequim, WA 98382.

http://www.fws.gov/refuge/dungeness/.

"631 acres of refuge include Dungeness Spit, Graveyard Spit, and portions of Dungeness Bay and Harbor. Dungeness Spit is 5.5 miles long and very narrow. The narrowest portions measure only 50 feet wide during high tides and sometimes breaches occur."[7] **Getting there:** Access via Kitchen-Dick Road to Lotzgesell Road. **Hours:** Dawn to Sunset. **Fee:** $3 per visit.

New Dungeness Lighthouse, in Dungeness National Wildlife Refuge, Sequim, WA 98382.

360-681-3494. http://www.newdungenesslighthouse.com/

Access to the Dungeness Lighthouse involves a 5.5 mile hike one way. (Check the tide tables before setting out!)

> **Tip:** 5.5 miles is longer than it seems but the destination and views are worth the trek. Boating and kayaking to the lighthouse are also possible.

Dungeness River Audubon Center & Railroad Bridge Park, 2151 W. Hendrickson Rd., Sequim, WA 98382. 360-681-4076. http://dungenessrivercenter.org/

Hours: 10a-4p. When the railroad line was discontinued, the railroad bridge over the Dungeness was converted into a foot trail that ties into the Olympic Discovery Trail. The rails and ties are gone; the bridge and trail now provide for comfortable walking through lovely scenery. The **Dungeness River Audubon Center** is located within the Railroad Bridge Park on the bank of the Dungeness River. The Audubon gives free field tours ("bird walk") every Wednesday, and the Center features taxidermy displays of the local fauna, including much more than just birds, an interpretive center and gift store. The

7   http://dungeness.com/refuge/. Accessed June 10, 2017.

website lists their schedule of events and classes for both youth and adults, along with suggested donation amounts, if any.

Morning Star Balloon Company,

468 Dorothy Hunt Lane (Sequim Airport), Sequim 98382

360-601-2433. www.nwplace.com; Email: airboss@nwplace.com

Ride a Hot Air Balloon into the Blue Hole for an aerial view ranging from Vancouver Island to the Olympic Mountains, the Salish Sea and the Strait of Juan de Fuca, the town of Sequim and the rural farms and fields of Dungeness Valley.

Olympic Game Farm, 1423 Ward Rd., Sequim, WA 98382

Phone: 360-683-4295; 1-800-778-4295.

http://www.olygamefarm.com/

Hours: Open every day 9a-3p, longer hours in spring, summer and fall. **Getting There**: From downtown Sequim, take Sequim-Dungeness Way north 2.5 miles (4 km). Turn left (west) on Woodcock Rd. and go 2.27 miles (3.6 km). Turn right (north) on Ward Rd. and go 1.4 miles (2.25 km) to address on the left. At one time the owners and inhabitants worked closely with Disney Studios producing wildlife films. The Olympic Game Farm officially opened to the public in 1972. Drive through the facility in your enclosed car and enjoy fairly close interaction with the animals. Feeding 100% whole wheat bread is permitted; bring yours or purchase at the farm. (Visitors recommend bringing two loaves.)

Sequim Museum and Arts Exhibit Center, 175 W. Cedar St., Sequim, WA 98382

360-681-2257. http://sequimmuseum.com/

Hours: Wed-Sat 11a-3p. Entry is free, though donations are welcome. **Getting There**: From the corner of Sequim Avenue and Washington Street (downtown Sequim), go 1 block north on Sequim Avenue. Turn left (west) on West Cedar Street to address, which is on left.

First Friday Art Walk in Sequim: First Friday every month – 5p-8p. The Museum and Arts Center presents the cultural history of the Dungeness Valley, including the recent find of mammoth fossils, as well as the artistic works of local artists.

Sequim Lavender Farms

These are some of my favorite lavender farms in Sequim, presented from east to west, and all of them can be toured during the **Sequim Lavender Festival** in mid-July of each year. Most of them (if not all) have gift shops that are open most days from June to September, and most offer U-pick lavender. Check the websites for exact details.

Purple Haze Lavender Farm, 80 Bell Bottom Rd., Sequim, WA 98382 888-852-6560;

360-683-1714. http://purplehazelavender.com

Summer Hours: 7 days/week, 10a-5p.

Email: info@purplehazelavender.com

Getting there: From East Washington Street, take West Sequim Bay Road going east. Turn right (south) on Bell Bottom Road to address. Farm is on the right.

Purple Haze Lavender Farm

Jardin du Soleil, 3932 Sequim-Dungeness Way, Sequim, WA 98382
360-582-1185. http://jardindusoleil.com

Scenic grounds, many lavender varieties, lovely gift shop. **Getting there:** From Highway 101, take the Sequim Avenue offramp and turn right (north). Continue north to address, farm is on right side of road.

Fat Cat Garden and Gifts, 21 Fat Cat Lane, Sequim WA 98382

360-681-6832. www.fatcat-lavender.com;

Hours: 9:30a-5p, closed Tues. Email: jeeandb@olypen.com.

Getting there: From Highway 101, take Carlsborg Road and turn right (north). At T intersection with Old Olympic Highway, turn right (east). Continue straight on Cays Road (Old Olympic peels off to the right) to Fat Cat Lane. Farm is on the right side of road at the corner of Cays and Fat Cat Lane. Ample gift shop. U-pick includes flowers and lavender. Take a stroll through the fields and gardens.

Washington Lavender, 965 Finn Hall Rd., Sequim, WA 98382

Phone: 360-452-4877; https://www.facebook.com/walavender; Email: info@walavender.com.

Hours: Mon-Sat 10a-5p.

Getting there: From Highway 101 in Carlsborg, take Carlsborg Road north to Old Olympic Highway. Turn left (west) at the "T" and go to Matson. Turn right (north) to Finn Hall Road. Turn left (west). Washington Lavender farm is on the right.

B&B Family Farm, 5883 Old Olympic Highway, Sequim, WA 98382

360-504-2585. www.bbfamilyfarm.com; Email: info@bbfamilyfarm.com

Getting there: From Highway 101, take Carlsborg Road and turn right (north). At the T intersection with Old Olympic Highway, turn left (west), to address. Farm is on the right side of road.

Victor's Lavender Celebration, 3743 Old Olympic Highway, Sequim, WA 98382

360-681-7930. http://victorslavender.com.

Getting there: From Highway 101 in Carlsborg, take Carlsborg Road north to Old Olympic Highway. Turn left (west) at the "T" and go to address, which is between Cameron Road and Barr Road.

If you just can't get enough of lavender and lavender farms, there ARE more lavender fields to see and lavender products to purchase! See Part 2C: Sequim Lavender Festival.

Sequim Bay State Park, 269035 Highway 101, Sequim, WA 98382

360-683-4235; Camping and group reservations: 888-226-7688. http://www.parks.wa.gov/582/Sequim-Bay

Hours: 8a-dusk, year around (day use). Picnic and Day-Use facilities available – and can be reserved either online or by phone at 888-CAMPOUT (888-226-7688). Enjoy beautiful forested surroundings with direct personal and boating access to Sequim Bay. Clamming, crabbing, oysters can be harvested in season with a permit. Check the website. Covered shelters, picnic tables, ball fields, and Interpretive activities.

Hardcore Hiking

Tubal Cain Mine Hike to B-17 Bomber Wreck and Buckhorn Lake:

Description: http://www.wta.org/go-hiking/hikes/tubal-cain-mine-and-buckhorn-lake

Map, Directions: https://www.fs.usda.gov/Internet/FSE_DOCUMENTS/stelprdb5359909.pdf

Forest Service Info: https://www.fs.usda.gov/recarea/olympic/recarea/?recid=47949

The trailhead is a 12.5 mile drive into the hills from Sequim. The hike to Tubal Cain Mine is 8.6 miles (13.8 km). At the 3.5 mile (5.6 km) mark, after some moderately difficult hiking is the B-17 wreck dating to 1952.

Sequim Restaurants

Alder Wood Bistro, 139 W. Alder, Sequim, WA 98382

360-683-4321. http://www.alderwoodbistro.com/.

Hours: Thu-Sat, Lunch 11:30a-3p; Dinner 4:30p-8:30p. **Getting there:** Very near the corner of Alder and North Sequim Avenue. Excellent food; a reservation would be wise.

Bell Creek Bar and Grill, 707 E. Washington St., Sequim, WA 98382

360-683-4825. https://www.facebook.com/BellCreekSequim/

Hours: Mon-Sat 8a-8p; Sun 8a-7p. **Getting there:** Cross street is South Brown Road, to the east of downtown Sequim.

Black Bear Diner, 1471 E. Washington St., Sequim, WA 98382

360-504-2950. **Hours:** Sun-Thu 7a-8p; Fri-Sat 7a-9p. **Getting there:** Located at the east end of Sequim very near the Holiday Inn. Good food, large portions, nice ambience.

Dockside Grill, 2577 W. Sequim Bay Rd., John Wayne Marina, Sequim, WA 98382

360-683-7510. http://www.docksidegrill-sequim.com/

Hours: Wed-Sun 11:30a-3p; 4p-9p; closed Mon-Tues. **Getting there:** From downtown Sequim, take East Washington Street heading east. Turn left on West Sequim Bay Road and travel east along Sequim Bay to the John Wayne Marina. Reservations recommended. It's right on the water, and the food is excellent.

Blondie's Plate, 134 S. 2nd Avenue, Sequim, WA 98382 360-683-2233. www.blondiesplate.com/

Hours: Sun-Thu 4p-9p; a reservation would be wise. Fri-Sat 4p-10p (reservations needed). **Getting there:** Blondie's is located in an old country church (*pictured*) which might have something to do with the heavenly food. Find it between West Washington Street and West Bell Street.

Emerald Northwest Grill and Public House, 179 W. Washington St., Sequim, WA 98382. 360-504-2083. https://www.facebook.com/ EmeraldGrillandPub/

Hours: Tue-Sun 11:30a-9:30p; closed Mon. No entry from Washington Street! **Getting there:** From Washington, turn south (towards the hills) on South Second Street and then left (east) to the parking lot behind Blondies. You'll see the entrance. Both the food and the brews are excellent.

Nourish Sequim, 1345 S. Sequim Avenue, Sequim, WA 98382

360-797-1480. http://www.nourishsequim.com/

Hours: Tue 11:30a-2:30p; Wed-Sat 11:30a-8:30p; Sun 11a-2:30p. **Getting there:** Located to the south just past Miller Road. Organic fare, fresh picked from local farms. You'll feel great after a meal.

Oak Table Café, 292 W. Bell St., Sequim, WA 98382

360-683-2179. http://www.oaktablecafe.com/

Hours: Every Day 7a-3p. **Getting there:** Located at the corner of West Bell Street and South Third Avenue. Why oh why does a delicious restaurant close at 3?

Old Mill Café, 721 Carlsborg Rd., Sequim, WA 98382 360-582-1583. http://old-millcafe.com/

Hours: Tue 8a-3p; Wed-Sun 8a-8p; closed Mon. **Getting there:** At Highway 101 and Carlsborg Road, turn right (north) and go to address. Restaurant is on left side of road. This place turns out some really fine food.

Pacific Pantry, 229 S. Sequim Ave., Sequim, WA 98382

360-797-1221.

http://places.singleplatform.com/pacific-pantry-artisan-deli/

Hours: Mon-Sat 11a-7p, closed Sun. **Getting there**: Located on Sequim Ave. 1.5 blocks south of Washington St. They prepare their own meats and make breads on site.

Sequim Kabob House, 173 W. Washington St., Sequim, WA 98382

360-504-2598.

Hours: Mon-Sat 10:30a-7p; closed Sun. **Getting there:** Located on the south side of Washington St between S. 2nd Ave and S. Sequim Ave. Authentic, flavorful Lebanese food.

Chinese

Dynasty Chinese, 380 E. Washington St., Sequim, WA 98382

360-683-6511. **Hours:** Tue-Sun 11a-9p

Fortune Star, 145 E. Washington St., Sequim, WA 98382

360-681-6888. **Hours:** Mon-Fri 11a-9:30p; Sat 12p-9:30p; Sun 11:30a-9:30p.

Mexican

Sergio's Family Mexican Restaurant, 271 S. 7th Avenue, Sequim, WA 98382

360-582-1006. FB: https://www.facebook.com/pages/Sergios-Haci enda/120562671294511

Hours: Mon-Sat 11a-9p; Sun 12n-8:30p. **Getting there:** Cross street is Washington Street.

Jose's Famous Salsa, 126 E. Washington St., Sequim, WA 98382

360-681-8598. http://josesfamoussalsa.com/

Hours: Tue-Sat 11a-7p. Fast food vibe. Order your tacos, burritos, etc., and help yourself to your choices of salsa at the salsa bar. Plus, purchase a bottle or three of Jose's Famous Salsa to go.

Thai

Sawadee Thai Cuisine, 271 S. 7th Avenue, Suite 31, Sequim, WA 98382

360-683-8188. https://www.facebook.com/pages/Sawadee-Thai-Cuisine/111652482204695

Hours: Thu-Tue: 11a-3p, 4:40p-9:00p.

Sequim Coffee Roasters, Kiosks & Coffee Lounges

Rainshadow Coffee Roasting Company, 157 W. Cedar St., Sequim, WA 98382

360-681-0560. http://www.rainshadowcoffee.com

Hours: Sun 9a-5p; Mon-Sat 8a-5p. The denizens of the Pacific Northwest love their coffee! Rainshadow is Sequim's own coffee-roasting company. They source top quality beans from small farms around the world and then roast them in small batches to order. Several blends offered.

Hurricane Coffee Company, 104 W. Washington St., Sequim, WA 98382

360-681-6008. https://www.facebook.com/hurricanecoffee/

Hours: Sun 8a-6p; Mon-Sat 7a-6p

Lodging in Sequim

Econo Lodge, 801 E. Washington St., Sequim, WA 98382

360-683-7113.

http://www.econolodge.com/hotel-sequim-washington-WA051.

A "green" hotel on the east side of Sequim. Offers free breakfast, is smoke-free and pet friendly.

Holiday Inn Express, 1441 E. Washington St., Sequim, WA, 98382

360-681-8749. http://hiesequim.com/

Olympic View Inn, 830 W. Washington St., Sequim, WA 98382

360-683-4195; Toll-free: 800-810-4195. http://olympicviewinn.com/

Sequim Bay Lodge, 268522 Highway 101, Sequim, WA 98382

360-683-0691; Toll free: 800-622-0691. www.sequimbaylodge.com.
Sequim Bay Lodge is located at the far east end of Sequim on Highway 101.

Sequim Quality Inn & Suites, 134 River Rd., Sequim, WA 98382

360-683-2800.   https://www.choicehotels.com/washington/sequim/quality-inn-hotels/wa151?pmf=tripbl&source=pmftripblaw

Sequim West Inn & RV Park, 740 W. Washington St., Sequim, WA 98382

Phone: +1-360-683-4144. http://sequimwestinn.com/

Sequim Cottages

Dungeness Bay Cottages, 140 Marine Drive, Sequim, WA 98382

360-683-3013.   http://dungenessbaycottages.com/.   Email: relax@dungenessbaycottages.com

Cottages are situated within a stone's throw of Dungeness Bay, and provide direct beach access and many other amenities.

Juan de Fuca Cottages, 182 Marine Drive, Sequim, WA 98382

360-683-4433.   http://www.juandefuca.com/ The Juan de Fuca Cottages, Suites and Lodge are situated right on the Dungeness Bay.

Rent kayaks, bicycles, and snowshoes at the facility, depending on the season and your interests.

Sequim Vacation Rentals

Brigadoon & Sequim Vacation Rentals, 61 N. Rhodefer Rd., Sequim, WA 98382

360-683-2255; 800-379-2256.

http://www.sequimrentals.com/list-vacation-rentals

Several vacation rental homes, by the day or by the month, in both Port Angeles and Sequim.

Sequim Bed & Breakfasts

Ambiance Bed & Breakfast, 774 Lost Mountain Lane, Sequim, WA 98382

360-683-2341. http://ambiancebnbwa.com/

Spectacular views of Strait of Juan de Fuca, luxurious suites, gourmet breakfast.

Purple Haze, 180 Bellbottom Road, Sequim, WA 98382

888-852-6560 or 360-683-1714. https://purplehazelavender.com/ info@purplehazelavender.com. This vacation rental is part of a working lavender farm.

Red Caboose Getaway B&B, 24 Old Coyote Way, Sequim, WA 98382

360-683-7350. http://www.redcaboosegetaway.com/

Private luxury rail cars situated around a Wildlife Habitat duck pond. B&B is not far from downtown Sequim.

Dungeness Barn House Bed & Breakfast, 42 Marine Drive, Sequim, WA 98382

360-582-1663. http://www.dungenessbarnhouse.com/

Secluded relaxing getaway surrounded by lavender and lovely gardens. Two well-appointed suites.

Lost Mountain Lodge, 303 Sunny View Drive, Sequim, WA 98382

360-683-2431; 888-683-2431. http://www.lostmountainlodge.com/

Romantic B&B suites and private cottages in acres of National Wildlife Federation Certified Habitat. Enjoy gourmet meals with ingredients from on-site organic gardens.

Sequim RV Parks

John Wayne's Waterfront Resort, 2634 W. Sequim Bay Rd, Sequim, WA 98382

360-681-3853.

http://www.johnwaynewaterfrontresort.com/index.html

Nightly, and weekly rates (stay 7 days, pay for 6). With individual cottages, RV sites and tent sites, this 'resort' is frequently full. We suggest you book your stay up to a year in advance. Find all sorts of John Wayne themed souvenirs and memorabilia in the office/mini-mart.

Sequim West Inn & RV Park: See full listing above under Lodging in Sequim.

Carlsborg

Carlsborg is a little town between Sequim and Port Angeles. It has its own US Post Office, but most of the area surrounding Carlsborg is technically considered a part of Sequim.

Find Carlsborg at the junction of Highway 101 and Carlsborg Road. You'll know it by the traffic light. Also at that corner are two gas stations (Chevron and Shell), one with a mini-mart, the other with a Blimpie franchise. There is also a Big 5 Sporting Goods store, should you need any last-minute sporting or camping supplies.

Fresh Groceries

The coup de grace for the junction of Highway 101 and Carlsborg Road is the **Sunny Farms Country Store**, located within a block of the intersection of Highway 101 and Carlsborg Road in the northeast quadrant. This is a typical country store that feels a bit like a farmer's market under a single roof. You can stock up on fresh produce, meats, vitamins, excellent salsa, ready-to-bake pizzas, and lots more, of course.

Sunny Farms Country Store, 261461 US-101, Carlsborg, WA 98382

360-683-8003. http://www.sunnyfarms.com/country_store.html

Carlsborg Restaurants

The Old Mill Café is located in Carlsborg on Carlsborg Road, but is listed with Sequim restaurants.

West of Carlsborg toward Port Angeles

Deer Park Campground. Deer Park Road intersects Highway 101 just before the Morse Creek "S" curve, and before Port Angeles. You'll see the Deer Park Theater and some auto dealerships at this corner. Take Deer Park Road to the south – this will be an exit on the *right* side of the road – and follow the signs. Deer Park Road travels eighteen miles up into the Olympic Mountains. The last nine miles are unpaved, narrow, and winding.

The campground is perched on a mountaintop at 5,400 feet in altitude. The snow doesn't clear out until close to June, and might return in mid-October. The road is subject to closure when conditions warrant, however walking in may be possible, a 7.6 mile (12.2 km) hike. Check the website for additional details.

- Campground status:

  https://www.nps.gov/olym/planyourvisit/campground
  status.htm

- Deer Park brochure:

  https://www.nps.gov/olym/planyourvisit/upload/Deer%20
  Park.pdf

- Obstruction Point Trail to Deer Park Campground:

  http://www.protrails.com/trail/577/olympic-national-
  park-deer-park-trail

Blue Mountain Peak. Drive upward on Deer Park Road a little farther, and you'll arrive at the top of Blue Mountain. Walk the Rainshadow Trail, a 0.5 mile (0.8 km) loop at the top of Blue Mountain with spectacular views – the Strait of Juan de Fuca to the north, and the Olympic Mountains to the south.

> **Next – Segment D: Hurricane Ridge in Olympic National Park!**

Getting there from the east: Enter Port Angeles on Highway 101 westbound. At the McDonald's, the westbound lanes become Front Street. Turn left (toward the hills) on Race Street. Road becomes Mount Angeles Road. At the Y, take the right-hand fork (Hurricane Ridge Road) and travel seventeen miles (27.3 km) into the hills to the Hurricane Ridge Visitor Center.

Getting there from the west: In downtown Port Angeles, the eastbound lanes of Highway 101 become First Street. Take First Street eastbound to Race Street. Turn right (toward the hills) and follow the directions above.

4D) Hurricane Ridge in the Olympic National Park

There's a reason why Hurricane Ridge is a top destination within Washington State's Olympic National Park: Stunning, and easily accessible, grandeur. Hurricane Ridge ranks number one on my list of must-see places on the Olympic Peninsula, and you might feel the same once you've paid it a visit.

The Visitor Center sits at just under one mile high: 5,242 feet (1.60 km). The mountain habitat is sub-alpine, with wind-battered and stunted stands of evergreens, and flowered meadows.

A late-spring view of the Olympic Mountain range.

Hurricane Ridge Visitor Center

Use the contact info of the Park Visitor Center in Port Angeles (Part 4E).

Summer: https://www.nps.gov/olym/planyourvisit/visiting-hurricane-ridge.htm

Winter: http://www.nps.gov/olym/planyourvisit/hurricane-ridge-in-winter.htm

Hurricane Ridge PDF Brochure: https://www.nps.gov/olym/plany ourvisit/upload/Hurricane.pdf

The Hurricane Ridge Visitor Center is 17 miles to the south (into the hills) of Port Angeles. This equates to a 35-45 minute drive from many of the Port Angeles hotels.

Entrance Fees: Olympic National Park fees apply, and are collected at the Heart o' the Hills Park entry kiosk. See Part 3F for additional details and situations:

- $25 for a 7-day pass for 1 vehicle and all occupants, or
- $50 for a year pass to Olympic National Park, or
- $80 for a year pass to all nationwide national parks (America the Beautiful Pass)

Check road conditions first.

This is especially important during the wintertime. Use phone or Twitter.

Phone: 360-565-3131 (recorded message). Twitter: http://twitter. com/HRWinterAccess

Hurricane Ridge Road is open 7 days a week during spring, summer, and fall. Winter hours are listed below.

Your experience begins before you arrive. Along Hurricane Ridge Road is a pull-out viewing area. If the weather is clear, a stop will reward you with an amazing view of Mount Baker, the Dungeness Spit, and the Strait of Juan de Fuca (*pictured above*).

Even if your only plan is to simply drive to the Visitor Center and back, the drive and the views at the Visitor Center would be well worth the trip. You'll find fantastic 360-degree views. To the south, dozens of glaciated and snow-capped Olympic Mountain peaks stretch the span of your view. A short stroll to the north opens views of the Strait of Juan de Fuca and a glimpse of the towns of Port Angeles and Victoria BC in the distance.

Hiking at Hurricane Ridge:

The area immediately surrounding the Visitor Center offers several very short loop trails, two of which are wheelchair-accessible with assistance. Two other trails may interest you:

- **The 1.6-mile trail to the top of Hurricane Hill.** The trail is partially paved. Reach this trail by driving beyond the Visitor Center to the trailhead at the end of the road. It's a wonderful hike with great views. We've seen folks in motorized wheelchairs on the paved portion of this trail. The paving peters out for the last half-mile or so, as the trail makes a final, steeper, push to the summit. Total altitude gain is 700 feet (213 m), a very doable hike for most healthy individuals. Remnants of snow remain on the ground near the trails through August, and possibly all year, depending on the season's weather.

- **The 2.8 or 3.8-mile (4.5 or 6.1 km) Klahhane Ridge Trail**. The first 2.8 miles takes you to the junction of the Klahhane Switchback trail. The last mile of this hike climbs 800 feet to Klahhane Ridge.

There are more hikes, of course. If you're a power-hiker, you'll find many miles of back-country trails and campsites available to you in season, many of them accessible from the Hurricane Ridge area. See the Hurricane Ridge PDF Brochure (linked above), or chat with a Park Ranger in the Visitor Center. Overnight backpacking trips require a Wilderness permit, obtainable at the Port Angeles Wilderness Information Center.

View of Olympic Mountain range from Hurricane Hill trail

Early summer is springtime high in the Olympic Mountains. You'll find innumerable wildflowers in their seasons. **There's also wildlife galore**. We've personally seen black-tailed deer, Olympic marmots, Steller's jays, robber jays, hawks, eagles, squirrels, chipmunks, snowshoe hares, Olympic grouse, and black bears in the distance.

The National Park Service provides and maintains picnic areas and restrooms at each of the more popular trail heads, including the Hurricane Hill trailhead.

Experience Olympic (www.ExperienceOlympic.com) offers eco-tours of the Hurricane Ridge area. More info in Part 2D.

While these pictures may give you some idea of the grandeur that can be experienced at Hurricane Ridge, nothing can truly replace being there and immersed in it yourself.

Hurricane Hill hikers in August.

Unique Fauna at Hurricane Ridge

Olympic Black Bear:

Hiking the extensive back country trails within the Olympic National Park is probably the best way to encounter the Olympic Black Bear, a subspecies of the typical American Black Bear. They do occasionally wander near Hurricane Ridge or down into the nearby lowlands surrounding the Olympic National Park.

This Olympic Black Bear found its way into an empty cow pasture in the southern foothills of Port Angeles.

Olympic Marmots:

The Olympic Marmot is found only on the Olympic Peninsula, mostly within Olympic National Park boundaries. It is a stocky critter as big as a large house cat.

Olympic marmot in a field on Hurricane Hill near its burrow

They make their home in both sub-alpine and alpine meadows, as well as on rocky slopes, all of which are found in the Olympic Mountain range. Marmots remain on the "Least Concern" list as 90% of the population lives within the protected Olympic National Park. Their numbers are currently estimated to be between 2,000 to 4,000 animals.

Hurricane Ridge in Winter

From mid-October and forward, 400+ inches, or thirty to thirty-five feet (9-10.67 m) of snow fall on Hurricane Ridge each winter. Despite the copious snowfall, the Visitor Center at Hurricane Ridge is usually open when the road is open. It provides a warm space, restrooms, and exhibits. A snack bar and rental shop are open 10a–4p during the winter season. Rent downhill and cross-country skis, and snowshoes.

Winter season typically lasts from late-November to late-March. The road to Hurricane Ridge is open from 9:00a to 4:00p every Friday through Sunday throughout the winter season, plus holiday Mondays.

Snowboarding at Hurricane Ridge

Winter Road Conditions:

Weather and road conditions DO close the road from time to time; it is wise to check the ONP "Road and Weather Hotline" before setting out. See Hurricane Ridge Visitor Center above.

Carry Chains:

This isn't just a suggestion, but a requirement for all vehicles traveling beyond the Heart o' the Hills entry point in winter. This includes your four-wheel-drive macho truck. If you will be driving a rental car, you'll have to obtain chains. Check with the car rental company about this. Or, Les Schwab Tire Center in Port Angeles at the corner of Highway 101 and Monroe Road can provide you with chains:

Les Schwab Tire Center, 2527 E. Highway 101, Port Angeles, WA 98362; 360-452-7691.

Winter Recreation Season:

The Winter Recreation season typically stretches from mid-December through the end of March. Hurricane Ridge doesn't provide world-class recreation, of course, but that's okay. It still provides an immeasurable amount of winter fun. For families, gently sloped wide areas provide hours of sledding, tobogganing, and tubing till the little tykes are plum tuckered out. There is no additional charge to use the kiddie slopes, other than the Park entry fee. (Additional fees apply to the ski lift areas.)

Snowshoeing, Cross country skiing:

Miles of high country open and partially forested country surround the Hurricane Ridge Visitor Center, should you like to step out and make your own paths on snowshoes or cross country skis.

Join a ranger-led Snowshoe Walk!

From mid-December through the end of March, 1.5-hour walks take place at 2 pm on Saturdays, Sundays, and holiday Mondays, weather permitting. Ground covered is less than a mile, and they'll provide both snowshoes and instructions. **Make reservations in advance by calling: 360-565-3136.** See additional info here: https://www.nps.

gov/olym/planyourvisit/hurricane-ridge-in-winter.htm (bottom of the page)

Hurricane Ridge Ski and Snowboard Area: www.hurricaneridge. com

For skiers and snowboarders needing more adrenaline, take advantage of rope tows and steeper hills. The ski area is open Saturdays, Sundays, and holiday Mondays from 10a–4p. Olympic National Park fees apply, plus ski lift rates for half- and whole-day usage. If you like, get yourself some ski or snowboard lessons while here. All the details are at the above link.

Hurricane Ridge is still clad in mountains of snow
on this perfect day in May

Next – Segment E: Port Angeles, WA!

Getting there from the east or west: Highway 101 runs through downtown Port Angeles.

Getting there from Hurricane Ridge: Return via Hurricane Ridge Road to Front Street. Turn left (west) and proceed to downtown Port Angeles.

4E) Port Angeles

If you're going to, or coming from, the north Olympic Peninsula, you'll likely stay in, stop at, or pass through Port Angeles. Which is great, because the authentic Pacific Northwest is embodied in its character. Port Angeles has a population of 19,038 according to the 2010 Census and is slowly growing. The Office of Financial Management estimates the 2015 population at 19,448.

Iconic view of Port Angeles from the vantage point of the bluff at Laurel Street, overlooking the Black Ball terminal and the Coho ferry leaving the Port Angeles harbor.

Port Angeles Map

Port Angeles, Washington has much to offer visitors and vacationers. It is surrounded by the beauty of the Olympic Peninsula and Strait of Juan de Fuca. It is also probably THE main hub for activities throughout the Olympic Peninsula. You may wish to allot more than a single day to your Port Angeles stay.

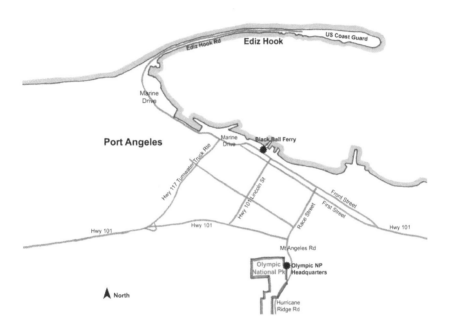

History of Port Angeles and Clallam County

The indigenous Klallam peoples have lived on the North Olympic Peninsula for millennia. Their territory stretched from the Hoko River west of the town of Sekiu, to Discovery Bay east of Port Angeles, and beyond. Some historians suggest the Klallam have lived here for over 2,700 years.

Two native villages are important to the history of Port Angeles. **Tse-whit-zen** was located at the base of Ediz Hook to the west of Port Angeles Harbor, while the village of **I'e'nis** was situated east of the harbor at the mouth of Ennis Creek, the name Ennis being an Anglicized pronunciation of I'e'nis.

The first Europeans to arrive in Port Angeles were Spaniards who came by naval boats. Captain Francisco de Eliza named the port in

1791: *Puerto de Nuestra Senora de Los Angeles.* A year later in 1792, this mouthful was shortened to the much more manageable and still current name, "Port Angeles," by the next naval captain to show up, a British captain named George Vancouver.

Evening view of Port Angeles from Ediz Spit

Downtown Port Angeles from Observation Tower

Washington Territory began to boom in the 1880s, and settlers poured into the Port Angeles area. Between the years of 1886–1890, the population grew from 300 to 3,000 enterprising individuals. The little trading post became a general store, hotels were constructed, and Port Angeles was officially incorporated. Clallam County governance was moved from New Dungeness near the Dungeness Spit to Port Angeles in 1890 after an overwhelmingly successful public vote. Port Angeles became the largest population center and also the hub of local commerce.

The town had its ups and downs. The nationwide Panic of 1893 arrived. Prices plummeted. The only bank failed, and when it did, the prominent businessman Gregers M. Lauridsen issued his own money for use **only** in his store. That detail notwithstanding, "Lauridsen Money," or "Port Angeles Money" if you prefer, circulated for ten years all over the Peninsula as an equivalent of US dollars.

Logging was one of the few money-earning enterprises in Port Angeles and Forks. With many square miles of old-growth forests choking the entire Peninsula, it was a clear bet that logging would provide a return to improved regional economy. A railroad line was built "from timber to mill," bringing the logs into Port Angeles for milling. The "Big Mill," built at the foot of Ediz Hook, served the area from 1914 until early in the Great Depression.

Despite the few fluctuations in fortune, logging boomed for years in Port Angeles and the west end of Clallam County. In the 1970s, environmental issues conspired against the industry. One by one, sawmills closed, thanks to activism over the northern spotted owl.

Today, logging is alive and well, though greatly diminished. Other industries have moved into the region to pick up the slack. The Big Mill now manufactures heavy recycled paper. Other manufacturing includes yachts and composite airplane parts. Tourism has increased in importance in the region, supporting hotels, restaurants, and attractions.

Port Angeles Information Center, 121 E. Railroad Avenue, Port Angeles, WA 98362

Phone: 360-452-2363. *(Pictured at right.)*

http://www.portangeles.org/.

The Info Center is sponsored and staffed by the Port Angeles Chamber of Commerce and is located just east of the ferry terminal near the waterfront. It's a great idea to stop by - they have free brochures galore, introductory videos, and people to talk to who can answer your specific questions about the various Port Angeles attractions and the area in general.

Additional Port Angeles Services

- **Port Angeles Newspaper:** Peninsula Daily News – http://www.peninsuladailynews.com/
- **Dungeness Line:** 800-457-4492 - https://olympicbuslines.com/
- **Rocket** ("Door to Door, SeaTac and More"): 877-697-6258 - http://gorocketman.com/

Port Angeles Yearly Festivals

Port Angelenos celebrate three yearly festivals. These are detailed in Part 2C.

- Juan de Fuca Festival of the Arts
- Dungeness Crab Festival
- Independence Day Parade on July 4th

Port Angeles Attractions

City Pier and Hollywood Beach: Near junction of North Lincoln Street and East Railroad Ave

The Port Angeles Pier is a prominent feature of the downtown Port Angeles waterfront. At the end of the pier is a four-story observation tower providing amazing views of the Olympic Mountains, downtown Port Angeles, Ediz Hook, and the Strait of Juan de Fuca. The buildings of Victoria, BC glimmer in the distance against the bulk of Vancouver Island. **Got kids?** They'll love the padded playground "pirate ship" near the City Pier parking lot.

Ediz Hook (also known as "The Spit")

Ediz Hook is a long, narrow, naturally formed spit of sand formed by the ocean tide action on the sand, silt and debris that washes into the Strait from local creeks. It is roughly three miles in length. The occasional harsh winter storm would disrupt the spit, however, it would rebuild itself in the weeks following the disruption. The City of Port Angeles eventually lined the Spit with heavy boulders on the side of the Strait of Juan de Fuca in order to prevent breakages. The tip of the Spit is now home to the Port Angeles Coast Guard Station.

Getting there: Follow Highway 101 into Port Angeles. The eastbound lanes (Front Street) empty onto Marine Drive. Continue straight on

Marine Drive through the paper mill and onto the Spit. You are free to drive the length of the Spit up to the Coast Guard Station.

Art Feiro Marine Life Center, 315 N. Lincoln St., Port Angeles City Pier, Port Angeles, WA 98362.

360-417-6254. http://feiromarinelifecenter.org/.

Hours: Every day 12–5p. The Feiro Marine Life Center is located at the entrance of the Port Angeles Pier at the north end of Lincoln Street in downtown Port Angeles. It contains various live marine life exhibits and participates in marine research. Inquire about presentations by marine experts. Adults and kids can participate in regular educational programs.

Conrad Dyar Memorial Fountain and Downtown Street Art: At First and Laurel Streets in Port Angeles and throughout the immediate downtown Port Angeles area.

Surrounding the fountain itself is a huge mural and benches; relax and rest, smell the sea-brine, and fathom the calls of seagulls. When you're ready, stroll through downtown Port Angeles and admire the murals, public art exhibits and sculptures displayed along Front Street and First Street in downtown Port Angeles, between Lincoln Street to the east and Oak Street to the west. Peek into the shops, and enjoy your day.

Port Angeles Heritage Tour, Port Angeles Information Center, 121 E. Railroad Avenue, Port Angeles, WA 98362. 360-452-2363, ext. 0.

www.portangelesheritagetours.com/

This insightful tour of old Port Angeles history dating to the late 1800s is also known as the **Port Angeles Underground Tour**. Tours last approximately 2 hours. Exact start times vary from summer to winter, however range between 10 or 10:30a and 2p. Check the website for hours, days, and prices, or call to arrange a private group tour.

Museum at the Carnegie, 207 S. Lincoln St, Port Angeles, WA 98362 *(Pictured)*

360-452-6779; 360-452-2662. http://www.clallamhistoricalsociety. com/

The Carnegie Museum chronicles even more Port Angeles history. Hours are Wednesday through Saturday, 1p - 4p. Admission is by donation. **Getting there**: Follow Highway 101 into Port Angeles and continue on South Lincoln Street to address.

Port Angeles Fine Arts Center and Webster's Woods Art Park, 1203 E. Lauridsen Blvd., Port Angeles, WA 98362. 360-417-4590; 360-457-3532. http://www.pafac.org/

Worthy indoor and outdoor art exhibits regularly presented. **Getting there:** Follow Highway 101 into Port Angeles and turn south (left) on Race Street. Turn east (left) on East Lauridsen Boulevard, and follow the signs to address. The Fine Arts Center is on the left side of the road.

Port Angeles Symphony Orchestra Presentation

http://portangelessymphony.org/.

The Symphony Orchestra started out in individual homes in Port Angeles in 1932 and has since expanded to an 80+ volunteer musician orchestra presenting an "ambitious yearly schedule." Concerts take place at more than one location in Port Angeles; check the website for details. Plus, with Saturday rehearsals free, you may get to listen in before heading out to your next leg of the Loop.

Olympic Discovery Trail Segments in Port Angeles: Hike or Bike

http://www.olympicdiscoverytrail.com/trail_maps.html

The Olympic Discovery Trail will eventually reach 126 miles long, spanning the distance from Port Townsend to La Push. Half of it is complete, offering several miles of Strait-side hiking or biking in Port Angeles.

- **Start at the downtown Hollywood Beach trailhead and head east.** The trail parallels the Strait for four miles. If you're lucky, you'll see otters, sea birds, bald eagles, and possibly the blows of a whale or two.

- **Start at the downtown Hollywood Beach trailhead and head west** along the Port Angeles Waterfront Trail onto the Ediz Hook. You can go all the way to the Coast Guard Station.

- **Start at the Morse Creek trailhead,** and take the trail either to the east or to the west. **Westward** crosses the creek over the bridge and continues to the Strait of Juan de Fuca, a one-mile (1.6 km) hike one way. The walk is scenic and peaceful. Once you arrive at the Strait, you'll be rewarded by views of Port Angeles and Canada in the distance. Nothing says you have to turn around at one mile – you can walk all the way to Hollywood Beach (downtown Port Angeles) and beyond if you so choose. **Eastward** will take you all the way into Sequim, if you so desire. **Getting there:** From Highway 101, turn in at Strait View Drive, just east of Port Angeles at the Highway 101 "S" curve.

Kayak in the Port Angeles Harbor and Strait of Juan de Fuca

The waters around Port Angeles offer fascinating kayaking, not to mention the likelihood of encountering sea otters, bald eagles, even large marine mammals. If you need to rent kayaks, check the companies listed in Part 2G. These companies may also offer local guided kayaking tours. How fun!

Visit Victoria, BC, on Vancouver Island (90 minutes away via ferry)

Coho Ferry leaving Port Angeles, heading to Victoria, BC

Arrive mid-morning in Victoria, spend a half-day exploring and enjoying, and then catch the last ferry back to Port Angeles. Details in Part 4F. For fares, sailing schedule, and reservations see Part 3E. (Walk-ons don't need reservations.) **Motion Sickness Sufferers:** See Part 5B.

Native American Port Angeles Attractions

Elwha Klallam Heritage Center, 401 E. First St., Port Angeles, WA 98362

360-417-8545. http://elwha.org/

Hours: Mon-Fri 8a-5p. This is an excellent place to learn more about the local Elwha Klallam tribe and their history, and to see ancient tribal artifacts. They have also put on display an exhibit on the recent removal of the Elwha Dam. The return of salmon to the Elwha River has been highly meaningful to the Elwha Klallam tribe.

Elwha River Casino, 631 Stratton Rd., Port Angeles, WA 98363

360-452-3005. http://www.elwharivercasino.com/ Check website for hours.

Getting there: Follow Highway 101 into Port Angeles on Front Street. Pass Lincoln Street and continue straight as Front merges with Marine Drive. Turn south (left) on Highway 117 (Tumwater Truck Route). Turn west (right) on West Lauridsen Boulevard, which will empty onto West Edgewood Drive. Continue to Lower Elwha Road and turn north (right). Continue to Kacee Way and turn west (left). Kacee turns into Stratton Road. Follow Stratton Road to address, following signs to casino.

Whale Watching

Whale Watching Cruises departing from the Landing Mall, 115 E. Railroad Avenue, Port Angeles. 360-293-4215; toll-free 800-465-4604. Contact: whales@islandadventurecruises.com. http://www.pawhalewatch.com/.

"Port Angeles is a premier destination for whale watching... Throughout the whale watching season the chance to view up to 5 kinds of whales is high, but it is the fall out of Port Angeles that gives way to some of the best viewing of humpbacks in the entire Pacific Northwest," according to GoWhaleWatch.com[8]. Catch a 4-5 hour whale-watching tour from Port Angeles from mid-May through November. See the website for details, exact dates, and to book your spot online.

Olympic National Park (ONP)

ONP Headquarters are located in Port Angeles:

Olympic National Park Visitor Center in Port Angeles, 3002 Mt. Angeles Rd., Port Angeles

https://www.nps.gov/olym/index.htm.

360-565-3130. The Olympic National Park Visitor Center provides an excellent introduction to your experience in the Olympic National Park. It has fascinating exhibits offering insight into the flora and

8   http://www.gowhalewatch.com/picking-a-departure-location.php

fauna of the Pacific Northwest, a short introductory movie and a book and gift store where you can purchase educational resources or guides for your Olympic National Park experience. Don't forget the old cabin exhibit and nature trail behind the Visitor Center building. **Getting there:** Follow Highway 101 from Sequim into Port Angeles. Turn left (south) on Race Street. Race Street turns into Mt. Angeles Road, continue to address. The Visitor Center is on the right side of the road.

Port Angeles Lodging

Port Angeles lodging is organized from east to west in each lodging category.

Olympic Lodge, 140 Del Guzzi Drive, Port Angeles, WA 98362. 360-452-2993;

800-600-2993. http://www.olympiclodge.com/ Elegant upscale lodging, probably the best that the Olympic Peninsula currently offers. Many amenities.

Days Inn Port Angeles, 1510 E. Front St., Port Angeles, WA 98362. 360-452-4015.   https://www.wyndhamhotels.com/days-inn/port-angeles-washington/days-inn-port-angeles/overview.

Located in East Port Angeles within a couple miles of downtown. Continental breakfast included.

Red Lion Hotel, 221 N. Lincoln St., Port Angeles, WA 98362

360-452-9215. www.redlion.com/portangeles

Located downtown on the waterfront and within a half-block of the ferry terminal. Unobstructed views of Hollywood Beach, Strait of Juan de Fuca, and the activities on the Port Angeles pier, plus direct proximity to the Discovery Trail (*pictured*).

Quality Inn Uptown, 101 E. Second St., Port Angeles, WA 98362

360-457-9434.   https://www.choicehotels.com/washington/port-angeles/quality-inn-hotels/wa099. Located at the top of the downtown bluff with great views to both mountains and harbor, within blocks of restaurants, shops, and the ferry terminal.

Port Angeles Inn, 111 E. Second St., Port Angeles, WA 98362

360-452-9285 or toll free: 800-421-0706. http://www.portangelesinn.com/

A touch of Bavaria centrally located in downtown Port Angeles. Many rooms have spectacular views of the waterfront.

Bed and Breakfasts

Colette's Bed & Breakfast, 339 Finn Hall Rd., Port Angeles, WA 98362

360-457-9197. http://www.colettes.com/

Very highly rated B&B on oceanfront estate; luxurious king suites with magnificent views, fireplaces, Jacuzzis, and private entrances. Located in the Agnew area west of Port Angeles proper. **Getting there:** Old Olympic Highway to Matson, north to Finn Hall Road. Turn west (left) to address.

Domaine Madeleine Bed & Breakfast, 146 Wildflower Lane, Port Angeles, WA 98362

360-457-4174. https://domainemadeleine.com/

Very highly rated B&B with nature-inspired decor located on the bluffs midway between Port Angeles and Sequim. Open year round. **Getting there**: Old Olympic Highway to Matson, north to Finn Hall Road. Turn west (left) to Wildflower Lane. Turn north (right) to address.

Eden by the Sea, 1027 Finn Hall Rd., Port Angeles, WA 98362

360-452-6021. http://www.edenbythesea.net/

Three spacious suites plus a cottage apartment on a bluff between Port Angeles and Sequim. Beautiful grounds, amazing view of both the Strait and the Olympic Mountains. **Getting there:** Take Old Olympic Highway

to Matson, north to Finn Hall Road. Turn west (left) to address. (*Pictured.*)

George Washington Inn, 939 Finn Hall Rd., Port Angeles, WA 98362

360-452-5207. www.walavender.com/ Email: info@walavender.com.

This B&B is a replica of Mt. Vernon. It is also a working lavender farm. Panoramic views in nearly all directions. **Getting there:** Old Olympic Highway to Matson, north to Finn Hall Road. Turn left. George Washington Inn is on the right.

Sea Cliff Gardens Bed & Breakfast, 397 Monterra Drive, Port Angeles, WA 98362

360-452-2322. http://www.seacliffgardens.com/

"Peaceful waterfront luxury" in a Victorian B&B on two acres of manicured grounds near natural forest. Located in the Agnew area, halfway between Port Angeles and Sequim. **Getting there:** Old Olympic Highway from either Port Angeles or Sequim. Turn north on Gunn Road, and then west (left) on Monterra Drive to address.

Five SeaSuns Bed & Breakfast, 1006 S. Lincoln, Port Angeles, WA 98362

360-452-8248. http://www.seasuns.com/

In Port Angeles at the corner of Lincoln Street and 10th Street.

A Hidden Haven Bed & Breakfast, 1428 Dan Kelly Rd., Port Angeles, WA 98368

360-452-2719. http://www.ahiddenhaven.com/

B&B with luxury cottages in a forested park setting by a pond is located a few minutes west of Port Angeles on Highway 112.

Vacation Rentals

Harborview Vacation Rental, 639 E. Park Avenue, Port Angeles, WA 98362

360-452-6014. https://www.vrbo.com/326027

Ideally located vacation rental very near downtown Port Angeles AND the Olympic National Park. **Getting there**: From Highway 101, drive into Port Angeles and turn south (left) on Race Street. Turn west (right) on East Park Avenue and go to address.

Explore other vacation rental options: https://www.vrbo.com/

RV Parks

Salt Creek Recreation Area

See full listing in Part 4G.

Olympic Peninsula/Port Angeles KOA, 80 O'Brien Rd., Port Angeles, WA 98362

360-457-5916 or 800-562-7558. http://koa.com/campgrounds/port-angeles/

Email: portangeles@koa.com. **Getting there:** Located about halfway between Sequim and Port Angeles, on the south side of Highway 101.

Elwha Dam RV Park, 47 Lower Dam Rd., Port Angeles, WA 98363

360-452-7054. http://www.elwhadamrvpark.com/

Walk to the Elwha Dam site. **Getting there:** From Highway 101, take Highway 112 to the north (right) and go about 0.5 mile (0.8 km) to Lower Dam Road. Turn right and go to #47. About ten minutes west of Port Angeles.

Crescent Beach and RV Park, 2860 Crescent Beach Rd., Port Angeles, WA 98363

360-928-3344. http://www.olypen.com/crescent

Park and stay within a stone's throw of an incredibly photogenic crescent-shaped sandy beach. **Getting there:** From Highway 101, take Highway 112 to the west. Turn north (right) on Crescent Beach Road, and go to #2860.

Shadow Mountain Grocery & RV Park, 232951 US-101, Port Angeles WA 98363

360-928-3043;   877-908-3043. http://www.shadowmt.com/

Located on Highway 101, 16 miles west of Port Angeles, just past Lake Sutherland at the Texaco station.

Port Angeles Restaurants

Bella Italia, 118 E. First St., Port Angeles, WA 98362 360-457-5442. http://www.bellaitaliapa.com/

Hours: Sun-Thur 4p-9p; Fri-Sat 4p-10p. Italian and Mediterranean Cuisine. **Getting there:** Located on First Street between Laurel Street and Lincoln Street.

Café Garden, 1506 E. First St., Port Angeles, 98362 360-457-4611. www.cafegardenpa.com

Hours: Off season: Open daily at 6:30a. Sun 6:30a-2:30p; Mon 6:30a-4p; Tue-Sat 6:30a-closing. June-Sep: open 7 nights per week. Casual family dining, lovely ambience. **Getting there:** Located at East First Street and Alder Street. Restaurant is on the south side of road.

C'est Si Bon, 23 Cedar Park Drive, Port Angeles, WA 98362. (360) 452-8888

http://www.cestsibon-frenchcuisine.com/index.html

Hours: Tue-Sun 5p-11p. C'Est Si Bon provides as close to a five-star French European cuisine and dining experience as you'll find anywhere on the Olympic Peninsula. The chef is herself French, trained and practiced in France. **Getting there:** Exit Highway 101 at Deer Park Road. Follow Deer Park Loop to address.

Chestnut Cottage Restaurant, 929 E. Front St., Port Angeles, WA 98362

360-452-8344. http://chestnutcottagerestaurant.com/ **Hours:** Every day, 7a-3p. Upscale American cuisine. **Getting there:** In east Port Angeles on Front Street (westbound Highway 101).

Downrigger's Waterfront Restaurant, 115 E. Railroad Avenue, Suite 207, Port Angeles, WA 98362. 360-452-2700. http://www. downriggerspa.com/

Hours: Sun-Thur 11:30a-9p; Fri-Sat 11:30a-10p. Northwest seafood, and more, all with a killer view of the Port Angeles Harbor. **Getting there:** Located at the intersection of North Lincoln Street and Railroad Avenue. Take the ramp up to the Downrigger's parking lot.

First Street Haven, 107 E. First St., Port Angeles, WA 98362 360-457-0352.   https://www.facebook.com/First-Street-Haven-100171 846704740/ **Hours:** Mon-Sat 7a-4p; Sun 8a-2p. Upscale American cuisine. **Getting there:** Located near the corner of E. First Street and N. Laurel Street.

Granny's Café, 235471 Highway 101, Port Angeles, WA 98363

360-928-3266. http://www.grannyscafe.net/

Hours: Peak Season: 8a-8p; Off Season: 8a-5p. Call ahead if you're not sure which "season" applies to your visit. **Getting there:** Granny's is west of Port Angeles and of the Elwha River, on the way to Lake Crescent and points west. Food is handmade by a passionate cook. **NOTE:** Everyone LOVES Granny's soft-serve ice cream.

H2O Waterfront Bistro, 222 N. Lincoln St., Port Angeles, WA 98362

360-452-4261. https://www.facebook.com/H2O-Waterfront-Bistro-403772299769962/

Hours: 11a-11p. Upscale, Pacific Northwest cuisine. **Getting there:** Located at the corner of N. Lincoln and E. Railroad Avenue.

Kokopelli Grill, 203 E. Front St., Port Angeles, WA 98362

360-457-6040. www.kokopelli-grill.com

Hours: Mon-Thur 11a-9p; Fri-Sat 10a-10p; Sun 2p-8p. Southwestern restaurant serving steak and seafood classics. **Getting there:** Located near the intersection of Front and Lincoln Streets.

La Belle Creperie, 222 N. Lincoln St., Port Angeles, WA 98362

360-452-9214. https://www.facebook.com/LaBelleCreperie/

Hours: Every day 8a-4p. Breakfast crepes. Lunch crepes. Dessert crepes. Memorable. **Getting there:** Located between Front and Railroad Avenue. If you have problems with lactose or gluten, this might not be the restaurant for you.

Michael's Fresh Northwest Seafood and Steakhouse, 117 E. First St., Port Angeles, WA 98362. 360-417-6929. http://michaelsdining.com/

Hours: Sun-Wed 4p-10p; Thur-Sat 4p-11p. Northwest gourmet cuisine (one visit might not be enough!). **Getting there:** Between Laurel and Lincoln Streets.

Next Door Gastropub, 113 W. First St., Port Angeles, WA 98362

360-504-2613. http://www.nextdoorgastropub.com/

Hours: Mon-Thur 11a-11p; Fri-Sat 11a-2a; Sun 10a-10p. "Eat, drink, gather." There doesn't seem to be anything "mundane" about the menu at the Gastropub or their seasonal microbrews. **Getting there:** Located between Laurel and Oak Streets.

The Coffee Cottage, 1921 W. Highway 101, Port Angeles, WA 98363

Hours: Mon-Fri 5a-6p; Sat-Sun 6a-6p. This cute little coffee shack with great coffee, tea, smoothies and snacks is on the right side of Highway 101 heading west, in the parking lot of an auto repair shop.

Toga's Soup House Sandwiches and Espresso, 122 W. Lauridsen Blvd., Port Angeles, WA 98362 360-452-1952. http://www.togassouphouse.com/home

Hours: Mon-Fri 7a-4p; closed Sat-Sun. Wonderful homemade soups, salads, sandwiches, in-house fresh baked goods. **Getting there:** Located on an in-town stretch of Highway 101; nearby cross street is South Oak Street. **Toga's Espresso** – enter behind the restaurant (Laurel to West Motor Road).

Turnip the Beet, 132 E. Front St., Port Angeles, WA 98362

360-797-1113. https://www.facebook.com/pg/turnipthebeet.pa/.

Hours: Mon-Thur 11a-11p; Fri-Sat 11a-3a; closed Sun. #7 on this "best of" list: http://www.onlyinyourstate.com/washington/wa-restaurant-gems/

Westside Pizza, 612 S. Lincoln St., Port Angeles, WA 98362

360-457-9900. http://www.westsidepizza.com/

Hours: Sun-Thur: 11a-10p; Fri-Sat: 11a-11p. Excellent pizza outfit. **Getting there:** Located at 7th and Lincoln.

Woodfire Grill, 929 W. 8th St., Port Angeles, WA 98363

360-452-0400. http://www.ldswoodfiregrill.com/

Hours: Mon – Thur 4:30p-8p; Fri-Sat 4:30p-9p. Stylish American tavern serves great food and does have a wood-fired grill and two fire pits outside. **Getting there:** In west Port Angeles near the corner of Eighth and C Street.

Mexican Cuisine

Fiesta Jalisco, 636 E. Front St., Port Angeles, WA 98362

360-452-3928. FB: https://www.facebook.com/Fiesta-Jalisco-Mexican-Restaurant-Port-Angeles-1463823407197227/. **Hours:** Mon-Thur 11a-9:30p; Fri-Sun 11a-11p. Authentic Mexican cuisine, full bar. **Getting there:** Located just east of downtown Port Angeles on Front Street (Highway 101 westbound).

Sergio's Hacienda and Cantina, 205 E. 8th St., Port Angeles, WA 98362

360-452-8434. https://www.facebook.com/Sergios-Hacienda-Cantina-Port-Angeles-100105863521888/. **Hours:** Sun-Thur 11a-9p; Fri-Sat 11a-10p. Authentic family Mexican restaurant, authentic food, reasonably priced, full bar. **Getting there:** Enter Port Angeles from east on Front Street and go to downtown. Turn south (left) on Lincoln, and then left into Sergio's parking lot before the 8th Street traffic light.

Asian Cuisine

Midtown Public House, 633 E. First St., Port Angeles, WA 98362

360-457-1647. https://www.facebook.com/MidtownPublicHouse

Hours: 4p-10p. "Asian Fusion" cuisine. **Getting there:** On north side of First Street at Eunice Street.

Chinese

Tendy's Garden, 920 E. First St., Port Angeles, WA 98362

360-452-3322.

http://www.tendyschinese.com/

Hours: Mon-Fri 11a-9:30p; Sat-Sun 11:30a-9:30p. Excellent Chinese cuisine. **Getting there:** Located between S. Race Street and S. Washington Street.

Japanese Cuisine

Okasan Japanese Restaurant, 1617 E. Front St., Port Angeles, WA 98362

360-417-3929.

https://www.facebook.com/Portangelesokasans/?fref=ts

Hours: Mon-Thur 11a-9p; Fri 11a-9:30p; Sat 12p-9:30p. Excellent Japanese cuisine. My faves: Variety of delicious sushi rolls and hot saki. **Getting there:** Near the intersection of Front Street and S. Penn Street.

Thai Cuisine

Jasmine Bistro, 222 N. Lincoln St., Port Angeles, WA 98362

360-452-6148. www.jasminebistropa.com

Hours: Mon-Fri: 11a-2:30p; 4:30p-8p; Sat: 11a-9p. Sun closed. "Home of authentic northern Thai and tapas cuisine." **Getting there:** Located between Front and Railroad Streets.

Sabai Thai, 903 W. 8th St., Port Angeles, WA 98363

360-452-4505. http://www.sabaithaipa.com/

Hours: Mon-Sat 4p-9p. One of the best Thai restaurants I've ever eaten at. **Getting there:** At the corner of West Eighth Street and South B Street.

Fast Food

Frugal's Burgers, 1520 E. Front St., Port Angeles, WA 98362 360-452-4320. http://www.frugalburger.com/

Hours: Sun-Thur 10:30a-10p; Fri-Sat 10:30a-11p.Really good hamburger joint, as far as fast food goes. **Getting there:** Located between S. Alder Street and S. Penn Street.

Frugal's

Fast Burrito, 940 E. First St., Port Angeles WA 98362

360-457-9272. www.fastburritos.com

Hours: Mon-Sat 7a-10p; Sun 9a-10p. Best carne asada burritos <u>ever</u>. **Getting there:** Located just east of Race Street near Tendy's Chinese Restaurant.

Got a Sweet Tooth?

Cock-a-Doodle Doughnuts, 105 E. Front St., Port Angeles, WA 98362

360-477-8144. http://www.cockadoodledoughnuts.com/ **Hours:** Tue-Sat 6a-3p; Sun 7a-3p; Mon closed. Handmade donuts … delish! **Getting there:** Near the corner of East Front Street and North Laurel Street.

Next – Segment F: Victoria, BC!

Victoria, BC is not part of the Olympic Peninsula, but it is oh so close - just twenty short miles (32 km) between Port Angeles and Victoria as the crow flies, close enough to warrant a visit from the Peninsula, if you are so inclined.

The Coho leaving the Port Angeles dock headed for Victoria, BC

Getting there requires a ninety-minute ferry ride on the Black Ball Coho ferry. Coho contact info is in Part 3E.

Getting there also requires a valid passport or enhanced driver's license.

4F) Victoria, BC, Canada

Victoria. Busy, but British-ly genteel. Victoria is truly amazing; she's magical, irresistible, delightful and wild, beautifully clothed in fir and flowers, embraced by the sun and the Salish Sea.

Victoria, Canada is situated on a calm inner harbor on the southern tip of Vancouver Island in British Columbia, Canada. This modern city is filled with Victorian and Edwardian architecture mixed with First Nations sculpture, buildings and totems. Nestled nearby are coffee bars, craft beer, and restaurants ranging from hip to funky to traditional. They vie for the attention of every flavor of foodie, serving tourists and locals alike.

Boathouses at Fisherman's Wharf in Victoria, BC's inner harbour

Victoria BC Map

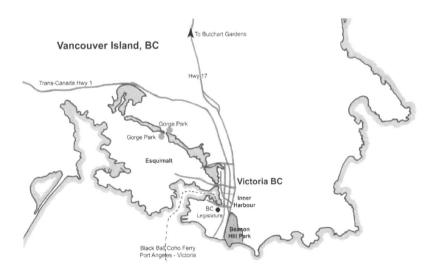

Downtown Victoria, BC

Downtown Victoria is walkable. If it's shopping you're after, head up Government Street to the modern Bay Centre mall and Market Square, catching all the little stores, boutiques, and tourist shops along the way.

Demographics of Victoria, BC, Canada

Since the discovery of this bountiful land, Europeans and Canadians have arrived to enjoy the easy lifestyle, pleasant climate and abundant beauty. Victoria itself embraces about 80,000 people, with a large population of retirees; the greater Victoria area, including her rural areas, total about 345,000.

The BC Provincial Legislature building in downtown Victoria

Victoria, BC, History

At its very beginning, it was home to several communities of Coast Salish peoples: the Songhees, the Saanich, and the Sooke, who had been settled in the area for several thousand years. They were there to greet the first European explorers, Juan Perez from Spain in 1774, and British Captain James Cook in 1778.

In 1843, James Douglas established a Hudson's Bay Company trading post on a site the Coast Salish peoples called Camosack, or "rush of water." Originally naming it Fort Camosun, it was also briefly known as Fort Albert, and later became Fort Victoria in 1846, in honor of Queen Victoria.

During the 1858 gold rush in Fraser Valley, British Columbia, Victoria became the hub for the arrival of gold-fevered miners from all over the world, where provisions for and transportation to the gold fields could be acquired. The population blossomed overnight from 300 to over 5,000. Victoria became the busiest seaport north of San Francisco, and the largest importer of opium from Hong Kong. (The opium trade was banned in 1908.)

Victoria also became the capital of the Province of British Columbia in 1871. As the city of Vancouver, on the mainland, rose to a more prominent role in shipping, manufacturing and commercialism, Victoria began to settle into her more genteel role as a seat of government, a popular tourist destination and a pleasant place to retire.

The Empress Hotel dominates Victoria's Inner Harbour

The Inner Harbour's wild scenery changed with the completion of the Parliament Buildings in 1897, and the Empress Hotel in 1908. The beauty and promise of the area also attracted industrial businessmen. Their legacies remain in such structures as Craigdarroch Castle, Hatley Park, Point Ellice House, Gatsby Mansion and Butchart Gardens.

Things to Do in Victoria, BC

Inner Harbour and Downtown Victoria:

Tea at the Empress, 721 Government St., Victoria, BC V8W 1W5 1-250-652-4422.

www.fairmont.com/empress-victoria/dining/afternoontea/

Cost: Can$51+/person. **Dress Code**: Sophisticated, smart casual, casual elegant

Yes, High Tea, also called Afternoon Tea, IS an event at the Empress. It is elegant and scrumptious. The setting is amazing, the service is impeccable. For an afternoon you are a celebrity. This is a popular event despite the cost; reservations will probably be essential.

Craigdarroch Castle, 1050 Joan Crescent, Victoria, BC V8S 3L5. 1-250-592-5323. www.thecastle.ca

Built by business tycoon Robert Dunsmuir in 1887 in the "Richardsonian Romanesque" style, this beautiful castle is filled with incredible stained glass and highly detailed woodwork typical of the 1880s. For architectural fans and history buffs, this may be one of the impressive things to do in Victoria. Well worth a visit.

Royal BC Museum, 675 Belleville St., Victoria, BC V8W 9W2. 1-250-356-7226. www.royalbcmuseum.bc.ca

Founded in 1886, this is a world-class, very thorough museum, several stories high, with numerous galleries featuring natural history, first peoples, modern history with native plant gardens and current exhibitions. See their website for past, current and upcoming exhibitions. This is a great family venue, and well worth the modest entry fee.

Royal BC Museum in Christmas-themed evening lights

IMAX Theatre, In the Royal BC Museum, 675 Belleville St., Victoria, BC V8W 1A1

1-250-480-4887. http://imaxvictoria.com/

Great IMAX venue for a thoroughly enjoyable, huge-screen mostly educational movie experience. Located within the Royal BC Museum. Check website for current shows and times.

Inner Harbour Tours, 792 Government St., Victoria, BC V8W 1W5. 1-250-708-0201. https://www.victoriaharbourferry.com/tours-services/harbour-tours It's an unforgettable perspective to see Victoria, BC from the water. At the same time you'll learn some of

Victoria's history and other information from knowledgeable captains functioning as tour guides. Besides, the boats are charming! The Harbour Tour season extends from March through October. Check the website for details.

BC Provincial Legislature Buildings, 501 Belleville St., Victoria, BC V8V 1X4

1-250-387-3046. www.leg.bc.ca/welcome

Tours are free. Request a tour online, or call the number above. Besides public or group tours, you can also follow a self-guided tour (available in 13 languages). Victoria, BC is the capital of the province of British Columbia, and the Provincial legislature buildings are right downtown bordering the Inner Harbour. Built in 1897, the beautiful and elegant architecture is representative of old Victoria.

The Government Buildings are beautiful day or night.

Whale Watching from Victoria, BC

Victoria is an excellent spot from which to go whale watching. It is usually a brief sail to whale feeding grounds off the shores of Victoria and around the San Juan Islands, and the chance of seeing any of multiple whale species is very good. Choose from 6 excellent whale-watch tour companies in downtown Victoria, all listed on Beautiful Pacific Northwest:

http://www.beautifulpacificnorthwest.com/victoria-whale-watching.html

Christ Church Cathedral, 501 Belleville St., Victoria, BC V8V 3G8. 1-250-383-2714. http://ChristChurchCathedral.bc.ca/.

The church is open for tours; entrance is free, though there is discreet opportunity to make a donation should you care to do so.

The Anglican Christ Church Cathedral has seen three iterations, the first dating to circa 1850. The gothic architecture in the current cathedral is remarkable, and well executed. The interior measures 93x140 feet; the towers reach to 122 feet above street level.

Beacon Hill Park, Douglas Street and Dallas Rd., Victoria, BC

Situated along the Strait of Juan de Fuca lie 200 acres of gardens, woodlands, walking trails, playgrounds, a petting zoo, water park and ponds. This is a great family-outing location, perfect for catching a sunset or the spectacular views south to the Olympic Mountains of Washington State.

Stroll (and shop) along Government Street, Downtown Inner Harbour area of Victoria, BC

Depending on the season and weather, a stroll along Government Street may be more entertaining than normally anticipated. Besides a multitude of restaurants, shops, First Nations crafts and souvenirs, you will find free viewing of chalk art (pictured - donations welcome, of course!), musicians (some with amazing talent, some not so much), booths with handicrafts of all sorts, and more. Here is where you'll find the requisite CAN$20 t-shirt, and for the less budget-constrained, exquisite jewelry, carvings, heirloom-quality photos, handicrafts, and more.

Chalk art in progress along Government Street

Roger's Chocolates, 913 Government St., Victoria, BC V8W 1X5

1-250-881-8771; 1-800-663-2220.

https://www.rogerschocolates.com/

Hours: Sun-Wed 9:30a-8p; Thur-Sat 9:30a-9p. Rogers' Chocolates had its start in Victoria, BC in 1885, and has now found international appeal. There are five stores in Victoria and Saanich Peninsula alone, offering a dizzying array of chocolates, flavor combinations, candies and confections.

Chinatown, at Fisgard Street south of Government Street

Authentic and the oldest Chinatown in Canada, though not as large as others in, say, San Francisco or Vancouver. Pass through or near the Gates of Harmonious Interest, down Fan Tan Alley and up and down either side of Fisgard Street. It's a historical area with interesting buildings formerly housing gambling clubs and opium dens, now filled with shops and restaurants.

Fisherman's Wharf, 1 Dallas Rd., Victoria, BC. 1-250-383-8300. www.fishermanswharfvictoria.com/ This is a fun place to take the family.

A ferry's-eye view of Fisherman's Wharf

Formerly a serious working wharf with eccentric characters roaming the docks (well, there's still that at the far end of the wharf), it is now surrounded by resorts and condos and full of colorfully painted floating homes and houseboats where you can feed the seals and enjoy great seafood or other ethnic chow. Get the highly touted fish-n-chips at Barb's, or snag an ice cream or mocha at Moka Joe's on the ground floor of the beautiful Shoal Point condo building. Check the website for other food and seafood offerings on Fisherman's Wharf. **Getting there:** On Belleville Street in front of the Coho Ferry, turn west and follow the road as it changes names to Pendray Street, Quebec Street, Montreal Street, Kingston Street, and Saint Lawrence Street. Turn west on Dallas Road – signs to Fisherman's Wharf are clear. You can also catch a Harbor ferry at the foot of the Empress Hotel.

Butchart Gardens, Saanich Peninsula

Butchart Gardens is a definite **must-see attraction** for any who appreciate a world-class garden continually maintained in impeccable condition by an army of 1,000+ gardeners during the growing season.

Autumn foliage in the Butchart Gardens Sunken Gardens

The only problem might be getting from Victoria to the gardens and back, AND returning to Port Angeles on the same day. If you're visiting during the summer season, Black Ball adds a fourth sailing, solving the problem. You can arrive and exit customs in Victoria at 10:15a, and take a bus (or taxi or rented car) to Butchart Gardens by 1:00pm or sooner. This allows for 3 or more hours to thoroughly enjoy the gardens, and then leave the park at 4:30p to return to Victoria.

Once in Victoria, you'll have enough time to enjoy a meal and a cold beer (or Irish coffee) at a pub of your choice before returning to the Black Ball Coho in time for the 7:30p departure. This schedule is very doable (I've done it comfortably), but your time in downtown Victoria will be limited. If this is okay with you, then go for it!

Or here's a HINT: If you're a beautiful-garden-aficionado, then spend a night. Enjoy your first day in downtown Victoria. Make your way to the Saanich Peninsula in the evening and secure lodging not far from Butchart Gardens. (I enjoyed the Waddling Dog Inn, listed under Hotels Near Butchart Gardens, below). Then be at the Butchart Gardens entrance gate *before* the 9:00am opening. You'll be happy I told you this little tip, because you'll miss the crowds, you'll have lots of time to enjoy the Gardens, and you can choose your next sailing time – either the 3:00p or the 7:30p return trip to Port Angeles.

Butchart Gardens, 800 Benvenuto Avenue, Brentwood Bay (Central Saanich Peninsula)

1-250-652-4422. www.butchartgardens.com

Jennie Butchart's vision of creating something beautiful from an exhausted limestone quarry is exquisitely fulfilled in flowing fountains, bountiful flowers and themed gardens. The gardens are open year round. You will not regret re-visiting these 55 acres of horticultural amazement during **each** of the four seasons, if possible.

Springtime brings an explosion of spring green and a rainbow of tulip blooms.

Summertime: Vivid blooms and spectacular fireworks displays every summer Saturday evening.

Autumn: Intensely vibrant fall colors overpower the senses during September through November.

Winter's barren beauty is supplemented by the Christmas Lights Display turning Butchart Gardens into a magical place after 4:30 pm throughout December and into January.

Victoria, BC Hotels

You may very well plan to return to Port Angeles on the same-day ferry. If, however, you want to extend your stay, here are some highly ranked historic B&B mansions, waterfront hotels, the world-famous Empress Hotel, and a few name-brand hotels. Just know that in the summer, rooms book up very quickly. Make your reservations early!

The Fairmont Empress Hotel, 721 Government St., Victoria, BC V8W 1W5

1-888-750-1414. http://www.fairmont.com/empress-victoria/

The Empress is an historic landmark in Victoria's Inner Harbour. The hotel itself opened on January 20, 1908 and has since, with consummate elegance, hosted the wealthy and famous, amidst many thousands of regular folk.

Abigail's Hotel, 906 McClure Avenue, Victoria, BC V8V 3E7

800-561-6565. www.abigailshotel.com

This boutique bed-and-three-course-breakfast hotel is for adults only (above age 13). It is located three blocks from downtown and the Inner Harbour. The historic 1930's Tudor building is a heritage property, beautiful, but no elevators.

Magnolia Hotel & Spa, 623 Courtney St., Victoria, BC V8W 1B8

1-877-624-6654. www.magnoliahotel.com

Boutique hotel in downtown Victoria, two blocks from the Inner Harbour, offering a mix of traditional and contemporary. Treat yourself to a massage and more at The Spa Magnolia. The on-site restaurant offers meals with a Mediterranean spin, with the Cicchetti

Bar offering tapas, wine and cocktails. Magnolia has been ranked #10 in the world with Conde Nast business travelers.

Oak Bay Beach Hotel, 1175 Beach Drive, Victoria, BC V8S 2N2

1-844-336-1458. www.oakbaybeachhotel.com

Stunning waterfront location near the village of Oak Bay on the east side of Victoria, an upscale hotel with full-service spa at the Boathouse Spa & Baths. Also offered are three dining choices: The Dining Room, the Snug Pub, and Kate's Cafe.

Embassy Inn, 520 Menzies St., Victoria, BC V8V 2H4

1-866-261-1161. http://www.embassyinn.ca/

Located near the Inner Harbour, just a little south of the Parliament Buildings.

Royal Scot Hotel & Suites, 425 Quebec St., Victoria, BC V8V 1W7

844-913-7905; 800-663-7515. www.royalscot.com/

Located about one block from the Inner Harbour, within walking distance to all the downtown attractions, restaurants, pubs and shopping.

Chateau Victoria Hotel & Suites, 740 Burdett Avenue, Victoria, BC V8W 1B2

1-250-382-4221; 1-800-663-5891. www.chateauvictoria.com/

Located in the heart of downtown Victoria, close to everything.

Huntingdon Manor Hotel, 330 Quebec St., Victoria, BC V8V 1W3

1-800-663-7557; 1-250-381-3456. www.huntingdonmanor.com/

Getting there: Step off the Coho Ferry. Walk 1/2 block to the right and then one block to the left. It's hard to get more convenient than this for the price, especially within the Inner Harbour district.

Huntingdon's incredibly helpful Heather. Note the complimentary newspapers and Victoria maps, all available in every hotel.

Strathcona Hotel, 919 Douglas St., Victoria, BC V8W 2C2 1-800-663-7476; 1-250-383-7137.

http://strathconahotel.com/

The Strathcona is a "Family-owned and Operated Entertainment Center," a full-service Victoria, BC hotel situated downtown in a renovated gold rush-era building. In addition to the hotel and a liquor store, the Strathcona also includes six additional facilities (night clubs, pubs). See website for details.

Hotels near Butchart Gardens

The following two hotels will put you close to Butchart Gardens, in case this option is important to you. For the record, Butchart Gardens is only a half-hour north of Victoria. Many more hotels are available in both the Victoria and the Saanich Peninsula areas.

Brentwood Bay Resort and Spa, 849 Verdier Avenue, Central Saanich, BC V8M 1C5

1-250-544-2079, 1-888-544-2079. www.brentwoodbayresort.com/

"Victoria's only five-star oceanfront boutique hotel, resort and spa." This resort hotel is located just minutes from Butchart Gardens on the Saanich Peninsula.

Quality Inn Waddling Dog, 2476 Mount Newton Cross Rd., Central Saanich, BC V8M 2B8

1-800-567-8466. http://www.qualityinnvictoria.com/

The Waddling Dog Inn is about 30 minutes from Victoria on the Saanich Peninsula, but it is also only 3.9 miles (6.3 km) east of Butchart Gardens. It is situated along Highway 17, and is very easy to find. The sports-bar eatery attached to the hotel serves excellent food and craft beer.

Victoria, BC Restaurants

Innumerable restaurants in Victoria! Listed are favorites.

Bard & Banker Scottish Pub, 1022 Government St., Victoria, BC V8W 1X7 (*Pictured.*)

250-953-9993. http://bardandbanker.com/

What a delightful place to stop and wet the whistle! The food is excellent, the crafted beer perfect, and the sidewalk seating is fabulous for warm summer days.

Blue Fox Café, 919 Fort St., #101, Victoria, BC V8V 3K3

250-380-1683. www.thebluefoxcafe.com

Reservations recommended. Excellent food, excellent service.

Canoe Brewpub, Marina & Restaurant, 450 Swift St., Victoria, BC V8W 1S3

250-361-1940. www.canoebrewpub.com

Located on the water at the foot of Chinatown, Canoe Brewpub serves handcrafted beer, burgers, seafood, and steak, featuring fresh ingredients from local suppliers. Watch the harbor in action while enjoying melt-in-your-mouth deliciousness.

Q at the Empress, 721 Government St., Victoria, BC V8W 1W5
http://www.fairmont.com/empress-victoria/dining/tea-at-the-empress/

Dress Code: Sophisticated, smart casual.

Reservations: Strongly recommended. Make your reservation via the above link.

Hours: 6:30a-11p every day. Open for breakfast, lunch, High Tea, dinner. Pacific Northwest cuisine sourcing local ingredients and the chef's personal herb and vegetable garden. Your meal will be fresh and unique.

Harbour House Restaurant, 607 Oswego St., Victoria, BC V8V 4W9

250-386-1244. http://victoriaharbourhouse.com/

This restaurant rates highly with me. They served the best salmon ever.

John's Place Restaurant, 723 Pandora Ave., Victoria, BC V8W 1N8

250-389-0711. www.johnsplace.ca

Though he was a gold medal winner in the 1976 Culinary Olympics, owner John Cantin says he's always loved honest diner food. He serves up Tex Mex or pancakes for breakfast, traditional clubhouse sammies for lunch; pasta, falafel or meatloaf for dinner. With his very creative menu, John has taken diner food up a few notches.

Murchie's, 1110 Government St., Victoria, BC

V8W 1Y2 250-383-3112. www.murchies.com

Murchie's is actually a purveyor of its own fine tea blends and roasted coffee beans. Murchie's is also a wonderful place to stop for refreshment. Stop here for late morning refreshment before heading out to enjoy the rest of the day in Victoria. The coffee is outstanding, and their sandwiches are special, even gourmet. Enjoy in house or take it to go. Murchie's brand teas and coffees are sold from space adjoining the dining area.

Nautical Nellie's, 1001 Wharf St., Victoria, BC

V8W 1T6 250-380-2260. www.nauticalnelliesrestaurant.com

Nautical Nellie's is located near the waterfront with a heated deck. It is a great place for excellent seafood or steak. The inside atmosphere is cozy and comfortable.

Next – Segment G: Strait of Juan de Fuca Highway (Highway 112) to Neah Bay!

Getting there from the east: The junction of Highway 101 and Highway 112 is 5.5 miles (8.8 km) west of downtown Port Angeles (Lincoln and Front Street).

But, as you head west on Highway 101 and just after Airport Road on Highway 101, you'll find one last very good chance to caffeinate yourself, and/or pick up snacks, teas, and smoothies at **The Coffee Cottage**. See Port Angeles Restaurants (Part 4E).

Getting there from the west: Heading east from Forks, it is possible to take Highway 113 north to Highway 112, joining it halfway through its transit along the Strait. This route works if your main goal is to visit Neah Bay and Cape Flattery, which ranks #3 on my Must-See list.

4G) Strait of Juan de Fuca Highway (Highway 112) to Neah Bay

Highway 112 intersects with Highway 101 at the far west end of Port Angeles. Immediately west of Laird Road, turn north on Highway 112, also called the Strait of Juan de Fuca Highway for reasons which will become obvious. Highway 112 is sixty-one miles (98 km) long, and its full length can be traveled in around two hours. (If you're coming from the west, take Highway 113 north at Sappho, which turns into westbound Highway 112.)

Map of the North Olympic Peninsula and Highway 112

The jewel at the end of Highway 112 is the Cape Flattery Trail to the end of the world, or as the Makah people assert, the *beginning* of the world. In fact, Neah Bay and Cape Flattery easily make it onto our short list of must-see destinations on the Olympic Peninsula.

These are the points of interest along Highway 112 starting at the east near Port Angeles, and ending in Neah Bay.

Salt Creek Recreation Area

A scant 4.25 miles along Highway 112 past the junction with Highway 101 in Port Angeles brings you to Salt Creek Recreation Area., which is a wonderful, mosquito-free place to camp. The locals get away by coming here for a weekend.

Salt Creek Recreation Area, 3506 Camp Hayden Rd., Port Angeles, WA 98363

360-928-3441. http://www.clallam.net/Parks/SaltCreek.html

Day Use Hours: Every day 8a-8p. **Getting there:** From Highway 112, turn north on Camp Hayden Road. Drive 3.5 miles (5.63 km). At the "Y," bear right on Tongue Point Park Road and go to the campground.

Or if you prefer, at the "Y," bear left, which will take you to a parking area near Crescent Beach.

The Salt Creek Recreation Area includes an excellent campground, playground, facilities for volleyball, basketball, softball, and horseshoes. Camp Hayden is also on site, including the remains of a WWII bunker. Foot trails take you from the bunker to the beach, and to Tongue Point and several lookout areas. The beach is a great place to scavenge for sea glass during low tide. There are also foot trails to nearby Striped Peak.

The **Tongue Point Marine Life Sanctuary** protects the many tide pools and tide lands along the rocky shores of the Strait of Juan de Fuca at Tongue Point. If the tide is out, you'll be in for a treat: views of remarkable diversity of sea life in the various tide pools. The colors can be hot and bright, in sharp contrast to the typical sandy grays of the seashore. At the same time, if you're lucky, there may be whales just offshore which may tempt you away from the tide pools.

At this spot where Salt Creek empties into the Strait of Juan de Fuca, Crescent Beach slopes incredibly gently for quite a distance into the water. The sun warms the shallow water, resulting in a perfect play area for both children and adults. Kayakers love the area.

There is something for everyone here, and you could literally spend all day here and not get bored.

Return to Highway 112 either by following Camp Hayden Road back to Highway 112, or by turning right (west) out of the parking lot and continuing west on Crescent Beach Road. If you choose this option, turn left on Agate Beach Road and follow it the short distance to "downtown" Joyce, WA.

Joyce, Washington

Joyce is little more than a fun little whistle stop, if that. There are no traffic signals, just a single two-lane country road, a gas station that is also a post office and country store, a very cool local museum that chronicles the area's past, and a couple restaurants.

Joyce Depot Museum in downtown Joyce

360-928-3568. http://www.joycewa.com/museum.htm

Hours: Memorial Day through Labor Day: Mon, Thurs-Sat 10a-4p. Rest of the year: Sat only,

10a-4p. Curator is Mary Pfaff-Pierce. **History:** The log building housing the museum used to be the train depot and was built in 1915. The railroad connected logging efforts around Deep Creek (near Pysht) and other points west to the port of Port Townsend in the east. The Spruce Railroad which ran along the north shore of Lake Crescent connected to this line. With the establishment of roads around the Olympic Peninsula, the railroad eliminated passenger service in 1930, and then was discontinued altogether in 1951. Logs moved via trucks from then on.

Joyce General Store, 50893 WA-112, Port Angeles, WA 98363

360-928-3568.

http://www.joycegeneral.com/;
https://www.facebook.com/
joycegeneralstore/

Hours: Every day 8a-8p. Joyce General Store houses a US Post Office, a general store, and a 76 gas station. Fuel your car, mail your post cards, pick up bottled water, chewing gum and snacks. As they say, "*If we don't have it, you don't need it.*"

Blackberry Café, 50530 WA-112, Port Angeles, WA 98363

360-928-0141.   https://www.facebook.com/pages/The-Blackberry-Cafe/218400148203658

Hours: Every day 7a-8p. Located near Joyce Bible Church. American cuisine; they serve a killer blackberry BBQ hamburger, and blackberry desserts are on the menu (in season).

On the Road Again

From Joyce to Clallam Bay is 36.5 miles (58.74 km) of mostly forested two-lane road. Very rural, very secluded. There WILL be logging trucks heading both ways. Do them a favor and pull to the shoulder of the road and let them pass. Don't worry about them holding you up later . . . not a chance! The guys driving these trucks are working hard to make a living, and you're on vacation, taking it easy, enjoying the ride and the sights. So just pull over. They'll whiz-rumble by and everyone will be happy.

Highway 112 along the Strait of Juan de Fuca

The road eventually heads to the coast, losing altitude as it goes. After a couple hairpin turns, the Strait comes into view. Over the next ten miles, Highway 112 tracks mostly along the coastline, offering long stretches of sandy and log-littered beaches and multiple easy entry points for beachcombing, picnicking, or simply walking the beach and grabbing photos of waves or whales.

Pillar Point

Pillar Point is a very scenic spot with parking and beach access. There is very little for you here unless at this point you really need to get out of the car and enjoy a break from the road. **Getting there:** From Highway 112 heading west, take Pillar Point Road to the right (north) less than a quarter-mile (0.4 km) to a parking area very near the Strait. Nearby, the Pysht River empties in a big "S" into the Strait of Juan de Fuca, as does the much smaller Indian Creek.

Eventually Highway 112 turns inland and comes to a "T" intersection and a stop sign. Here Highway 112 takes a right turn and continues traveling northwest. (Just so you know, turning left at the "T" puts you on Highway 113, which terminates to the south at Highway 101.) From the junction of Highway 113 and Highway 112, it is approximately six miles (9.66 km) to Clallam Bay.

Clallam Bay and Sekiu, Sister Cities

2.5 miles (4 km) separate these two towns which hug the shores of the Strait of Juan de Fuca at opposite ends of the small crescent beach that edges Clallam Bay. Get to either town via boat, or via Highway 112, the only road in the area that goes anywhere at all.

A quick way to acquaint yourself with the area is to stop by the Visitor Center located on Highway 112 in "downtown" Clallam Bay. Look for it on the north (right) side of the road where it bends sharply as it continues heading west.

Clallam Bay Visitor Center, Highway 112, Clallam Bay, WA 98326

360-963-2339. http://www.clallambay.com/tourism/visitors-center/.

Hours: Apr-Oct 9a-5p

Sekiu is in the background, from the vantage point of Clallam Bay

About Clallam Bay and Sekiu:

- Clallam Bay population as of 2010: **363**

- Sekiu population as of July 1, 2016: **28**. Yep, twenty-eight.

- Sekiu is pronounced "**SEE-cue**"

- The two towns share a Chamber of Commerce: www.clallambay.com/. Check the website for fishing information and local fishing derbies and contests.

- With an average rainfall of **ninety-five inches per year**, don't be surprised if a little rain falls on your parade. The good news is that July and August tend to be considerably drier than the rest of the year, with less than eight inches falling during the three months of summer. On the other hand, winter, spring, and autumn rainfall ranges on average from 23.79 inches to 37.95 inches per season. See rainfall charts in Part 5H.

- The average year-round temperatures in Clallam Bay range from forty-one degrees F (5 C) in December to 58 F (14.4 C) in August. Being right on the water, the weather CAN be chilly throughout the summer, although maximum temperatures can certainly reach into the low eighties for a few days in July.

- The area is at least partially dependent on tourism. Logging and fishing contribute to local industry. Clallam Bay is the general location of a county prison (deep in the back woods).

Fishing is a main reason for Sekiu's existence. If fishing interests you, there's Sekiu Charters.

Sekiu Charters, 444 Front St., Sekiu, WA 98381

360-640-4857. www.sekiucharters.com/

Fish for halibut, salmon, bottom-fish and more, out of Sekiu or Neah Bay with Robert Abner and his 32' sport fisher, *The Phoenix*. Robert has twenty years of experience fishing these waters, and can take up to six anglers, providing all the gear.

Lodging in Clallam Bay and Sekiu:

Curley's Resort & Dive Center, 291 Front St., Sekiu, WA 98381

360-963-2281 or 800-542-9680.

http://www.curleysresort.com/

Curley's offers dive and fishing information, boat/kayak rentals, and scuba equipment rentals/sales/supplies. Lodging consists of basic motel rooms or cabins.

Winter Summer Inn B&B, 16651 Highway 112, Clallam Bay, WA 98326 360-963-2264. http://www.wintersummerinn.com/

This is a traditional bed and breakfast in a charming home with a view of the Strait of Juan de Fuca. Gourmet breakfast is included. Some rooms have a private bath, others have a half-bath and shared shower.

Straitside Resort, 241 Front St., Sekiu, WA 98381

360-963-2100. http://olsons-resort.com/;

https://www.facebook.com/straitside/

Part of the Mason/Olson Resort. Motel rooms, some with kitchenettes.

Mason's Olson Resort, 444 Front St., Sekiu, WA 98381

360-963-2311. http://olsons-resort.com/

Great fishing location, rustic motel/cabins/camping sites, moorage also available.

Chito Beach Resort, 7639 Highway 112, Sekiu, WA 98381

360-963-2581. www.chitobeach.com/

Open April through October, Chito Beach Resort is located eight miles west of Sekiu. You can reserve one of six charming and rustic waterfront cabins. Each comes with a full kitchen with all supplies, linens, picnic table, charcoal grill, HDTV, wireless internet, and use of the grounds, including outdoor games.

The Inn at Neah Bay, 1562 WA-112, Sekiu, WA 98381

360-374-2225. http://www.theinnatneahbay.com/

Four miles east of Neah Bay, and owned and managed by the proprietors of Excel Fishing Charters. Your stay is discounted 20% if you also go fishing with Excel.

Restaurants in Clallam Bay and Sekiu

By The Bay Café, 343 Front St., Sekiu, WA 98381

360-963-2998. https://www.facebook.com/cafebythebay/

Hours: Mon-Thur 8a-8p; Fri 8a-9p; Sat 7a-9p; Sun 7a-8p. Tripadvisor ranks this restaurant #1 of one restaurant. Yes, there really is just one restaurant in Sekiu. I've eaten very well here. The place is not big, but it has earned its "favorite" status with locals and visitors.

By the Bay Café, Sekiu   *Breakwater Restaurant, Clallam Bay*

Breakwater Restaurant, 15582 WA-112, Clallam Bay, WA 98326.

360-983-2428. https://www.thebreakwaterrestaurant.com

Summer Hours: Sun-Thur 7a-9p; Fri-Sat 7a-10p. American cuisine, many menu choices. Restaurant is on Highway 112 and a stone's throw from the water's edge, resulting in great views as you dine.

Ozette Lake in Olympic National Park

Highway 112 meets with Hoko-Ozette Road 2.25 miles (3.66 km) beyond the turnoff to Sekiu. To get to Ozette Lake, travel the entire twenty-mile length of Hoko-Ozette Road. You will have seen many similar wooded miles along Highway 112, but it is Ozette Lake and the hike to the coast that makes this drive eminently worthwhile.

Weathered, mossy boardwalk section of the Ozette Triangle Trail.

The **Ozette Triangle Trail** is a nine mile (14.5 km) round trip hike of three, three-mile (4.8 km) legs: One leg travels from Ozette Lake to Sand Point on the Pacific Ocean. The second traverses the shoreline to Cape Alava, and the third leg returns to Ozette Lake. The land is some of the most primordial I've ever seen: forsaken, wet, but beautiful rain forest. Old mossy boardwalks put in place by the Park Service decades ago. A multitude of mushroom species on every side, some of them purple. Completely fabulous. Hundreds of seabirds—gulls, harlequin ducks, hooded mergansers, even bald eagles—congregate at the Pacific Coast. Fog might hang low over the beach at midmorning, but the afternoon is likely to be fog-free, even if the overhead cloud cover remains.

The **Ozette Ranger Station and Ozette Campground** are situated next to Ozette Lake and operated by the Olympic National Park. It gets busy in the summer. More info here: https://www.nps.gov/olym/planyourvisit/camping.htm

Ozette Beach and Pacific Ocean near Flattery Rocks NWR

Return to Highway 112 by backtracking the same way you came. Turn left (west) toward Neah Bay. From this point, Highway 112 tracks closely along the shore of the Strait of Juan de Fuca, providing multiple opportunities to pull over, access the beaches, and picnic, beachcomb, or simply get the knots out of the joints by walking.

Shipwreck Point

Shipwreck Point is a great spot to explore. **Hours:** Sunrise to sunset. Discovery Pass not needed.

Located a few miles east of Neah Bay at mile post 6, this 472-acre State Natural Resource Conservation Park is secluded with three miles (4.8 km) of tide pools, and old-growth coastal forest rimming the water. The road along these three miles provides multiple turn-outs so you can park and enjoy the views. If the tides are fully out, use the main beach access point to walk along the beach and check out the many tide pools.

The Whale Trail includes Shipwreck Point, and there is an informational plaque at the main beach access point. Much of Hwy 112 is higher than the beach; this will be the best vantage point for catching sight of gray whales, humpbacks, or passing orca whales. Sea otters might be cavorting in the kelp beds just offshore.

Neah Bay and the Makah Indian Reservation are just six miles (9.66 km) to the west.

Neah Bay, Washington

Highway 112 ends at the Makah village of Neah Bay, turning into the town's main drag, Bay View Avenue. You will have arrived at the distant corner of the northwest Olympic Peninsula, the tip of the wedge of land where the Strait of Juan de Fuca meets the Pacific Ocean. It's truly a spectacular place.

This entire remote corner is the 46.89 square mile (121.45 sq. km) Makah Indian Reservation.

Makah is pronounced Mah-KAH.

Neah Bay Marina, Makah Indian Reservation

On a clear day, Vancouver Island, Canada, is easily visible to the north across the Strait of Juan de Fuca.

The Makah Marina is the central point in town, filled with fishing vessels and rimmed with businesses. Fishing, and sometimes canoeing and whaling, are essential activities in this community.

The remote village of Neah Bay is considered the "*beginning of the world*," according to the Makah, or "Cape People," who have occupied these parts for longer than anyone can remember. Get a (simple) map of the area here: www.neahbaywa.com/map.pdf.

Cliffs of Cape Flattery, with Vancouver Island in the distance.

Additional Details about Neah Bay:

- Neah Bay population as of 2010: **865**. Population estimates in 2014 suggest a current Neah Bay population of 1,002.

- The town is named for Chief Dee-Ah, pronounced NEE-ah in the Makah tongue

- The tribe celebrates its culture, extended family, connections to related tribes, and US citizenship with a yearly festival, **Makah Days**. Visitors are welcome; see Part 2C.

- Fishing and tourism support the local economy.

- The Neah Bay Chamber of Commerce represents both tribal and private businesses at the west end of the North Olympic Peninsula: www.neahbaywa.com/

- The Coast Guard has a presence in Neah Bay. The Coast Guard also has a cutter named the *Neah Bay*. The cutter is stationed in Cleveland, OH.

- Average rainfall in Neah Bay is a cool 99.5 inches per year. Rain preparations are recommended!

Things to Do in Neah Bay

A Makah Recreation Pass ($10) is required for most activities and attractions inside the Makah Indian Reservation. Passes are good for an entire year, and can be obtained at the locations listed here: www.Makah.com/activities/.

Makah Museum and Research Center, 1880 Bayview Avenue, Neah Bay, WA 98357

360-645-2711. www.MakahMuseum.com/

Hours: Daily 10a-5p; closed New Year's Day, Thanksgiving and Christmas and possibly during inclement weather. **Entrance Fee:** Adults $5.00; Senior Citizens (62 and older), Students and Military $4.00; children five and under are free.

The Makah Museum is on the left just before you roll into Neah Bay proper. It is a world-class museum depicting life in a long house, and other aspects of Makah life in the past, such as hunting, fishing, and plying the waters of the Pacific in long canoes. A revolving exhibit includes photos, carvings, clothing and baskets. The museum is also home to ancient artifacts dating back 500 years, recovered from an archeological site of a Makah village in Ozette, WA. The ethnobotanical garden has been developed containing many native plants and outdoor exhibits. So many things to see! Need souvenirs? No problem: they also offer a wonderful gift shop, of course.

Cape Flattery Trail

The Cape Flattery Trailhead is on Cape Loop Road. From Bayview Avenue (Highway 112) in Neah Bay, turn left on Fort Street. Go three blocks to 3rd Avenue and turn right. Go one block and turn left on Cape Flattery Road. Cape Flattery Road turns into Cape Loop Road after 3.2 miles (5.1 km). Keep going for 4.5 miles (7.23 km) on Cape Loop Road. When the road forks, stay to the left, but by then, you will already see the parking lot and probably lots of cars at the trailhead. **A Makah Recreation Pass** is required to park at the trail head.

Sign in the parking lot marking the way to the Cape Flattery Trail

From the trailhead, the Cape Flattery Trail starts out fairly steeply downhill for a short piece, then wends its way for 0.75 mile (1.2 km) through quintessential Pacific Northwest rain forest to its terminus on a 100-foot bluff overlooking the Pacific Ocean. The hike takes about twenty minutes one way and is an easy walk, with the exception of the climb back up to the road. It passes through various sections of boardwalk, packed earth (depending on the weather, this could read "puddles"), and steps, winding through cedar, fir and fern. As you near the end of the trail, you find several side trails to vantage points toward the west, north, and northeast.

View of a spindly sea stack from one of the fenced viewpoints along the Cape Flattery Trail

At the far end of the Cape Flattery Trail, you will have arrived at the westernmost point of the lower forty-eight states. From an elevated platform you are rewarded with panoramic views taking in the Pacific Ocean, Tatoosh Island and its lighthouse, and in the distance, Vancouver Island. Sea lions, seals, puffins, seabirds, otters, and migrating whales populate the area and might be seen from various railed platforms at the edges of the towering cliffs across which you have just hiked. Dramatic sea stacks are alive with sea birds and sea gulls clinging to cliff edges. Wild waves below have crashed against these cliffs for millennia, undercutting and eroding their bases, creating rocky caves and coves below. Stand still and wait for a moment or two; you'll feel the power of the waves under your feet.

Tatoosh Island sits just off the tip of Cape Flattery and is clearly visible. It is topped by the Tatoosh Island Lighthouse. The lighthouse was first constructed in 1857 by the US Coast Guard, who purchased the island from the Makah Nation. Named for a chief of the Makah Nation, Tatooche, the island was used as a summer base for hunting whales and salmon fishing. The lighthouse is now automated and the Island has returned to the Makah Nation, who maintain the grounds that once were, and still are, considered highly sacred.

Tatoosh Island and Lighthouse

Makah Days

http://makah.com/activities/makah-days/

Makah Days is a reunion festival that occurs yearly on the weekend closest to August 26. Tribal members who live elsewhere, and other related tribes are invited to come together for a three-day festival commemorating thousands of years of ancient Makah culture and the anniversary of becoming US citizens. There are tournaments and physical and endurance tests, traditional dancing, talent shows, fireworks, and salmon bakes. These and additional activities are meant to *"honor our ancient Makah customs and traditions and commemorate the history of our Tribe."*[9] The general public is more than welcome to come and join the fun. Do browse the street fair. **HINT:** If you plan to stay overnight, the tribe suggests you book a room early in the planning stages of your visit, as the rooms in Neah Bay fill up very fast. If there's no room at the inn, none in Sekiu or Clallam Bay, and no plans to camp, you could try finding room in Port Angeles or Forks.

Neah Bay Lodging

There are more options than just the following, especially if camping with a tent or RV, including moorage at the Makah Marina. Check the Neah Bay website for additional possibilities: www.makah.com/business/. Plus, if rooms are full in Neah Bay, there may be lodging available a few miles away in Sekiu.

Hobuck Beach Resort, 2726 Makah Passage, Makah Indian Reservation, Neah Bay, WA 98357

360-645-2339. www.hobuckbeachresort.com/

---

9   https://issuu.com/pnwmarketplace/docs/i20160511155640598/174, Special Sections - North Olympic Peninsula Guide, Spring-Summer 2016 Accessed June 15, 2017

Hobuck Beach Resort is located just south of Neah Bay along Hobuck Beach, with easy beach access and spectacular views. You'll find tent camping, full hook-up RV sites and a variety of fully supplied cabins, plus free showers, picnic tables and wireless internet. Hobuck Beach Resort fills up *fast*.

Cape Motel and RV Park, 1510 Bay View Avenue, Neah Bay, WA 98357

360-645-2250. http://cape-resort.com/

Cape Motel and RV Park is located in downtown Neah Bay overlooking the Makah Marina, and is a scant fifteen-minute drive to Pacific Ocean beaches and other sites.

Butler's Motel, 910 Woodland Avenue, Neah Bay, WA 98357

360-640-0948. Simple rooms have all you need, including TV and HD channels, coffeemakers, mini-fridges, microwaves. Pet friendly. RV hookups. Reservations are probably essential, even in the offseason.

Neah Bay Restaurants

Linda's Wood Fired Kitchen, 1110 Bay View Avenue, Neah Bay, WA 98357

360-640-2192. https://www.facebook.com/LindasWoodFiredFood49/

Hours: Wed-Mon 12p-8p. Closed Tues. Serves Italian, American, pizza, soups, salads.

Pat's Place, 1111 Bay View Avenue, Neah Bay, WA 98357

Unofficial FB page: https://www.facebook.com/pages/Pats-Place/439387872767943

Hours: Tue-Wed 12p-6p; Thur 12p-5:30p; Fri 12p-6p; Sat 12p-5:30p. Closed Sun-Mon.

Pat's Place serves Indian fry bread and tacos along with other Mexican and American cuisine. You may even get pie for dessert.

Makah Mini-Mart, 925 Bayview Avenue, Neah Bay, WA 98357

360-645-2802. http://makah.com/business/

Hours: Sun-Thur 7:30a-9p; Fri-Sat 7:30a-11p. Summer: Open an extra hour in the evening.

Gas station and mini-mart. Deli and pizza.

The Warmhouse, 1431 Bay View Avenue, Neah Bay, WA 98357.

360-645-2077.

https://www.facebook.com/The-Warmhouse-168510479985200/.

Hours: Sun-Thur 7a-7p; Fri-Sat 7a-8p. The Warmhouse offers American cuisine for breakfast, lunch, and dinner, including seafood, steaks, burgers.

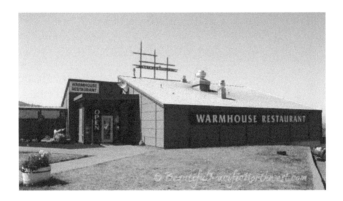

Shi Shi Beach in Olympic National Park

Like the Ozette beaches, Shi Shi (pronounced **"Shy Shy"**) is a captivating place, a crescent beach with plentiful sea life, sea stacks, and tide pools. It makes for a particularly dramatic beachscape.

Getting there: From Bayview Avenue in downtown Neah Bay heading west, follow the yellow lines on the pavement onto Cape Flattery Road. Travel 2.5 miles and turn left on Hobuck Road, which crosses the Wa'atch River. After the bridge keep going straight, following the signs for the Fish Hatchery. The signs will put you on Tsoo-Yess Beach Road, and this will turn into Fish Hatchery Road. Once you're on Fish Hatchery Road you'll find the Shi Shi Beach Trailhead within a quarter of a mile. The trailhead is a scant 6.4 miles (10.28 km) from Bayview Avenue in downtown Neah Bay.

The Shi Shi Beach Trail is a bit more than two miles long (4.5 miles/7.24 km round trip); an easy, almost flat hike through the same type of rain forest as that at Cape Flattery. The trail is well maintained, but apt to be wet and slippery. It is a combination of boardwalk and earth. The 1.7 miles (2.7 km) of trail on the Makah Reservation are pet-friendly, however, no pets are allowed once one enters the Olympic National Park, leaving Rover pretty much out of luck, assuming you will hike all the way to Shi Shi Beach.

Once on the shoreline, it is another 2.3 miles (3.7 km) one way to the Point of Arches surrounded with dozens of sea stacks: a glorious walk that will saturate the senses with scenery, sea life, and pungent briny breezes. On the way to Point of Arches you'll ford Petroleum Creek and pass the Shi Shi camping area.

Camping on Shi Shi Beach IS permitted. You will need permits.

- You will need a Makah Recreation Permit to park in designated parking spots on the Makah reservation (one pass per vehicle). There is parking at the trailhead, but overnight parking is located about one mile before the trailhead, across from Tsoo-Yess Beach, and costs $10/ night). Sorry, no room for RVs.

- You will also need an Olympic National Park pass (Part 3F).

- You will also need an ONP wilderness permit.

It IS possible to hike along the beach all the way to Rialto Beach. If this is on your list of to-dos, be sure to take a tide chart and topographical map with you, so you don't get caught by the tides.

Plan for 1-2 days to hike 15 miles from Shi Shi Beach Trailhead to the Ozette Trailhead, and another 3-4 days to cover the 20 miles along the coast from Ozette to Rialto Beach. Campground reservations may be required! For more info see: https://www.nps.gov/olym/planyourvisit/north-coast-route.htm

Return to Highway 101

I always have a hard time pulling myself away from the beginning of the world. All I can say is: it is so, so magical. I hope you have time for it in your schedule.

To head back to Highway 101, return to Highway 112 and go east:

- All the way to Port Angeles and the junction of Highway 101, or . . .

- Take Highway 113 by going straight at the junction of Highway 112 and 113, all the way to Highway 101 at the little hiccup in the road known as Sappho.

Next – H: Elwha Valley in Olympic National Park!

Getting there from the east: Olympic Hot Springs Road intersects Highway 101 three miles (5 km) west of the Highway 112 junction (west of Port Angeles) and immediately east of the Elwha River. If you're traveling west from Port Angeles and cross the bridge over Elwha River, you've gone too far.

Turn onto Olympic Hot Springs Road, which is the main road in Elwha Valley.

Getting there from the west: The Elwha Valley is 11.5 miles (18.5 km) east of Lake Crescent. Take Highway 101 eastbound, cross the Elwha Bridge, and immediately turn right (south) on Olympic Hot Springs Road.

4H) Elwha Valley in the Olympic National Park

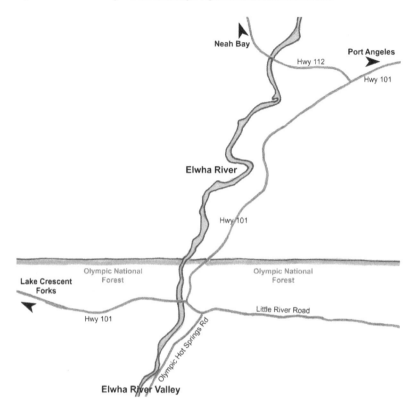

The Elwha Valley is home to **Madison Falls**, the wild Olympic Hot Springs, the bones of Glines Dam, and all sorts of hiking trails and cool scenery. **But: Road Closures are Possible!**

The problem is: the Elwha River has been a bit ornery lately. Flooding and river course changes over the last couple years mean the Elwha cannot currently be relied upon to remain inside its banks. The river flooded badly at the end of 2015, and washed out the road past the Olympic National Park (ONP) entry kiosk. The road remained closed for over a year. It finally opened in early 2017 – and then closed again due to more flood damage and repair work. So while Madison Creek Falls is consistently open for visiting, the road beyond the falls may or may not be open to vehicles, though you can certainly hike or bike in if you wish. **Check current road conditions here**: https://www.nps.gov/olym/planyourvisit/current-road-conditions.htm

Madison Falls

Madison Falls, or Madison Creek Falls. The falls go by both names, with the former apparently being the current official version. Whatever you call it, it's definitely worth a visit! Find the falls just nine or so miles (14.5 km) west of Port Angeles. It is within the Olympic National Park limits; however, the Park's fee area commences just a few meters beyond the Madison Creek Falls parking lot. You can visit the falls any time, no entrance fee required.

Madison Falls

Height of the Falls: Various sources offer differing heights for Madison Creek Falls. The "official" surveyed height is **76-feet tall** (23 m), according to the World Waterfall Database. Some of this measurement may include sections of waterfall immediately above the main, dramatic, waterfall.

Getting there: From Highway 101 west of Port Angeles and at the east end of the Elwha Bridge, turn south on Olympic Hot Springs Road and travel for two miles (3.22 km). The turn off to the falls is well marked. If you arrive at the Olympic Park entrance kiosk, you've gone too far (but you won't miss it).

Amenities at Madison Falls:

- Ample picnic area in view of the snow-capped Olympic Mountain Range *(pictured next page)*

- "Facilities" - a non-flushing hole under a toilet seat in a typical vented restroom.

- Completely paved trail to the falls, including railings in some areas, not that the exceedingly short trail is anything less than level or smoothly paved.

- Two benches for sitting and enjoying

- Temperate rain forest ambience, including and certainly not limited to giant trees and giant tree stumps, ubiquitous moss, and the nearby presence of the Elwha River.

- Beautiful views and surrounding countryside

Madison Falls is a very cool attraction, and a whole lot more impressive in person than on paper. We highly recommend a look-see.

Glines Canyon Dam Spillway Overlook

Glines Canyon Dam was removed in 2013. But Olympic Hot Springs Road still goes by the spillway overlook point and its ample parking lot. It's an impressive view. The spillway can also be reached from Whiskey Bend Road on the east side of the Elwha.

Whiskey Bend Trail

Just past the Elwha Ranger Station, Whiskey Bend Road branches to the left. 500 feet (152.4 m) on Whiskey Bend Road takes you to the trailhead for the Pacific NW Trail and Hurricane Ridge.

View of Geyser Valley along the Elwha River Trail

Olympic Hot Springs Road crosses over and then parallels the Elwha on its west bank, while Whiskey Bend Road parallels the river on the east bank. Drive 4.2 miles (6.76 km) to the Whiskey Bend Trailhead. Whiskey Bend Trail will connect you to several scenic and historic areas.

Goblin's Gate

Goblin's Gate is a twenty-foot wide (6.1 m) gorge, a part of the Grand Canyon of the Elwha where the river takes a sharp right and squeezes through "the throat of a monster." The jagged sides of the chasm resembled pained goblin faces to the explorers of the Seattle Press Expedition in 1889, hence the name.

Goblin's Gate

Getting there: Take the Whiskey Bend Trail to the Geyser Valley Trail 1.7 miles (2.74 km) past the Whiskey Bend trailhead. Follow the Geyser Valley Trail to Goblin's Gate.

Grand Canyon of the Elwha

Despite being nowhere near the width and scope of the one-and-only Grand Canyon, it is still quite impressive to witness the Elwha River pound its way through a narrow, steep-sided scenic gorge, given that the Elwha is typically seen coursing in an "S" shape through a wide valley.

Getting there: From the Whiskey Bend trailhead, take the Geyser Valley trail 3.5 miles (5.6 km), 0.5 miles (0.8 km) past Humes Ranch. This trail ends at the **Dodger Point Bridge**, a suspension bridge which spans the Elwha River at the point where it exits the Grand Canyon.

Humes Ranch Homestead

The Humes Ranch Cabin was originally the homestead of William Humes, who came from New York intending to head to the Klondike. He, his brother and a cousin decided to stay in the Elwha Valley. The

National Park Service acquired the property, restored the cabin, and maintains the pastures as did the Humes family. The site was added to the US National Register of Historic Places in September 1977.

Getting there: From the Whiskey Bend trailhead, take the Geyser Valley trail three miles (4.8 km) and then take the Humes Ranch loop of the trail.

Humes Ranch Homestead (Photos courtesy Rachel McLarty)

Olympic Hot Springs

Twenty-one tepid-to-hot alkaline mineral water springs bubble up in a bank of Boulder Creek, which feeds into the Elwha River. At one time there was a resort here, but the place fell into disrepair once the lease with the National Park Service expired in 1966. The buildings have long been removed, but the rock-lined shallow soaking pools remain. Hikers enjoy soaking in the warm pools in various states of dress or undress, whether in summer or winter. Winter road closures due to snowfall add an additional four miles (6.44 km) to your hike.

It might be smart to bring a bathing suit and a towel or two. And if you can find a dry spot, or branch, on which to hang whatever clothes you've decided to remove, all the better. You'll be less soggy (or chilled) for your hike back to civilization.

Getting there: Take Olympic Hot Springs Road, keeping to the right when Whiskey Bend Road peels off to the left. Keep going six miles

(9.66 km). When the road ends, the Boulder Creek Trailhead begins; follow it up to the hot springs. The hike is an easy 2.5 miles (4 km) to the hot springs. The trail is maintained, and offers a 200 feet (61 m) elevation gain.

Park Service warnings read as follows: "*Water quality of the hot springs is not monitored and may contain high levels of fecal coliform bacteria. Bathe at your own risk. Nudity is common.*" Thought you might like to know!

Camping:

Camping is available at the nearby Boulder Creek Campground. Get a permit at the Wilderness Information Center in Port Angeles, no reservations needed (Part 3F).

> **Next – Segment I: Lake Crescent in Olympic National Park!**

Getting there from the east: Lake Crescent is eighteen miles west of Port Angeles on Highway 101.

FYI: There is a Texaco fuel station just east of Lake Crescent near Lake Sutherland along Highway 101. The next gas beyond Lake Sutherland is thirty-three miles away (53 km) in Beaver, WA.

Getting there from the west: Lake Crescent Lodge is twenty-six miles (41.5 km) east of Beaver, WA on Highway 101.

4I) Lake Crescent in Olympic National Park

Eighteen miles to the west of Port Angeles, Washington is a stunning, nine-mile-long lake carved by ancient glaciers. The area is so picturesque, you may just want to sit and admire the views for a while. The views are impressive, even from the turnouts at the side of the lake. The steep mountainsides make for a dramatic backdrop to the deep turquoise water.

Or, you may want to return more than once to the lake and really let the beauty sink into the soul.

Cable-layers have unofficially measured the lake at a depth of 1000+ feet. Low oxygen levels and great depth result in water that is so deeply turquoise that, one must see it to believe it.

Lake Crescent Map

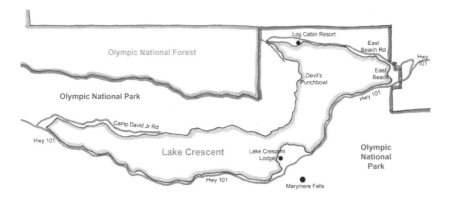

Lake Crescent History

Lake Crescent is integral to the history of the Pacific Northwest and the west end of the Olympic Peninsula. To hear the native tribes tell it, Lake Crescent was formed when Mount Storm King became unhappy with the Klallam and Quileute tribes who were fighting at its feet. It therefore hurled a mighty rock which became wedged at the outlet of the lake, raising the level of the water. What we do know is that an enormous landslide split the lake into two about 7,000 years ago. The east tip of the lake became a separate lake, now named Lake Sutherland.

By the late 1890s, the agriculture and timber industries were on the rise, especially in the Forks and surrounding areas, resulting in a slow but steady influx of settlers. The Log Hotel was built in 1895 on the north shore of Lake Crescent.

In 1900, there were no through-roads connecting Port Angeles and parts east with Forks and settlements to the west. The road from Port Angeles ended at East Beach on Lake Crescent. People arriving at Lake Crescent either from the north or the east needed to hop on a ferry for transport to points around the lake. Ferries stopped at East Beach, at the Log Hotel on the north shore, at Singer's Tavern (which is now Lake Crescent Lodge) and at Fairholme at the far westerly point of the lake.

By 1922, Washington State Road 9, now called Olympic Loop Highway (Highway 101), had advanced along the south shore of Lake Crescent. For years it was a gravel road. The entire loop was completed by 1931.

Singer's Tavern becomes Lake Crescent Lodge

In 1915, Avery and Julia Singer built a bungalow-style lodge and tavern and named it **Singer's Tavern**. The Singers owned and managed the tavern and lodge for thirteen years, the first six of which a ferry boat ride was the only way to get to the tavern. Upon the extension of the Olympic Loop Highway (now Highway 101) to the tavern in 1922, customers could finally reach the tavern by automobile.

Between 1927 and 1951, Singer's Tavern changed hands several times. In 1938, President Franklin D. Roosevelt created the Olympic National Park, which encompassed the entire mountainous interior region of the Olympic Peninsula.

View of Lake Crescent looking east from the Log Cabin Resort

The National Park Service purchased Singer's Tavern in 1951 and renamed it Lake Crescent Lodge. It is now listed on the National Register of Historic Places.

Log Cabin Resort History

On the north side of the lake is the Log Cabin Resort. The Resort began as the Log Hotel, originally a two-story log cabin built in 1895 by Mr. Saunders of Port Townsend, WA. The Log Hotel was the first hotel on the shores of Lake Crescent. It was built entirely of peeled cedar logs, with an observation tower, main lounge with large fireplace and dining room with bedrooms on the upper level.

The Log Hotel burned down in 1932. The current Log Cabin Resort was built on the site in the early 1950s, which by then had become part of the Olympic National Park.

Indian Valley Attractions, Food, Lodging

From Lake Crescent east to the Elwha River, Highway 101 runs through a steep-sided valley known as Indian Valley. This area has no attractions, per se; folks go to Lake Crescent for a destination with wonderful attractions. But, in the middle of this valley just east of Lake Sutherland is its claim to fame – the wonderful Granny's Café. See Port Angeles Restaurants.

The Indian Valley Motel, right next door, is also a part of Granny's. If you're interested in getting a jump on the next day's itinerary, spending the last night of a Port Angeles visit here might be a good plan.

Things to do around Lake Crescent, WA

Lake Crescent is at the epicenter of several worthy attractions and activities. For starters, here are two links; the first to the Olympic National Park "Visiting Lake Crescent" information, and the second to the Park's Lake Crescent brochure, which is a PDF:

https://www.nps.gov/olym/planyourvisit/visiting-lake-crescent.htm

https://www.nps.gov/olym/planyourvisit/upload/Lake-Crescent.pdf

- **Stops, Picnics, and Photos.** If you'd like to snap a few photos and just enjoy the beauty over a picnic, Highway 101 offers several large scenic turnouts right off the highway, all with terrific views. Or, add a picnic table to your views at no extra charge at **East Beach** or **La Poel** Picnic Area.

- Very near Lake Crescent Lodge is the **Storm King Ranger Station**.

- A few footsteps away from the ranger station is the trailhead for the trail to **Marymere Falls**.

- If you're after some serious hiking, the trailheads for two additional hikes are reached via the Marymere Falls Trail: **Mount Storm King Trail** and **Barnes Creek Trail.**

Storm King Ranger Station

360-928-3380 (or call the park's main phone number: 360-565-3130).

Hours: Daily 8a-dusk, and subject to closure due to season or weather.

Getting there: From Highway 101 heading west from Port Angeles, follow the signs and turn in at the Lake Crescent Lodge complex (near Highway 101 mile marker 227658). Follow the subsequent signage to the Storm King Ranger Station, which sits near a large parking lot.

The ranger station building is an "excellent example of early North Peninsula log construction." The renovated log cabin is listed on the National Register of Historic Places. Besides a visit to this historic building, a ranger will be on hand to answer any questions you may have.

Marymere Falls Trail

The trailhead is clearly marked, and passes *under* Highway 101 in a large corrugated tin tunnel. At the end of the 0.8 mile (1.29 km) hike, you arrive at Falls Creek and Marymere Falls, an impressive waterfall that tumbles 119 feet. The water continues on to join Barnes Creek before emptying into Lake Crescent.

Marymere Falls and the trail are located within the Olympic National Park. The surrounding forest is temperate rain forest. You'll see typical temperate rain forest characteristics:

- Huge trees, some of them old-growth
- Evidence of long gone nurse trees

- Epiphytes, mushrooms, ferns
- Moss-draped branches everywhere
- Native wildlife on quiet days

The trail tracks near, and over, Barnes Creek on both a foot bridge and a single-log bridge with handrails. The hike is a very easy one, more like a stroll for nearly all of the distance. Before you reach Marymere Falls, you'll pass near a second, shorter falls, the Barnes Creek Waterfall. Should you wish to explore these falls, beware the devilishly thorny Devil's club bushes growing in the area.

It is only at the last few hundred feet that the trail begins a steady climb on stairs which will take you to an upper observation point near the top of the falls. By the time you

Marymere Falls

think you might *start* getting winded, Marymere Falls will be already in sight. The forest and waterfall are inspiring, refreshing, serene. It is a place to revel in, to rest, enjoy, contemplate, marvel and relax.

East Shore Beach: "Ye Ole Swimming Hole"

East Shore Beach is a picnic area and swimming beach. Bring your own towels! Amenities include picnic benches, fire pits and rustic restrooms. Average summertime air temperatures hover near the seventy-degree F (21 C) mark, even in July and August. The steep hillsides limit the amount of time the sun can warm the water, meaning water temps rarely rise above "exceptionally cold." This doesn't faze the locals who have no qualms about plunging into the frigid water and enjoying lovely swims.

Once upon a time, a tiny Klallam village sat on Lake Crescent's East Beach. Much later, in the very early 1900s, the East Beach Hotel and a ferry service operated at East Beach. In the 1920s, the gravel road that would become known as Highway 101 advanced far enough to link East Beach to Singer's Tavern and then Fairholme. The road eliminated the need for the ferry and the hotel owner moved his business to Fairholme.

Today, there remains no trace of any of this history, just a little sandy stretch of lakeshore enjoyed all summer for swimming, frolicking and picnicking.

East Beach in mid-May

North Shore: Spruce Railroad Trail

The Spruce Railroad was built along the north shore of Lake Crescent in the late 1930s in order to transport spruce trees for use in World War II. The war ended before the railroad line was completed, and the effort was abandoned. Today, the ties have been removed and the rail bed turned into a walking trail.

- The trail is four miles long one way, eight miles total.
- Grade variation is just 100 feet. This is a very easy hike.

- The hike is very scenic; much of it hugs the lake, which can be seen for most of its length.

- Dogs, horses, and bikes ARE allowed.

- **Bonus feature**: A long dark **train tunnel!** Bring a flashlight. Tunnel hiking is optional—the Spruce Railroad Trail itself goes past the tunnel opening.

- **A second bonus feature**: The very cool and enormously popular **Devil's Punchbowl.** A rock wall ring, hence "punchbowl," makes a nearly sheer plunge into a pool that is at least 100 feet deep. The water is an incredibly deep turquoise color. On warm summer days this is a great spot to climb the rock walls and cliff-jump into the punchbowl. Or just swim a little. The punchbowl is a one-mile stroll from the east trailhead.

There are two trailheads to the Spruce Railroad Trail: one at each end. From Camp David Jr Road at the west end of Lake Crescent, and from East Beach Road which intersects Highway 101 at the east end of Lake Crescent. The trail travels nearly the entire length of the lake.

Devil's Punchbowl, Spruce Railroad Trail

A Quick Heads-Up: If you search online for this trail, Google will send you to the Camp David Jr Road trailhead, which is fine if that is where you'd like to start your hike. In reality, most hikers prefer starting at the east trailhead, which is nearer to Port Angeles, and just a mile (1.6 km) from the Punchbowl.

North Shore: Pyramid Mountain Hike

From Highway 101 at the west end of Lake Crescent (Fairholme), take Camp David Jr Road to the right (north) and travel 3.22 miles (5.19 km) to the trailhead. Note that the Pyramid Mountain Trail is closed in winter. *Check trail conditions* as this 3.5-mile hike crosses a scree field and avalanches occasionally happen. (http://www.nps.gov/olym/planyourvisit/wilderness-trail-conditions.htm#CP_JUMP_450763.) The trail is periodically closed if conditions are deemed unsafe for hiking. If open, however, the 2,600-foot climb in altitude will bring you to great views of the Strait of Juan de Fuca, Lake Crescent, and the surrounding regions.

Lodging Around Lake Crescent:

Two lodges and a campground sit directly on the shores of Lake Crescent, all of them serviced through the Olympic National Park:

- **Lake Crescent Lodge** and its restaurant, The Lodge, on the South Shore directly off Highway 101.
- **Log Cabin Resort** and its restaurant, Sunnyside Café, located on the North Shore on East Beach Road.
- **Fairholme Campground**, located on Highway 101 at the west end of Lake Crescent. The Fairholme Store offers "mini-mart" fare as well as equipment rental and other supplies.

Lake Crescent Lodge, 416 Lake Crescent Rd., Olympic National Park, WA 98363

855-802-6418. http://www.olympicnationalparks.com/lodging/lake-crescent-lodge/

Hours: The resort is open from early May through New Year's Day. Check website for exact dates. The Roosevelt Fireplace Cabins are open on weekends only during the winter season; all other rooms are closed for the winter, as is the restaurant.

Lake Crescent Lodge on a very pleasant September day

The Lake Crescent Lodge is beautifully situated among maples and evergreens at Barnes Point on a sandy shore of Lake Crescent. It is a rustic resort hotel and restaurant that also offers recreation and relaxation on Lake Crescent in the Olympic National Park. Today this historic lodge looks just as it did 100 years ago when it was known as Singer's Tavern.

A massive stone fireplace, a huge lobby filled with period antiques, and an inviting sun porch overlooking the lake provide heartwarming ambience. This is an excellent vacation spot from May to New Year's Day, not to mention a great home base for day-tripping due to easy access to popular sites such as Mount Storm King, Pyramid Mountain, Spruce Railroad Trail, Marymere Falls and Barnes Creek trails.

Accommodations at Lake Crescent Lodge:

1. **Rooms in the Lodge itself.** Your room will be on the second story of the main Lodge. Because the lodge dates to 1915, the rooms share a central bathroom and shower.

2. **Singer's Tavern Cottages**, listed on the National Register of Historic Places, were designed and built to resemble the original cottages constructed in 1915. One- and two-bedroom cottages each include privacy and a porch with lake and mountain views.

3. **Roosevelt Fireplace Cabins** are located along the shoreline of Lake Crescent, each one with a fireplace. These historic cabins are very popular and offer spectacular views.

4. **Storm King Rooms** are a more contemporary version of serene and restful. Each room has a balcony or porch, and the usual amenities although without TV or telephone.

5. **Marymere Rooms** are situated alongside Lake Crescent just a short distance from the historic lodge. No extra charge for the wonderful mountain and lake views.

6. **Pyramid Mountain Rooms**, surrounded by towering trees, peace and quiet, provide perfect ambience from either porch or balcony.

Log Cabin Resort, 3183 E. Beach Rd., Olympic National Park, WA 98363

(855) 289-2638.

http://www.olympicnationalparks.com/lodging/log-cabin-resort/

The Log Cabin Resort may not necessarily be fancy, but the rustic accommodations are buoyed by location, location, location. The sunny north shore of Lake Crescent is beautiful and peaceful.

Large green lawns sweep from the resort down to the lake, perfect for playing, both for kids and adults.

Along with RV sites and tent camping sites, choose from five types of lodging. All are non-smoking, and none have internet access; get your internet access in the lobby.

1. **Lakeside Chalets:** Waterfront, mountain views, private bath, double bed and double futon downstairs with double bed in loft. Mini fridge, microwave, and coffee pot but no cooking utensils. Close walk to restaurant. Max of six people. No pets. *(Pictured.)*

2. **Lodge Rooms:** Waterfront, mountain views, two queen beds, private bath. Max of four people. No pets.

3. **Camper Cabins:** Two double beds, electricity, picnic table, fire ring. No plumbing; communal restrooms with showers are available nearby. Max four people. Pets allowed.

4. **Rustic Kitchenette Cabins:** Original 1920s cabins with two double beds, private bath, kitchenette with appliances but no cooking or eating utensils. Max four people. Pets allowed.

5. **Rustic Sleeping Cabins:** Primitive cabins built in 1928, lake and mountain views, electricity, private baths, with a variety of sleeping options for three to four people. Pets allowed.

Other amenities include two restaurants (below), laundry facilities and general store. Internet access is limited. Rates range from $85-$200 per night. The resort is open during mid-May to early October only, so check the website for details on dates and rates.

Fairholme Campground and Store

On Highway 101 at the west end of Lake Crescent. Camping season is May to October; reservations are first-come, first-served, National Park Pass needed. Cost is $20/night, plus $10 per use of dump station. Sites available for RVs up to twenty-one feet. See the website for additional amenities: https://www.nps.gov/olym/planyourvisit/camping.htm.

Restaurants around Lake Crescent

The Lodge at Lake Crescent Lodge

360.928.3211.

http://www.olympicnationalparks.com/lodging/dining/lake-crescent-lodge/

Hours: Open for the season April 28-October 31. Times of operation vary, so please call or check the website.

Walk into the Lake Crescent Lodge and you'll see part of the restaurant, **The Lodge**, toward the back right of the large lobby area. Seating areas overflow into the wrap-around covered porch with lovely views of Lake Crescent and the surrounding forest and hills. You may also enjoy watching some of the activities on the lake and pier as you dine.

The Lodge has earned the WA Wine First Award for fine dining, and is also a certified Green Restaurant. The menu includes gourmet meals for breakfast, brunch, lunch and dinner in this romantic lakeside setting.

The restaurant closes between early January and late April. Full operating hours and menus are on the site: http://www.olympicnationalparks.com/lodging/dining/lake-crescent-lodge/

Sunnyside Café at Log Cabin Resort

http://www.olympicnationalparks.com/lodging/dining/log-cabin-resort/

Hours: Breakfast buffet between 8a-11a, children under 4 eat free. Lunch 12p – 4p;

Dinner 5p – 9p.

The Sunnyside Café, casual and comfortable, is situated in the main lodge with a wide open view of Lake Crescent. Lunch and dinner menus are online, and feature soups, salads, sandwiches, burgers, pizza, pasta and desserts. Reservations are not required but are recommended.

Lakeside Deli at Log Cabin Resort

The Lakeside Deli offers a casual menu of "grab-and-go" items, the better for continuing recreational activities, or enjoying the views from the lawn beside the lake.

**Next – Segment J: Sol Duc Valley
in Olympic National Park!**

Getting there from the east: The entrance to the Sol Duc Valley (Sol Duc Hot Springs Road) is on Highway 101, two miles west of the Fairholme General Store at the western tip of Lake Crescent Lodge.

Getting there from the west: The entrance to the Sol Duc Valley (Sol Duc Hot Springs Road) is 18.74 miles (30 km) east of Beaver, WA, on Highway 101.

If you need it, there is gas and a mini-mart in Beaver. See Part 4K.

4J) Sol Duc Valley in the Olympic National Park

The Sol Duc Valley is #6 on our Must-See list of attractions for excellent reasons. This singular valley gives one a nearly complete taste of the Pacific Northwest. Depending on the season, you might get to view salmon spawning, take a half-mile loop walk through an ancient and verdant rain forest, hike less than a mile through nearly level rain forest to a dramatic mini-gorge and waterfall, and then soak in  pools fed by thermal hot springs. If you have the time—possibly six or eight hours *if not more*—this is a wonderful destination to visit.

The Sol Duc Valley offers four major attractions:

- **The Salmon Cascade is at around the seven mile (11.5 km) mark**. Timewise you'll need, what, fifteen minutes? An hour and a half or more? It will depend on whether or not the salmon are present, and how fascinated you are with the salmon spawn.

- **The Ancient Grove Walk is at around the 9.25 mile (14.8 km) mark.** You can blitz the trail in fifteen minutes, or you can linger and lollygag a bit, especially at the spot where the trail traverses the edge of a high bank of the Sol Duc River. This is a beautiful stroll with impressive views of the Sol Duc River.

- **The Sol Duc Hot Springs Resort is around the twelve mile (19.4 km) mark.** Here you can soak away the trail dust and sore muscles to your heart's content in civilized fashion. Then, enjoy a nice meal, whether it's lunch at the Poolside Deli, or dinner in the Resort at the Springs Restaurant.

- **The Sol Duc Falls trailhead is around the 13.7 mile (22.1 km) mark.** Reach the Sol Duc Falls with a short 0.8 mile (1.29 km) hike one way. The falls are cool; you will probably want to hang out a bit, snap photos, and explore a bit. You can also hike the three miles (4.8 km) back to Sol Duc Hot Springs Resort along Lover's Lane trail, past Lover's Lane Falls. (This will work well if you can leave your car at the resort and get a ride up to the Sol Duc Falls trailhead.)

More info on visiting the Sol Duc Valley:

https://www.nps.gov/olym/planyourvisit/visiting-the-sol-duc-valley.htm

Sol Duc Valley Brochure: https://www.nps.gov/olym/planyourvisit/loader.cfm?csModule=security/getfile&PageID=176483

Salmon Cascade

The salmon spawn is one of those very nearly inexplicable events. Pacific salmon begin life in fresh water, migrate to the salty ocean for years, and then return to the exact gravelly stream of their birth to spawn and die.

All 5 species of Pacific salmon native to the Pacific Northwest spawn in the Sol Duc River: **Chum salmon** (or keta, calico or dog salmon after the canine teeth the males grow while spawning), **chinook salmon** (also called king, blackmouth, or spring salmon), **pink salmon** (or humpback or humpies), **coho salmon** (also known as silver salmon), and **sockeye salmon** (also known as red salmon as they turn bright red during during the spawn).

To get to their spawning beds, they must leap over the Salmon Cascade. Chinook salmon spawn around June-July. The best time to see coho salmon jumping at the Salmon Cascade is early October, but depending on the seasons, species and rainfall, salmon might be seen any time after August through the end of November.

Elderly couple walking to the Salmon Cascade overlook

Stand at the elevated Salmon Cascade viewing area which overlooks the Sol Duc River. It offers a clear view of the river cascading over the jumbled rocks of a mini-waterfall. Or, clamber over many root beds and down to the edge of the Sol Duc for a closer view of the river thundering over the Salmon Cascade. This makes for excellent photos of salmon fighting upstream against all odds.

I like standing on the river bank rocks and watching as the water literally gushes over the rocks. Over and over again, the salmon leap upwards. There is a pattern: most of the salmon leap up against the far bank of the stream, sometimes bouncing off the rocks with a slap and falling back into the river.

Even as the salmon clear the first hurdle, there are several more hurdles that they must leap. If they can land in a pool of water, even if turbulent, they can rest for a few moments, and then take more leaps upward and onward. It makes for great life lessons.

Sol Duc Salmon Cascade

There is no 'quit' in these salmon. They persevere against the obstacles, leaping again and again until they get it right.

Between the cascade and the Sol Duc Falls which is too high for leaping, the salmon will find miles of shallow river bed in which they can spawn and die.

How do salmon know how to get back to their birth stream?

While the exact mechanisms that guide the salmon are not clearly understood, it is believed that their guidance systems may be a combination of sensitivity to the earth's magnetic field *and* their sense of smell, which is very strong. Scientists think the earth's magnetic signals (*magnetoception*) guide the salmon to the general position of the river where they were born. As they approach, they follow the scents pouring out of their natal stream, finding the entrance to the river and the exact tributary and stream in which they were born.

Salmon don't always end up in their exact birth stream 100% of the time, studies show. A few salmon may end up in a nearby stream, thereby helping to ensure sufficient genetic diversity of the species. It also helps ensure that creeks with disrupted environments will eventually become repopulated with new runs of salmon.

Pictured: Pink salmon run in the Dungeness River

Salmon are known as a *keystone* species, because the entire ecosystem around the salmon spawning streams is dependent upon the nourishment that salmon provide. The ocean nutrients: nitrogen, sulfur, carbon and phosphorus, are transferred to the forest and its inhabitants upon the death of the salmon each year. *"Salmon continue to surprise us, showing us new ways in which their oceanic migrations eventually permeate entire terrestrial ecosystems" (Science Daily 2008).*

Ancient Grove Walking Trail

Continuing 1.5 miles toward Sol Duc Hot Springs and Sol Duc Falls, you arrive at the Ancient Grove, an easy 0.6 mile walking trail looping through a dense forested area that represents a temperate rain forest quite well.

The Ancient Grove walk is easy. It is level, and a boardwalk is provided through marshy areas. You'll see dense trees, mossy vistas, as well as a wider view of the spawning grounds of the Sol Duc River beyond the Salmon Cascade. You'll find

everywhere scenes typical of Washington temperate rain forests: thick moss drenching everything; trees of all sizes that have surrendered to age and to the buffeting of nature, now lying on the forest floor. You may also see saplings of a new generation getting a start on top of moss-covered deadfalls.

Sol Duc Falls

You're hiking in the forested Sol Duc Valley along the Soleduck Trail; hopping over rivulets, noting various fungi species, and enchanted by sightings of trillium blooms. Douglas fir and red cedar tower above. You pass an old log shelter, built years ago for the use of passers-by. The air is cool and refreshing, perhaps misty or drizzly.

You begin to hear a soft thunder. Soon the sound is unmistakable; there is a waterfall ahead. A couple more bends in the trail, and there it is: a chasm in the ground, a bridge to the other side, and the Sol Duc River

Sol Duc Falls in early April.
Spring runoff pounds over
the precipice

thundering over the Sol Duc Falls into the chasm to continue its way toward the Pacific.

From trailhead to falls is just 0.8 miles (1.29 km) of mostly level and well-kept trail. The terrain is beautiful. Smaller rain forest tributaries flow around and over moss-covered boulders looking like so many damp green marshmallows. It's a magical trek, the memory of which will take years to fade.

Sol Duc Hot Springs Resort

12076 Sol Duc Hot Springs Rd., Port Angeles, WA 98363

Reservations: 866-476-5382; Email: info@visitsolduc.com. http://www.olympicnationalparks.com/lodging/sol-duc-hot-springs-resort/

The resort is open seasonally between approximately March and October. Check the website for exact dates and road conditions. A stay at the resort includes entry to the hot pools. **Campsites:** Located nearby with water and electrical hookups. Reservations are recommended at these sites and entry to the pools is extra. *(Pictured: Sol Duc cabins)*

Campers or day visitors can purchase access to the pools. Check the website or call for current prices.

Resort Amenities

The highlight: Commercial pools fed by natural hot springs, long known by local native peoples for their healing properties. With one freshwater pool and three mineral pools with temperatures ranging from 50-104 degrees, resistance is futile. Give in and sink into the luxurious mineral waters, soak in the warmth and feel every muscle relax.

- On-site restaurant (below), café, gift shop, grocery store
- The resort does not have a full spa but does offer massages for a price.
- **NO electronic connectivity**: No TV, no radio, no telephone, and no Internet are provided in cabin rentals. All the better for full relaxation.

Nearby Hiking Trails:

- **Lover's Lane** hike is a 5.8 mile (9.33 km) moderate hike from the resort to Sol Duc Falls.

- **Mink Lake** hike is 2.6 miles (4.2 km) one way up to Mink Lake, a lovely alpine lake tucked into the forested hills.

- **Deer Lake** hike is 3.8 miles (6.1 km) one way up to a beautiful high mountain lake.

After your hike, return to the resort or continue upward on trails to the Little Divide, High Divide, and beyond if you wish. Wilderness Permits are needed for overnight hiking/camping, obtainable in Port Angeles (Part 4E).

More info: https://www.nps.gov/olym/planyourvisit/sol-duc-river-trail.htm

Eagle Ranger Station:

Located on Sol Duc Hot Springs Road. It is irregularly staffed, but if a ranger is there when you are, you'll get access to plenty of Olympic National Park and temperate rain forest information.

Springs Restaurant at the Sol Duc Resort

Springs Restaurant has you covered for breakfast and dinner; eat lunch at the Poolside Deli. See website for menus: http://www.olympicnationalparks.com/lodging/dining/sol-duc-hot-springs-resort/.

- Breakfast is served 7:30a - 10:00a
- Lunch at Poolside Deli served from 11:30a - 4:30p
- Eat in style for dinner from 5:30p - 9:00p

Brief History of the Sol Duc Hot Springs Resort

The therapeutic hot springs were introduced to an early settler, Theodore Moritz in the 1880s. He homesteaded the area and spread the word about these amazing waters.

Seeking relief from his own ailments, timber baron Michael Earles visited the hot springs, considered himself cured, and decided to make a worthy investment in the healing of others. In 1910, Earles purchased the property and poured a half-million dollars into his new four-story, 164-room hotel and resort.

After its opening in 1912, it became known as one of the best spas in the United States. Heated by steam from the hot springs, it contained the latest in modern amenities such as electric lights and telephones, bowling alley, billiard room and theater. The gardens were luxurious with fountains and tennis courts, golf links and croquet grounds. Vegetables, cattle and chickens were grown on-site for use in the resort's restaurants.

Folks came from all over the country, even as far as Europe, to soak in this luxury. At only $2.50 per day, it was considered very reasonable, despite the two-day journey to get there.

Four years later in 1916, a fire completely destroyed all of it. It took a few years to rebuild, but a more humble structure rose from the ashes.

Much later, in 1966, the resort was purchased by the National Park Service. The Sol Duc Hot Springs Resort gained fresh new life in the 1980s. Today it is a rustic and quiet retreat providing respite from mainstream life.

Next – Segment K: Forks

Getting there from the east: Forks is on Highway 101, 34.6 miles (55.7 km) west of Lake Crescent Lodge, and 56.3 miles (90.6 km) from Port Angeles, WA.

Getting there from the west: Forks is twenty-seven miles (43.5 km) west of Ruby Beach, and 67.3 miles (108.3 km) west of Quinault, WA.

4K) Forks, Washington

Yes, there IS a town named Forks in Washington State!

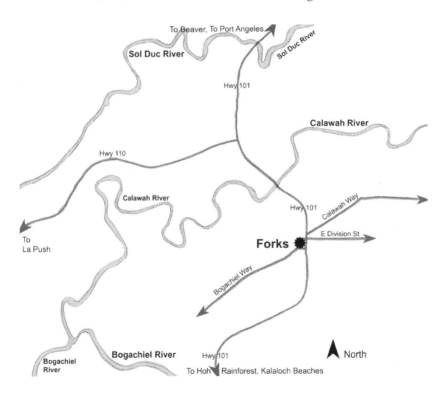

Forks is a small town of roughly 3,600 people in the heart of Washington State's Pacific Northwest temperate rain forest. It is located in a prairie but surrounded by dense forests. Three rivers converge nearby: the Bogachiel, Calawah, and Sol Duc, hence the name "Forks." Forks is also the main center of commerce throughout the entire west end of Clallam County, which comprises most of the northern part of the Olympic Peninsula of Washington State. From Aberdeen to the south, and Port Angeles to the north, you'll find precious little along the highway other than trees, trees, and trees. And the town of Forks.

Forks is a working town, a small village lost in the heart of billions of board-feet of rain forest. But given that it is situated in close proximity to many attractions both to the north and the south, Forks makes a terrific home base for a rain forest vacation. Be sure to allow enough time to see and do all that you desire.

People love to visit Forks for many reasons. The greatest draw might be the sheer beauty and enjoyment of the primordial temperate rain forest, or the nearby Pacific Ocean beaches. Additionally, *The Twilight Saga* series by Stephenie Meyer placed the town on the map in 2007.

The city of Forks does welcome you!

Forks Weather

The weather in Forks is—typically—rainy! No surprise there. Forks receives on average 100 inches of rain every year. However, the summer months are *much less likely* to be rainy. The dynamics of the Olympic rain shadow that keep Sequim and Port Townsend dry are the same dynamics that result in copious rainfall over Forks, and the Quinault and Hoh rain forests.

In Forks, moisture rolls in off the Pacific Ocean, passes over Forks and collects against the Olympic Mountain Range directly to the east of Forks, WA. But, there is SO MUCH moisture aloft that the entire region receives the overflow rainfall. The western slopes of the Olympic Mountains receive 140-170 inches per year, while the towns in the lowlands nearer the coast still receive ninety-five or more inches of rainfall per year, from Aberdeen and Hoquiam in the southwest to Neah Bay in the northwest Olympic Peninsula.

Forks Average Yearly Rainfall: 99.54 inches

Forks Average Yearly Rainfall per Season

- Winter: 44.53 Inches (113.11 cm)
- Spring: 18.9" (48 cm)
- Summer: 8.99" (22.83 cm)
- Fall: 47.2" (119.89 cm)

Forks Weather Records

- Record maximum rainfall in a single year: **162.14 inches (411.84 cm)** in 1997
- Record maximum rainfall in a single month: **41.70 inches (106 cm)** in January 1953
- 2 months with **ZERO rainfall**: August 1916, July 1922

Forks Average Monthly Rainfall

- January: 18.27" (46.4 cm)
- February: 12.72" (32.3 cm)
- March: 13.54" (34.4 cm)
- April: 9.21" (23.4 cm)
- May: 5.79" (14.7 cm)
- June: 3.90" (9.9 cm)
- July: 2.48" (6.3 cm)
- August: 2.49" (6.3 cm)
- September: 4.02" (10.2 cm)
- October: 1.81" (30 cm)
- November: 18.62" (47.3 cm)
- December: 16.77" (42.6 cm)

Whether or not you check the weather forecast before traveling to Forks, don't forget an umbrella or rain gear. Just in case.

History of the Town of Forks

What is a nice little town like Forks doing in the middle of a rain forest? Well, we're glad you asked! Here is the short version of Forks' 150-year history.

Before the establishment of a town in the middle of a rain forest, the Quileute Indian tribe lived throughout the west Olympic Peninsula, from the region south of Ozette Lake to

Herd of Roosevelt elk grazing at dusk in a cow pasture near Forks, WA

the land north of the Quinault River, including the area that Forks now occupies.

In the midst of their densely forested territory, they had an ingenious way of attracting the elk herds they hunted for meat: they created prairies by concentrating their tree-harvesting efforts in certain areas. They felled trees by burning and then used the wood for their homes and canoes. The resultant large open prairie drew the elk herds which love to forage on the grasses, bushes, berry-brambles and several fern species blanketing every open meadow.

Periodic intentional burning of the prairies stimulated the growth of the tender ferns, and also helped to perpetuate the prairie.

The Quileutes had created several prairies in this fashion; it was the prairie wedged between the forks of the Calawah and the Bogachiel Rivers twelve miles from La Push at the coast that attracted settlers to the region and helped to name the town of Forks. This prairie was a mile wide and three miles long.

The First Settlers

The first families of settlers began arriving in the mid-1800s, joining a few undaunted trappers were already living in this "prairie upstream," as the Quileutes called the area. Over the next several decades and spurred by homestead grants, settlers made their way to the Forks prairie the only way they could: via boat to the shores of the Olympic Peninsula and then inland on primitive, muddy foot paths.

They were farmers, not loggers. Besides the vegetables, grains and forages needed by the community, the settlers attempted to grow and market hops. The crop grew very well, however the difficult logistics of getting the hops to market—transporting it either over land to Port Townsend 100 miles away over those same muddy trails or via boat—proved daunting. More often than not, the hops rotted before they reached market.

Forks Timber

It was inevitable that a town choked by trees would soon turn to those trees as a source of income.

By the 1900s, timber camps were in full swing. A brutal hurricane and tornado in 1921 (winds to 170 miles per hour) flattened nearly 20% of the forests surrounding Forks Prairie. The ready availability of so many board-feet of wood just lying on the ground spurred timber-harvesting efforts.

Ancient two-man chainsaw displayed in the Forks Timber Museum.

On August 28, 1945, the town officially incorporated under the uncomplicated name of "Forks." By the 1970s, Forks had earned the moniker, **"Timber Capital of the World."**

Timber harvesting is much declined since the 1970s for several reasons, some of them environmental. As governmental legislation crippled the industry, mills were forced to close. The number of logging companies declined from seventy in 1980 to fourteen in 2001. The number of forest-related jobs diminished and unemployment soared. People left town to find their fortunes elsewhere, and the population dropped.

Forks Today

Today, the Forks population has rebounded somewhat. The current estimated population of Forks, WA is roughly 3,600 residents, which is more than its population during the timber heyday. Timber is still a significant industry even if greatly reduced.

The Twilight Saga and Tourism in Forks

The publication of Stephenie Meyer's *The Twilight Saga*, a series of four teen novels set in and around Forks created a boom in tourism for the little town of Forks.

Forks may be the timber capital of the world, but for the last decade it has also been the setting of imagined battles between werewolves and vampires, including a very sweet love story between Bella, a human, and Edward, an immortal vampire. It is actually a wonderful story highlighting unconditional love one for another, which no doubt drives some of the popularity of the saga, and as a result, tourism to Forks. In fact, houses and locations throughout the region have been identified that represent the places and events in the various *Twilight Saga* books. Guided *"Twilight* Tours" help "Twi-Fans" relive the touching love story.

Lifesize Twilight Character Cutouts: take your photo with one or all at the Forks Chamber of Commerce!

Forks Attractions

Twilight Tours by TeamForks, 130 S. Spartan Avenue, Forks, WA 98331

360-374-5634. www.teamforks.com/

Enjoy the full tour with Twi-fans of all the *Twilight* locations in and around Forks, including an evening hot dog roast on the beach. Or if your time is limited, take the two- to-three-hour local tour. Transportation is in a comfortable large van.

Forks Chamber of Commerce, 1411 S. Forks Avenue, Forks, WA 98331

360-374-2531; http://forkswa.com/visiting-forks/

The good folks at the Forks Chamber of Commerce are a wealth of information about Forks, its history, and the surrounding rain forest and other activities available to the visitor. They also offer information on Forks *Twilight* tours and have some *Twilight* souvenirs for sale.

Forks, WA Chamber of Commerce, with "Bella's truck" parked out front

Forks Timber Museum, 1421 S. Forks Avenue, Forks, WA 98331

360-374-9663. http://www.forkstimbermuseum.org/

$3.00 admission fee. The Forks Timber Museum is located next to the Chamber of Commerce. It is fitting that a timber museum is housed in a very old log house. Get a fascinating peak into the history of both Forks and the local timber industry.

Forks Lumber Mill Tour, 1411 S. Forks Avenue, Forks, WA 98331

360-374-9663. The Forks Chamber of Commerce manages tours of a working saw mill in Forks. Admission is by donation. You'll be taken by van to the various sites of the tour. Allow several hours, or a half-day depending on how closely you like to manage your time. This interesting and informative tour will teach you about logging, milling, and sustainable forest management.

Lake Pleasant County Park, W. Lake Pleasant Rd., Beaver, WA 98305

360-417-2291. http://www.clallam.net/Parks/lakepleasant.html

Lake Pleasant (*pictured above*) is ten miles east of Forks in the tiny village of Beaver. There's the lovely little lake with a couple piers and a boat launch, a grassy park, picnic tables, and a huge sand box with swing sets and play equipment. This is a really great *as-needed* stop.

Other Nearby Attractions:

- **Olympic National Park Beaches—Rialto Beach, Second and Third Beaches—and the Quileute Indian Reservation** are all near La Push, WA, which is just fourteen miles from Forks (Part 4L).

The Quileute Marina in La Push, with sea stacks in the background

- **Neah Bay, WA, at the end of Highway 112, extreme northwest corner of the Olympic Peninsula.** See Part 4G.

- **Hoh Rain Forest in the Olympic National Park.** The Hoh Visitor Center is thirty-one miles (50 km) south of Forks. See Part 4M.

Recreational Opportunities near Forks

- Hiking, kayaking, bicycling, through forest, rivers, beaches, or mountains

- Back-country, kayaking, rafting and cycling tours are all available

- Fishing guides can accommodate both expert and novice fishermen
- See Part 2D, 2G, and 2H for rental, tour, and guide companies.

Forks Lodging

Olympic Suites Inn, 800 Olympic Drive, Forks, WA 98331 800-262-3433. www.olympicsuitesinn.com

Olympic Suites Inn is situated near the Calawah River in Forks.

Dew Drop Inn Motel, 100 Fern Hill Rd., Forks, WA 98331

360-374-4055. www.dewdropinnmotel.com

The Dew Drop Inn Motel is located in downtown Forks toward the south end, near Pacific Pizza and the Forks Outfitters.

Forks Motel, 351 S. Forks Avenue (Highway 101), Forks, WA 98331

360-374-6243; 800-544-3416. www.forksmotel.com

Located downtown on Highway 101.

Pacific Inn Motel, 352 S. Forks Avenue, Forks, WA 98331.

360-374-9400; Reservations: 800-235-7344.

www.pacificinnmotel.com

Located downtown on Highway 101.

B&Bs in Forks

Fisherman's Widow B&B Inn, 62 Steelhead Avenue, Forks, WA 98331

360-374-5693. http://fishermans-widow.com/

This B&B is located on the bank of the Sol Duc River north of Forks.

Huckleberry Lodge Cabins, 1171 Big Pine Way, Forks, WA 98331

360-374-4090. www.huckleberryforks.com/

Located walking distance from the Calawah River. Reminiscent of a very upscale KOA.

Miller Tree Inn, 654 E. Division St., Forks, WA 98331

360-374-6806; 800-943-6563. http://millertreeinn.com/

Close to downtown Forks; this place is designated as *Twilight's* Cullen House in Forks. Yep, I can see that.

Misty Valley Inn, 194894 Highway 101, Forks, WA 98331

877-374-9389. Email: mystyinn@olynet.com. http://mistyvalleyinn. com/

Lovely B&B with four rooms (all with private baths) located just east of Forks.

Vacation Rentals in Forks and west end

A Cozy River House Riverfront Escape 1 & 2, Steelhead Avenue, Forks, WA 98331

360-374-4046. http://www.acozyriverhouse.com/

Two separate three-bedroom, two-bath units situated on the bank of the Sol Duc River minutes from downtown Forks.

Wood Street Guest House I & II, 60 Wood Avenue, Forks, WA 98331

360-640-4469. Two-bedroom guest house, and separate one-bedroom guest house. In Forks at the north end of town.

Olympic Peninsula Vacation Rentals:

http://www.opvacationrentals.com/. Vacation cabins in and around Forks, WA and the Olympic National Park. Six different properties, homes away from home that can sleep ten or more. They fill fast, typically booking several seasons in advance.

Forks Restaurants

Mocha Motion, 260 S. Forks Avenue (Highway 101), Forks, WA 98331

360-374-4094.

https://www.facebook.com/mochamotioninc/?rf=121344154584402

Hours: 5a-7p. Located on Highway 101 in the middle of Forks. Yes, it is a "coffee shack," a nice one. Yes, it has two windows, one for northbound and one for southbound. And yes, the coffee is really good. I stop here every time I pass through town, if possible.

Forks Coffee Shop, 241 S. Forks Ave, Forks, WA 98331

360-374-6769. https://www.facebook.com/pages/Forks-Coffee-Shop-Family-Restaurant/159915157374971.

Hours: 7 days, 5:30a-8p. American diner cuisine. Breakfast here is great.

Forks Outfitters Thriftway Food Store, 950 S. Forks Ave, Forks, WA 98331

360-374-6161. http://www.forksoutfitters.com/

Hours: 8a-10p. Groceries, deli, the works. And while you're at it, you can obtain just about anything else you might need or have forgotten, from sleeping bags to socks, and more.

JT's Sweet Stuffs, 80 N. Forks Avenue (Highway 101), Forks, WA 98331

360-374-6111.

https://www.facebook.com/pages/Jts-Sweet-Stuffs/100513003342007

Hours: 10a-6p. Candy, fudge, ice cream. And also soup and sandwiches. It's a win win!

Pacific Pizza, 870 S. Forks Avenue, Forks, WA 98331

360-374-2626.

https://www.facebook.com/pages/Pacific-Pizza/115494468473492

Hours: 11a-10p. Best pizza on the peninsula, I'm told. And more than just pizza. Get Italian dishes if you're not in the mood for pizza. It is fairly informal: Order at counter, serve yourself drinks and salad from salad bar, and seat yourself; they'll bring your pizza/food order to you.

Plaza Jalisco, 90 N. Forks Ave, Forks, WA 98331

360-374-3108.

https://www.facebook.com/pages/Plaza-Jalisco/113758075321174

Hours: Sun-Thur 11a-9p; Fri-Sat 11a-10p. Typical and tasty Mexican cuisine.

Sully's Burgers, 220 S. Forks Avenue, Forks, WA 98331.

360-374-5075.

https://www.facebook.com/pages/Sullys-Drive-in/181739955307370.

Hours: 11a-9p

This is a small-town burger joint with many tasty menu options. This is another of my favorite haunts in Forks. Check out the pleasant little gift shop inside the restaurant.

Taqueria Santa Ana, 80 Calawah Way, Forks, WA 98331

360-374-8606.

https://www.facebook.com/pages/Taqueria-Santa-Ana/145659 868863963

Hours: 10a-9p. Billed as Mexican fast food. Small Mexican taco shop/ restaurant has returned to well-regarded former owners. People are thrilled.

Food in nearby Beaver:

Hungry Bear Café, Milepost 206, US-101, Beaver, WA 98305

360-327-3225. https://www.facebook.com/pages/Hungry-Bear-Cafe/ 173170046066422

Hours: Sun-Fri 6a-8p; Sat 6a-10p. Located west of Lake Crescent on Highway 101 near the small village of Beaver. The Hungry Bear Café can be relied upon to serve you decent all-American diner food by waitresses who are good at their jobs.

Next – L: La Push and Beaches via Highway 110!

Getting there from east or west: Highway 110 intersects with Highway 101 nine miles (14.5 km) east of Forks proper, and 7.27 miles (11.6 km) west of Beaver, WA.

You'll find gas and groceries in Beaver, a stone's throw from Lake Pleasant:

Lake Pleasant Grocery and Gas Station, 200361 US-101, Beaver, WA 98305

360-327-3211. **Hours**: Mon-Sat 5a-7p, Sun 7a-7p.

4L) La Push and Beaches via Highway 110

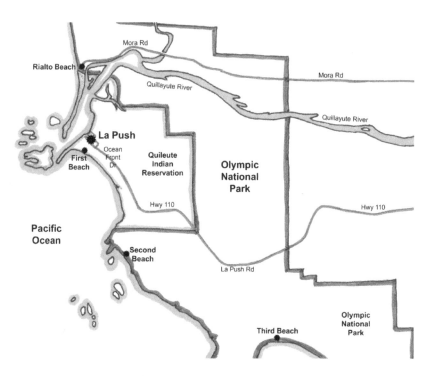

From its junction with Highway 101, Highway 110 travels twelve miles (19.3 km) and terminates at the Quileute Indian Reservation of La Push. Highway 110 is also the road you take to visit any of four beaches in the area: **Rialto Beach, Third Beach, Second Beach, and First Beach**, which is the only beach NOT in the Olympic National Park. The wide, full-flowing Quillayute River separates Rialto Beach from La Push and the nearest beaches to the south: First, Second, and Third Beaches.

Rialto Beach (Olympic National Park)

Rialto Beach, situated on the north bank of the Quillayute River and within the Olympic National Park, is a long sandy crescent littered with drift-logs and sea stacks. Walking is easy.

Getting there: From the junction of Highway 110 with 101, travel eight miles (12.8 km) along Highway 110 to Mora Road, and then turn right on Mora Road to go to Rialto Beach. Mora Road takes you to the Rialto Beach parking lot, which is practically on the sand. No hiking is required to get to the beach. You might not even have to step around a drift log, though there will certainly be lots of drift logs littering the beach.

Rialto Beach on a stormy day loses none of its magic

Two miles north of the parking lot is the **Hole-in-the-Wall**, a volcanic-pocked sea arch and one of the best places in the Olympic National Park for exploring tide pools. Hike north along the beach for 1.66 miles (2.66 km) to get there. If you can be there at low tide, you can walk through the hole in the wall and study the various sea creatures and tiny ecosystems in the tide pools. If you can time your hike just right, you might be able to capture photos of the setting sun shining through the Hole-in-the-Wall.

Mora Campground and Ranger Station are also along Mora Road and located two miles from Rialto Beach. Camp year-round in ninety-four total sites; first-come, first-served. $20/night and an extra

$10 per use of dump station. The Mora Ranger Station is on site. More info at these links:

- https://www.nps.gov/olym/planyourvisit/camping.htm
- https://www.nps.gov/olym/planyourvisit/upload/mora.pdf
- https://www.nps.gov/olym/planyourvisit/visiting-mora-and-rialto.htm

First Beach; La Push, WA in Quileute Indian Reservation

First Beach is in La Push at the end of Highway 110, or as the road is called in La Push, Front Street, or Ocean Front Drive. This is the only beach in this area NOT within the Olympic National Park.

Turn in at the **Quileute Oceanside Resort**; there are places close to the beach for day-use visitors to park. A day use parking pass is needed; cost is **$5**, you can obtain it in the Resort office. The pass is valid anywhere in La Push. Or, you can park at the Second Beach trailhead along the highway and walk down to the beach along the Olympic Discovery Trail paralleling the road.

First Beach, in La Push, WA on the Quileute Indian Reservation, WA

First Beach is another excellent walking beach, easily accessible without the need for a hike. Enjoy the beach, views of James and Little James Islands, and the **La Push Marina**. It is very scenic. Lodging is available within a stone's throw at the excellent Quileute Oceanside Resort which fronts First Beach in La Push (book well in advance!). Or, if you're ready to move on, drive into Forks, which is fourteen miles (22.5 km) to the south, or to Port Angeles, which is sixty-nine miles (111 km) to the north.

Quileute Nation: http://www.quileutenation.org/

Indian Country Etiquette: https://quileutenation.org/indian-country-etiquette/

Quileute Oceanside Resort: http://www.quileuteoceanside.com/

Lodging in La Push

Quileute Oceanside Resort & RV Park, 330 Ocean Drive, La Push, WA 98350

360-374-5267. http://www.quileuteoceanside.com/

The Quileute Indian Tribe welcomes you to this luxury resort literally on the shore of the Pacific Ocean. Deluxe and standard cabins, camper cabins, and two full-service RV parks. **Getting there:** From Highway 101, take Highway 110 all the way into the Quileute Indian Reservation to the address. The resort is on the left side of the road.

Lodging near Highway 110 and Mora Road

Quillayute River Resort, 473 Mora Rd., Forks, WA 98331

360-374-7447. http://qriverresort.com/

Suites, fireplaces, heated bathroom tiles, organic skin products, strong wi-fi.

Three Rivers Resort, 7764 La Push Rd., Forks, WA 98331

360-374-5300. http://www.threeriversresortandguideservice.com/

Located at La Push Road and Mora Road.

Manitou Lodge, 813 Kilmer Rd., Forks, WA 98331

360-374-6295. http://www.manitoulodge.com/

Westernmost B&B in the Lower Forty-Eight, located on ten acres of coastal rain forest west of Forks. Getting there: From Highway 101 take Highway 110 (La Push Road) to Mora Road. Turn right and go to Kilmer Road. Turn right to address.

La Push Restaurant

River's Edge Restaurant, 41 La Push Rd., Forks, WA 98331

360-374-0777. FB: https://www.facebook.com/riversedgelapush/

Hours: 7 days, 8a-7p. Dine with an amazing view near the La Push Marina. On the menu is incredibly fresh seafood: salmon, crab, steelhead, and much more, including house-made desserts.

Second Beach (Olympic National Park)

National Park Service - Second Beach Trail:

https://www.nps.gov/olym/planyourvisit/second-beach-trail.htm.

Second Beach is located south of First Beach, within the Olympic National Park. Get to the beach via a 0.7 mile (1.1 km) moderate hike to the shore from the well-marked trailhead at Highway 110 (La Push Road). If you arrive at First Beach, you will have passed the trailheads to both Second and Third Beaches.

At Second Beach, you'll find wonderful hard-sand beach to the south. Tide pools (at low tide) are to the north. Beach camping IS allowed; wilderness camping permits required (Part 3F).

Third Beach (Olympic National Park)

National Park Service - Third Beach Trail: https://www.nps.gov/olym/planyourvisit/third-beach-trail.htm

Third Beach is yet another sandy crescent accessed by a 1.5-mile (2.4 km) easy hike to the beach. The Third Beach trailhead is on La Push Road (Highway 110), close to La Push, WA. Allow time to make the hike to the beach, and time to stroll the beach. Pack some food with you and stay awhile, because this is a truly magnificent beach, complete with copious sea stacks and a waterfall. Camping IS permitted on the beach. (Wilderness camping permits required – see Part 3F.)

Third Beach in La Push, WA has it all: sea stacks, waterfall, sandy beach, tide pools, and plenty of driftwood cast up on the beach.

Next - M: Hoh Rain Forest in Olympic National Park!

Getting there from the east: The Upper Hoh Road intersection with Highway 101 is 13.02 miles (21 km) south of Forks. Turn east (left) on Upper Hoh Road.

Getting there from the west: The Upper Hoh Road intersection with Highway 101 is 13.77 miles (22 km) north of the Ruby Beach entrance on Highway 101. Turn east (right) on Upper Hoh Rd.

4M) Hoh Rain Forest in the Olympic National Park

Rain Forest Central!

The entire stretch of Highway 101 between Forks and Aberdeen is "temperate rain forest central." The Hoh Rain Forest, Yahoo Lake, and Queets and Quinault Rain Forests are equally soaked in rain forest ambience.

The Hoh Rain Forest, a premier example of North America's temperate rain forest, is **#2 on our list of Top-7** destinations. To get to the Hoh Rain Forest Visitor Center from Highway 101 traveling south from Forks, WA, travel a scant fifteen miles, and turn left (east) onto Upper Hoh Road. The signage directing you to the Hoh Rain Forest should be clear. The road eventually changes names to Hoh Valley Road, and ends at the Visitor Center. You will have traveled about thirty-one miles (50 km) from downtown Forks.

The Nightmare Tree: Moss-laden Big Leaf maple tree in the Hoh Rain Forest

The Hoh Rain Forest encompasses twenty-four miles of low elevation forest along the Hoh River. This coastal temperate rain forest is one of the largest in the U.S. Though parts of the area outside the Park have been logged over the last century, inside the Park there is plenty remaining of the quiet mystery of moss, fern and lichen and the awe-inspiring native Sitka spruce and western hemlock. These giants can reach sizes of over 300 feet high and twenty-five feet in diameter.

Conditions Producing a Coastal Temperate Rain Forest

On the Olympic Peninsula, the combination of proximity to the Pacific, moisture-laden air, and the precipitous rise of the mountains work together to produce the abundance of rainfall needed for temperate rain forests.

As moist sea air rises over the south and western slopes of the Olympic mountain peaks, the air quickly cools, triggering 100% relative humidity and then rainfall. The air that flows over the peaks to the lee side of the Olympics (mostly to the northeast) has lost much of its moisture and is often dry. (See Rainshadow map under Sequim, Part 4C.)

The Olympic Mountains are tall enough to trap most of the moisture on the windward side, or south and west-facing slopes. This is where you find the rain forests of the Hoh, Queets, and Quinault Valleys, and to a lesser extent Sol Duc, while the surrounding lowlands nearer the coast, including Forks, La Push, and Aberdeen, still receive more rainfall than most other towns across the United States.

In the Pacific Northwest, areas that receive 100 inches of rain or more annually are considered rain forest.

The Hoh embodies all that is a temperate rain forest. The surrounding terrain gets lots and lots of rain: 144–172 inches (12-14 feet or 366-437 cm) annually, on average.

Unique Flora and Growth Traits in the Hoh and other Temperate Rain Forests

Nurse Trees

When a tree falls, perhaps by high winds, it can take up to 100 years to decompose, leaving plenty of time for its remains to support the next generation. These are commonly called nurse trees because their decaying structures nourish seedlings that sprout on top of the log until they are nearly giants themselves.

Colonnades and Stilt Trees

Stands of colonnade trees result from the saplings that have grown up single file along the length of a fallen nurse tree.

The nurse tree that thundered to the ground a millennium ago is long gone, but you can certainly imagine where it would have lain all those many years. In its place is a colonnade of Sitka spruce.

As these saplings grow, their roots sink into and stretch around the nurse tree, thickening and strengthening as the tree grows. When the nurse tree has finally disintegrated, the empty hole where the nurse tree once lay becomes evident. Trees that got their start on a nurse tree sometimes look like they are standing on stilts because of the hole circumscribed by the massive roots.

Oregon Oxalis

Oregon oxalis, also known as redwood sorrel, is a hallmark of Pacific Northwest temperate rain forests. It loves the shade, and can be found nestled at the base of, and spreading out underneath, the canopy of conifers and other large trees, especially Douglas fir. Springtime is when you are likely to see their tiny white to pink star-shaped blooms.

Oregon Oxalis   *Epiphytic Moss*

Epiphytes

Epiphytes are plants that grow on another plant without being parasitic. Mosses, lichens and certain fern species can grow so heavy on big leaf maple trunks and branches as to topple trees or break off limbs. There are areas in the rain forest where it seems that mosses of some sort or another cover everything, from the forest floor to the bark on trees.

Fauna in the Hoh Rain Forest

The Olympic National Park is home to the largest un-managed herd of Roosevelt elk in North America– roughly 5,000 individuals. The elk subspecies, *Cervus Canadensis roosevelti*, was named after President Theodore Roosevelt, who saw the need to protect the elk from excessive hunting. Olympic National Park's initial working title was "Elk National Park," as it was intended that a large national park would protect these once-threatened animals from extinction. Today the elk population which was decimated due to overhunting in Roosevelt's day hase rebounded, and their populations are now stable.

In addition to elk: Chickadees, wrens, woodpeckers, nuthatches and thrushes, Pacific chorus frogs, black-tailed deer, cougar, Olympic black bear (at higher elevations), bobcats, raccoons, and enormous banana slugs all thrive in the Hoh Valley.

Hoh Visitor Center is the Hub of the Hoh

This is because most of the walking and hiking trails are accessible at or near the Hoh Visitor Center. Stopping at the Visitor Center can be very helpful – ask all your questions about the amazing rain forest or obtain local up-to-the-minute information about trails. Check out the rain forest exhibits, get your wilderness permit, and purchase a gift or souvenir.

The Hoh Visitor Center, Hoh Valley Rd., Forks, WA 98331

(360) 374-6925

https://www.nps.gov/olym/planyourvisit/visiting-the-hoh.htm

Hours: Check current hours by calling (360) 374-6925. Open daily in summer; open weekends during the off-season. Closed January and February.

PDF Brochure of the Hoh Rain Forest: https://www.nps.gov/olym/planyourvisit/upload/hoh.pdf

Hoh Rain Forest Trails

You have your choice of five trails within the Olympic National Park's Hoh Rain Forest, ranging from easy to difficult. All will lead through rain forest mosses dripping from maple trees, creeping over fallen trees and carpeting the forest floor. Look for "nurse" trees nurturing the next generation of distinguished sentinels.

- **The Mini Trail** is 0.1 mile (161 m), flat and paved, accessible for those who need assistance.
- **The Hall of Mosses Trail**. This 0.8 mile long (1.29 km) trail begins with an initial incline then levels off to a comfortable loop through "halls" of mosses.

- **The Spruce Nature Trail** is a 1.2 mile (1.93 km) loop providing another opportunity to marvel at rain forest mystery and beauty. This hike will take you to the bank of the Hoh River and then back to the Visitor Center.

These short trails are wonderful for giving the essence and magic of the Hoh Rain Forest. It is not a waste of time to stroll all three of them.

The Hoh Mini Trail is level and paved.

Hardcore Hiking Trails

Two additional trails are for the experienced and well-conditioned hiker. They may include fording rivers and/or traversing glaciers.

- **The South Snider-Jackson Trail** (also called the Hoh Lake Trail) originates six miles (9.66 km) west of the Visitor Center at the Olympic National Park entrance station. Its **11.8 mile** (19 km), 2,700-feet (823 m) ascent and descent will take you to the Bogachiel River.

- **The Hoh River Trail** starts near the Hoh Visitor Center. In **17.3 miles** (27.84 km), you'll climb 3,700 feet (1,128 m) to Glacier Meadows on the shoulder of Mount Olympus.

  https://www.nps.gov/olym/planyourvisit/hoh-river-trail. htm

  Diehard hikers can hike beyond Glacier Meadows to the Mount Olympus Blue Glacier. Find the Blue Glacier trailhead 0.9 miles (1.45 km) beyond Glacier Meadows. Along the way catch glimpses of the High Divide and Mount Tom. Backpackers will need a wilderness permit for overnight stays (available along with bear canisters at the Port Angeles Wilderness Information Center – call 360-565-3100).

  Or, if you like, hike only as far as Five Mile Island, an area just 5.3 miles (8.53 km) along the Hoh River Trail (10.6 miles or 17 km counting the return hike). Altitude gain is negligible. This is a lovely hike, and sightings of elk are somewhat likely. But, it will feel really long if you're unused to hiking. For more info on hiking the Hoh River Trail to Five Mile Island, check this link:

  http://www.wta.org/go-hiking/hikes/hoh-river

Lodging in or near the Hoh Rain Forest

Hoh Campground

The Hoh Campground is situated within the Hoh Rain Forest surrounded by lush rain forest, and is open year round. It is wheelchair accessible with flush toilets and potable water.

Eighty-eight campsites, first-come, first-serve. Show up, and if there's room, you can have a spot. Many campsites on A Loop and C Loop border the Hoh River, which snakes along beyond the trees in this photo. RVs up to twenty-one feet. Flush toilets and potable water. The campground IS handicap accessible.

Hard Rain Café

The Hard Rain Café on Upper Hoh Road also provides camping and an RV Park. Ten RV spots that handle larger rigs with difficulty. If you're lucky, maybe you can snag the one cabin available for rent. See listing below. Additionally, check their website for their recreational ideas.

Department of Natural Resources (DNR) Campgrounds

360-374-6131. http://www.dnr.wa.gov/OlympicPeninsula.

These DNR campgrounds are located outside but near the Hoh Rain Forest. First-come, first-served. Discover Pass required. Dogs okay on leash.

- **Hoh Ox Bow Campground:** Eight primitive campsites tucked into an "S" curve in the Hoh River.

- **Willoughby Campground:** Three campsites along the Hoh River.

- **Minnie Peterson Campground:** Nine primitive campsites on the bank of the Hoh River. Accommodates RVs up to sixteen feet

Bogachiel State Park, 185983 Highway 101, Forks, WA 98331

360-374-6356.

www.parks.state.wa.us/478/Bogachiel/

Bogachiel State Park is located six miles (9.25 km) south of Forks on Highway 101, and 7.5 miles (12 km) north of the Upper Hoh and Highway 101 intersection. The park is small, has a rain forest vibe, and is lovely for stretching the legs, day-use picnicking during a long road trip, and overnight camping. Its campsites are ideal for tenting and small RVs. You'll need a **Discover Pass** for day use (Part 3F), a fee that is incorporated into the camping fees should you choose to spend the night. This is a great camping alternative if the Hoh Campground is full.

On the other hand, stop here only on an "as-needed" basis, as there is nothing remarkable here if you don't need a pit stop, and you intend to stop at the Hoh, Queets, or Quinault Rain Forests.

Other Lodging in the Area:

Civilized lodging can be found in Forks, WA (Part 4K).

Food near the Hoh

The nearest (and only) restaurant by the Hoh Rain Forest is the Hard Rain Café, located on Upper Hoh Road. (You will pass it on the way into the Hoh Rain Forest.) Forks is your only other quasi-local source of food, if you have not brought your own. See Part 4K for restaurants in Forks.

Hard Rain Café and RV, 5763 Upper Hoh Rd., Forks, WA 98331

360-374-9288. http://www.hardraincafe.com/index.htm

Not open year round; typically opens in early April. **Hours**: 9a-7p. No reservations required. Breakfast, lunch, dinner, hamburgers, salmon burgers, smoked salmon, German Chocolate (Ya, sie sprechen Deutsch), snacks and meals to-go. It's not fancy, but the food is good.

Recreation in the Hoh

Peak 6 Tours and Rainforest Paddlers, 4883 Upper Hoh Rd., Forks, WA 98331

360-374-5254; Toll-free: 1-866-457-8398.

http://www.rainforestpaddlers.com/

Guides for rafting and kayaking on the Hoh and Quillayute Rivers, equipment rentals (boat, kayak, bicycles). Equipment sales, in case you need a kayak to go.

Next - N: Kalaloch Beaches in Olympic National Park!

All Kalaloch beaches are located on or along Highway 101.

Getting there from the north: Ruby Beach is thirty-two miles (51.5 km) south of the Hoh Rain Forest Visitor Center, and twenty-seven miles (43.5 km) from Forks.

Getting there from the south: Kalaloch Lodge and Beach are thirty-one miles (50 km) north of Amanda Park, WA near Lake Quinault.

4N) Kalaloch Beaches in the Olympic National Park

The entire fifteen-mile stretch of sandy beach from Ruby Beach south to South Beach at the southern point of the Olympic National Park is actually considered to be Kalaloch Beach, singular, with multiple access points. Several of these access points are unimaginatively named using consecutive numbering, for example, Beach 1, 2, 3, 4. All of these beaches are within the borders of the Olympic National Park.

"*Kalaloch*," pronounced *KLAY-lock*, means "good place to land" in the local Quinault tongue, and we think you'll agree after you've landed here yourself. Smooth sandy beaches, except for the driftwood that litter them, stretch for miles.

All of these Olympic National Park beaches—Ruby Beach, Beach 4, Beach 3, Kalaloch Beach, Beach 2, Beach 1, and the South Beach Campground—are easily accessible, expansive, and sandy, with various assortments of the following: fascinating tide pools, wildlife, birdwatching, sea stacks, spectacular sunsets, and storm watching if the weather obliges, and it just might, the whole area being temperate rain forest.

Ruby Beach

Beach Camping: "*Campgrounds at Kalaloch and South Beach are the only places to camp on the southern coast of Olympic National Park*" (quoted from first link below). Enjoy day use only of the beaches from Ruby Beach to South Beach; there is no overnight or primitive camping permitted on any of these beaches. (Unlike the beaches around Rialto Beach, where beach camping IS permitted between the Quillayute River and Ellen Creek.)

Check these Olympic National Park web pages for additional information on the Kalaloch beaches, the Olympic Coast National Marine Sanctuary, hiking the southern beaches, the tide pools, and more.

- Main info page:
  https://www.nps.gov/olym/planyourvisit/visiting-
  kalaloch-and-ruby-beach.htm
- Kalaloch Beaches Brochure:
  https://www.nps.gov/olym/planyourvisit/upload/
  Kalaloch.pdf
- Tide Pools:
  https://www.nps.gov/olym/planyourvisit/tidepool-
  activities.htm
- Tide pool safety:
  https://www.nps.gov/olym/planyourvisit/tides-and-
  your-safety.htm

Ruby Beach

Ruby Beach is one of my Top-7 destinations on the Olympic Peninsula, which is convenient, as it is located right on Highway 101 as the highway meets the Pacific Ocean south of the Hoh River. Ruby Beach is so named for the relatively high concentration of granular garnets in the sand. In the right light, they say, the sand glows pinkish. This beach is one of THE most photogenic beaches on the Washington shoreline, though I have thoroughly enjoyed photographing each of the beaches.

If you can, plan your visit to Ruby Beach at low tide, so you can cross Cedar Creek, which drains into the Pacific Ocean between the trail and the stretch of beach with all the sea stacks. (Or roll up the pant legs and hoof it barefoot.)

Beach 4

Approximately four miles south of Ruby Beach on Highway 101 is the Kalaloch Beach access point known as Beach 4. The beach is well marked. Turn off the highway to the west into a parking lot and take the short trail to the beach.

Beach 4. There are very cool tide pools in those rocks.

Beach 4 is known for excellent tide pools (*pictured*), which you'll find in the crevices of the rocky outcrops to the north of the beach access point. There are no facilities at Beach 4.

Beach 3

The access point for Beach 3 is located about 0.7 mile (1.12 km) south of Beach 4. Parking is provided alongside Highway 101 in a wide turnout paved for that purpose. The trailhead is marked with a small brown sign proclaiming "Beach 3," and an arrow indicating the way. The trail descends on dirt, gravel, and wooden stairs, losing approximately 100 feet in elevation to the beach. It's not terribly hard or far, and the short hike is a beautiful one. The beach itself is littered with drift logs and practically begs one to scavenge for drift wood, shells, or rocks. There are no facilities here.

Kalaloch Beach

Kalaloch Beach and Kalaloch Lodge are roughly two miles past the turn-off for Beach 3 on Highway 101 in the southern stretch of Olympic National Park beaches. The beach is a spectacular one for walking, beachcombing, and marine life viewing. Additionally, the **Kalaloch Nature Trail** offers an easy one-mile (1.6 km) looped hike through nearby rain forest. Find the trailhead on Highway 101 approximately 1100 feet (335 meters) south of the entrance to the Kalaloch Campground.

Kalaloch Creek Nature Trail: The Kalaloch Creek Nature Trail is a one-mile (1.6 km) easy looped hike through coastal rain forest. Altitude gain is only forty feet (12 m), and stairs are provided where needed. The trailhead is located halfway between the campground and the lodge on the east side of the road (away from the ocean); there is room to park on the side of the road if you're not parked already at the lodge or campground.

Kalaloch Beach at the mouth of Kalaloch Creek

Kalaloch Campground: https://www.nps.gov/olym/planyourvisit/camping.htm.

170 total sites. See the website for all the details. While there, you can watch for murres, puffins, and bald eagles, and keep an eye out for

whales. Stroll the beach and check out the astonishing "tree of life" or a spectacular sunset.

Kalaloch Tree Cave: Suspended over a cave in the bluff to the north of Kalaloch Lodge is a tree, most of whose roots end uselessly in the air. The few roots extending into the soil hold the tree in the air while the soil has eroded below it. The tree has been dubbed the "tree of life," and it is a sight to behold. One of these decades the whole thing is bound to tumble to the sand, but until then, a look-see is a great reason to go strolling on Kalaloch Beach by the bluffs at the foot of the campground.

Kalaloch Lodge

Kalaloch Lodge, 157151 Highway 101, Forks, WA 98331

360-962-2271; toll free: 866-662-9928. http://www.thekalalochlodge. com/

Kalaloch Lodge sits on the edge of a driftwood strewn coast on Highway 101, about forty minutes south of Forks (ninety minutes south of Port Angeles). Kalaloch Lodge provides an ideal position for watching both sunsets and storms.

Get yourself a room in the lodge itself, or opt for a delightful cliffside cabin with wood-burning stove (wood included). The cabin sleeps six, along with a sitting area, dining area, and a very adequate kitchen, plus bathroom and shower.

Creekside Restaurant at Kalaloch Lodge: http://www.thekalaloch lodge.com/Dine.aspx

Dining Reservations: 360-962-2271 ext. 4007

Summer Hours: Breakfast 7a-11a; Lunch 11a-5p; Dinner 5p-9p. **Winter Hours:** 8a-8p.

Breakfast, lunch and dinner are served at the Creekside Restaurant. The food is outstanding with ingredients sourced locally, and the dining room offers spectacular views of the Pacific Ocean.

You can also include the purchase of a sack lunch with your room reservation. They make it fresh for you in the morning so you can take it with you on a rain forest hiking expedition or sandy beach stroll. (There are very few food options around the Hoh Rain Forest!)

Beach 2

Beach 2, Beach 1, and the South Beach Campground are 1-, 2-, and 3 miles (1.6, 3.2, 4.8 km) south of Kalaloch Beach, at the southern tip of the Olympic National Park shoreline. The access trails are, in each case, short and well-marked at Highway 101 as long as you are watching for the signs.

The hike to Beach 2 is short, and involves fording a creek and crossing a short foot bridge. In the wintertime, that creek may be running bank to bank, meaning you'll need some decent rubber boots to cross without getting your feet wet. Nevertheless, the beach is worth the short hike.

Spruce trees and burls at Beach 1

Beach 1

The short trail to Beach 1 traverses a short but fascinating stretch of forest filled with spruce trees afflicted by the spruce gall, resulting in a heavy concentration of large spruce burls. In fact, the ONP created a "Spruce Burl Trail" through the affected forest, with explanatory plaques.

South Beach Campground

The South Beach Campground is perched on a bluff offering spectacular and unobstructed views of the Pacific Ocean. https://www.nps.gov/olym/planyourvisit/camping.htm.   Park   entrance fee applies (Part 3F). The campground is open from May through September; reservations are first-come, first-served. See the website for more info and fees.

The South Beach **day-use area** immediately south of the campground entrance is green and grassy, with picnic tables, an outhouse, and gorgeous views. The photo above was taken from the day-use area.

South Beach Campground on the bluff, expansive beach below.

Multiple trails lead down to the beach itself where you can walk for miles to the north and back. (The Quinault Indian Reservation is just 1442 feet or 0.27 miles [0.44 km] to the south.) A 2.76 mile (4.43 km) hike to the north will bring you to the mouth of Kalaloch Creek at the foot of Kalaloch Lodge.

Strolling or Hiking any of the Olympic National Park Beaches

Take a hike and take your time. Look for wildlife, bird species, and whales. (Whale migration seasons are March/April and October.)

Be sure to take a topographic map with you if you plan extensive hikes, as some areas are more easily accessible than others. Some offer passage during high tide, others do not. If you're not careful, it is possible to get caught or stranded by a high tide.

Essential tools:

Be sure to take a topographic map with you if you plan extensive hikes, as some areas are more easily accessible than others. Some offer passage during high tide, others do not. If you're not careful, it is possible to get caught or stranded by a high tide. See Part 3H for links to a recommended topographical map.

Local Tide Table: http://www.saltwatertides.com/dynamic.dir/washingtonsites.html—choose the location nearest to you, then enter the date at the bottom of the page.

(You may also like to use a smartphone app – see Part 5E.)

> **Next – Segment O: Queets Rain Forest in Olympic National Park!**

Getting there from the southeast: On Highway 101, the Queets River Road intersection is 17.7 miles (28.5 km) miles west of Amanda Park, WA.

Getting there from the north: On Highway 101, the Queets River Road intersection is 12.5 miles (20 km) south of Kalaloch Lodge.

Queets River Road is the northern access point to the Queets Rain Forest.

4O) Queets Rain Forest in Olympic National Park

From Highway 101, Queets River Road is your access point into the Queets Rain Forest in the Olympic National Park. The point of intersection is 7.5 miles (12 km) south and then east of the Queets River.

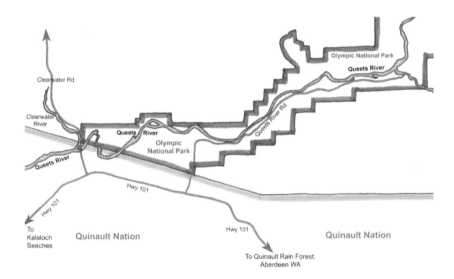

   The small native Quinault town of Queets sits on the south bank of the Queets River at the Highway 101 bridge over the Queets. You will likely not see too much of the town itself, but you *will* see the Queets Trading Post just beyond the Queets River at the corner of 101 and Jackson Heights Drive.

Queets Trading Post, 402 Jackson Heights Drive, Forks, WA 98331

360-962-2003.

https://www.facebook.com/pages/Queets-Trading-Post/117664184926656

If necessary, fuel the car, and get snacks and more at the convenience store.

Clearwater Valley to Yahoo Lake

The next point of interest is **Clearwater Road** which is just five miles (8 km) from the Queets Trading Post. Clearwater Road turns north (left) and follows the Clearwater River north along the Clearwater Valley for miles. Given that you are surrounded by epic rainforest destinations like the Hoh, Queets, and Quinault Rain Forests, I'm not sure that most folks would give the Clearwater Valley a second thought. It is rain forest, but it is also a managed forest, meaning, harvested by periodically leveling it to the ground.

Just keep pressing on, I say. **EXCEPT, Yahoo Lake.** If camping high in the Olympics by a remote but beautiful little alpine lake next to almost no one else is a thing for you, then a little detour along logging roads high into the hills to **Yahoo Lake** might be just right!

Yahoo Lake: https://www.dnr.wa.gov/OlympicPeninsula (at bottom of page)

Getting to Yahoo Lake: From Highway 101 just southeast of Queets, take the Hoh Mainline/Clearwater Road to the left (north). Clearwater Road tracks generally alongside the Clearwater River. Travel around fourteen miles (22 km), and then take NF-C3000, a logging road, to the right (east), and go 0.8 miles. Turn right on NF-C3100 Road (one lane paved, then gravel. Google Maps may continue to label this road C-3000). Continue 6.1 miles to the Yahoo Lake trailhead: a 500-foot boardwalk trail from the parking area to the lake. I'm told it'll take you a little more than an hour to make the drive.

Yahoo Lake is nestled in the notch of several mountain ridges at 2,400 feet altitude. The campground offers four sites. Besides the pristine quietness and beautiful surroundings, it is also possible to walk all around the lake. The facilities are fairly primitive. Bring water and toilet paper. What else you can do while here? Whitewater paddling, swimming, fishing. Another bonus to the location is the ability to tie in with some serious long-distance high-country hiking trails.

The Queets Rain Forest

From the junction of Clearwater Road and Highway 101, continue heading south, and east, another 2.5 miles (4 km) to Queets River Road. Pass the Queets-Clearwater Elementary School which is clearly visible from the highway and watch for the big brown sign one-half mile (0.8 km) before the turnoff stating: "**OLYMPIC National Park – Queets Valley Lower – LEFT 1/2 MILE**." The road will be a gravel one, but fairly well maintained.

Queets River Road exists in two segments due to a road washout several years ago. The lower segment is easy to get to; it's the stretch of road that intersects directly with Highway 101.

Turn left (north) onto Queets River Road. In less than half a mile (0.8 km), the road enters the Olympic National Park and its raw rain forest along the Queets River.

Olympic National Park Queets Rain Forest Area Brochure can be downloaded:

https://www.nps.gov/olym/planyourvisit/upload/Queetsnew access-2.pdf

Queets River Valley in the Olympic National Park

While the Hoh and Quinault Rain Forests are wet and beautiful, there is the distinct presence of humanity there, which is not bad at all, of course. In contrast, the Queets River Valley is a rain forest at its most wild and rugged, even neglected. It is as though one must prepare, not for bears or wolves, but for pterodactyls and T. Rex. The crunching of Queets River Road gravel supports the illusion, though the fact that you're riding in a decidedly twenty-first century vehicle will bring you back to reality.

The road heads straight for the Queets River, then bends to the northeast, generally tracking along the southern shore of the Queets River for many miles. As the road turns east, it crosses the Salmon River, which empties into the Queets. A little farther brings the traveler to the Hartzell Creek boat ramp. While the banks of the Queets are generally steep, here is where you can walk out (or possibly drive!) onto the sand bars. It is also when you'll suddenly wish you had high waders so you would not necessarily be confined solely to sandy gravel.

Queets River and Olympic Mountains

The Queets riverbed is amazingly wide. The river itself, milky blue with glacial melt, meanders in dramatic S-curves around and over sandbars and gravel. Tree bones litter the sandy river bed, washed downriver for miles and miles. I have no doubt that during spring runoff the river rages in bank-to-bank torrents. The views of distant snow-capped mountains against the backdrop of the Queets River are magical.

The road travels for 7.23 miles (11.64 km) along the main trunk of the Queets to the bank of the lower fork of the Queets River, and then abruptly ends due to the flood washout. The far end of Queets River Road is 4.79 miles (7.70 km) long and perfectly navigable, but to get there, you have to go back to Highway 101, travel 7.03 miles (11.3 km) farther south, and then turn left (north) on West Boundary Road.

Queets River at the Hartzell Creek boat ramp

Getting to the far end of the road: West Boundary Road (NF-21) turns into NF-2405. Travel roughly 7.84 miles on 2405, most of which is paved. At the junction of NF-2422 bear left, staying on 2405, which will end at Queets River Road. From Highway 101 to Queets River Road is 9.24 miles (14.87 km). The road goes in either direction; turn right (east) to go to the ranger station.

It's worth it! What's really cool about this stretch of the road is that it takes you to the Queets Ranger Station (usually unmanned) and the trailhead to **Sam's Loop Trail**. This is a three-mile (4.82 km) narrow foot trail through primordial and magnificent old-growth rain forest. Because the area is so remote, hikers may see the local herd of Roosevelt elk, and also black bear in springtime. (Be wary!) **TIP:** Bring rubber boots as some stretches of the trail are perennially waterlogged. Glorious. Here is how the Washington Trails website describes this trail: http://www.wta.org/go-hiking/hikes/sams-river

---

Next – Segment P: Quinault Rain Forest in Olympic National Park!

Getting there from the south: Quinault Lodge Is forty-four miles (71 km) north of Aberdeen, WA.

Getting there from the west: Quinault Lodge is 20.5 miles (33 km) east of the Highway 101/Queets River Road Junction.

4P) Quinault Rain Forest in the Olympic National Park

"Valley of the Rainforest Giants"

The Quinault Rain Forest region extends from the Pacific Ocean to the Olympic Mountains. A large part of this area includes the Quinault Indian Reservation, but the public areas are preserved within the boundaries of the Olympic National Park and Forest surrounding Lake Quinault and the Quinault River Valley. North Shore Road,

South Shore Road, and Graves Creek Road provide access deeper into the rain forest and into the mountains to lower elevations.

The Quinault Rain Forest receives on average twelve feet (3.66 m) of rain every year. This surely contributes to the fact that a large number of record-sized giant trees grow within the confines of the Quinault Valley.

The Olympic National Park Quinault brochure can be downloaded:

https://www.nps.gov/olym/planyourvisit/upload/quinault.pdf

Amanda Park, Washington

The village of Amanda Park, population 252 (2010 census), is a Quinault tribal town, and indeed, the lake itself is administered by the Quinault Indian Nation. It straddles the west end of Lake Quinault and the Quinault River as it leaves the lake and meanders its way to the Pacific Ocean.

Quinault River as it flows out of Lake Quinault in Amanda Park, toward the Pacific Ocean.

For a village in the middle of a rain forest getting an average of 129 inches (329.66 cm) of rain per year, the month of July is surprisingly dry. An average of less than one inch (2 cm) of rain falls in July. June and August both average 3.3 inches (8.4 cm). Ideally, you'll want at least a little rain to fall during a visit to a rain forest—it keeps the moss green and the trees vibrant.

The town, small as it is, does have a few amenities for the traveler. There's a gas station, mercantile, a market, an inn and RV park, an internet café with info center, and a pizza joint that elicits varied opinions of quality. All of these enterprises are on or very close to Highway 101.

Quinault River Village Internet Café and Visitor Information Center, 6094-B US Highway 101, Amanda Park, WA 98526

360-288-0571.　　http://www.quinaultrainforest.com/Quinault-WA/information-center.html

Hours: Mon-Fri 8a-4p; Sat-Sun 7a-4p. Being a visitor center, these folks know everything about everything, and are more than happy to help you resolve all your questions so you can have a great visit in the Quinault Valley. They are situated just north of the Quinault River Bridge in downtown Amanda Park. Along with answers and free wi-fi, they also serve espresso, American cuisine, beer, and wine.

Bear Hunting, Salmon and Steelhead Fishing

The hunting and fishing are apparently outstanding! However, because the activities take place on the Quinault Reservation (which includes the lake itself), you are required to have an accompanying Quinault tribal member. Get in touch with fishing and hunting guides at one of these websites:

- Quinault Tribal http://www.quinaultindiannation.com/
- Quinault River Inn http://quinaultriverinn.com/fish/

Lodging, RV Park

Quinault River Inn, 8 River Drive, Amanda Park, WA 98526

360-410-2237. http://quinaultriverinn.com/

Amenities include a complimentary fitness center on site. Rates vary with seasons.

Town of Quinault, Washington

The village of **Quinault** hugs the south shore of Lake Quinault, which is probably the main focus for tourism, and the Quinault Rain Forest. Olympic National Park's Lake Quinault Lodge is here. Quinault also offers a gas station, a museum, several miles of easy to moderate looping rainforest and lake hiking trails, a ranger station, and several lodges, restaurants, and campgrounds.

Things to Do

See as many champion big trees as you have time and conditioning for. Quinault Valley isn't called "Valley of the Rainforest Giants" for nothing. Six "biggest-of-their-species" trees live here. The largest western red cedar, largest Sitka spruce, and co-largest Douglas fir are very easy to get to.

The largest yellow cedar in the USA is six more miles up the trail from Irely Lake on the North Shore. The largest mountain hemlock and largest western hemlock are thirteen and fourteen miles up the trail in Enchanted Valley. Download and print this PDF overview: http://www.quinaultrainforest.com/pdf/GIANTSpg.pdf and then stop at the ranger station or the Quinault Information Center for more information and directions.

This world-record Sitka spruce tree grows just a quarter-mile (0.4 km)
from South Shore Drive in Quinault.

North Shore to South Shore Loop Drive. A hugely popular activity is completing the North Shore-South Shore loop around Lake Quinault. This is also a great opportunity to eat that boxed lunch you picked up at Kalaloch Lodge (or purchased in Amanda Park or brought on your own).

North Shore Road travels to the east along Lake Quinault through parts of the Olympic National Park and past a few more lodging opportunities. The road continues along the banks of the Quinault River through old-growth forest. The road is paved for quite a few miles along North Shore Road, then becomes a gravel road until the transition to South Shore Road. **FYI:** The road is not suitable for trailers and RVs.

After fourteen miles (22.5 km) it crosses the Quinault River. Changing names to South Shore Road, it transits west along the south bank of the Quinault River and lake, passes through the village of Quinault, WA in the Olympic National Forest, and rejoins Highway 101.

The total length of the Quinault Loop drive is 27.25 miles (42.86 km), and will probably take longer than anticipated due to road conditions along the gravel stretches of the drive. In fact, because of the various points of interest and trailheads along both North and South Shore Drives, you might like to simply plan a full day (or more) for your tour into the Quinault rain forest.

North Shore scenic spots, from west end to east end:

- **Quinault Big Cedar Tree:** about 1.5 miles (2.4 km) along North Shore Road is a turnout and sign for a short hike to an enormous western red cedar tree. This hike is short but strenuous, because it takes you up the side of the mountain.

- **Quinault Rain Forest Ranger Station** (Olympic National Park)**:** Open part-time in the summer as staffing allows. If no ranger is present, you can still follow two self-guided hikes with trailheads at the station:

  ◻ **Maple Glade Rain Forest Trail:** a flat, half-mile (0.8 km) loop through temperate rain forest rich in moss-draped big-leaf maples

  ◻ **Kestner Homestead Trail:** 1.3-mile looped trail to the old Kestner homestead on the north shore of Lake Quinault. The homestead is listed on the National Register of Historic Places in Grays Harbor County, WA.

- **Irely Lake Trail:** Find the trailhead on North Shore Road beyond the turnoff that would bring you to South Shore Road. The hike is 1.1 miles (1.77 km) one way, a fairly easy hike to a scenic lake. Find the trailhead 0.25 miles before the North Fork Campground. If you like, you can keep hiking onward and upward to Three Lakes. On your way, you'll pass a record-setting Alaska yellow cedar tree.

Lake Quinault on a misty winter morning

South Shore scenic spots, from east end to west end:

- **Bunch Falls** (near road)

- **Fletcher Canyon Trail:** Trailhead is on South Shore Road 1.4 miles from the North Shore-South Shore bridge. This is a 4.1 mile round trip (6.6 km) moderate hike through rain forest with 1100 feet of elevation gain to a high point of 1450 feet (442 m) in altitude. Bonus: Fletcher waterfall. Another bonus: you may encounter one or more small herds of Roosevelt elk.

- **Merriman Falls** (not far from the road)

- **Gatton Creek Trailhead**, near the Gatton Creek Campground. 1.6 mile (2.6 km) easy to moderate hike. Walk along South Shore Road to return to the trailhead. Bonus: Gatton Creek Falls. **TIP:** Taking Wrights Canyon Road (gravel) into the forest will get you to within 0.3 miles (0.48km) of the falls. Park and walk to Gatton Falls – those 0.3 miles should be wheelchair accessible.

- **Quinault National Recreation Trail System** https://www.fs.usda.gov/Internet/FSE_DOCUMENTS/stelprdb5363543.pdf

- A series of looped and sometimes interconnected trails of varying lengths, most being very easy hikes. These trails are roughly centered on Willaby Campground to Gatton Creek Campground in Quinault. They climb into the rain forest south of South Shore Road, looping around and tracing the shoreline of Lake Crescent. Most of the trailheads are on South Shore Road. There are MORE hiking opportunities than are listed here! Download the map from the link above, and if necessary obtain more information and maps at the Quinault Forest Service Ranger Station.

  - **Rain Forest Nature Trail** (0.5 mile loop) (0.8 km): *"The Quinault Rain Forest in a nutshell."*

  - **Falls Creek Loop** (starts and ends at Falls Creek Campground): 1.5 mile (2.4 km) loop.

  - **Trail of the Giants** connects Falls Creek Trail with the Gatton Creek Trail. This 1.5 mile (2.4 km) trail takes you through stands of gigantic Douglas fir.

  - **Quinault Rain Forest Trail, Quinault Loop Trail**, and **Quinault Lodge Trail,** with trailheads near Lake Quinault Lodge and the Ranger Station.

Lake Quinault Museum, 354 South Shore Rd., Quinault, WA 98575

360-288-2317

http://www.quinaultrainforest.com/Lake-Quinault/Lake-Quinault-museum.html

Hours: Memorial Day to Labor Day, Tue-Sun 11a-4p. Winter hours vary –call for a tour.

Fee: Donation. Museum is housed in the old Quinault Post Office building built in 1918 and used as a post office all the way up to 1981. It houses a large collection of photos and local artifacts, including a couple twenty-four-foot cedar dugout canoes. You'll learn both about local history and the lives of the native Quinault peoples.

Olympic National Forest Ranger Station, 353 South Shore Rd., PO Box 9, Quinault, WA 98575 360-288-2525. https://www.fs.usda.gov/recarea/olympic/recarea/?recid=47695

Ranger station is located directly to the east of Lake Quinault Lodge on the South Shore. Obtain Wilderness (Backcountry) Camping Permits for all of Olympic National Park here, plus assistance planning your trip such as trail info, trail conditions, and any safety concerns.

Summer Schedule (Memorial Day-Labor Day): Mon-Sat 8a-4p; Sun 9a-4p. **Winter Schedule:** Mon-Fri 8a-4:30p. Closed for lunch, and hours subject to change. Water and restrooms available when open.

Guided Tours of the Lake Quinault Rain Forest

http://www.olympicnationalparks.com/things-to-do/tours-of-lake-quinault-rainforest/

Tours leave from Lake Quinault Lodge and take approximately four hours. Travel in a fourteen-passenger tour coach with interpretive guide. **Highlights:** Beauty and tranquility, with improved understanding of environmental interconnections. Wildlife sightings may include elk, bear, and multiple bird species. Check the website for times and rates.

Boat Tours of Lake Quinault

http://www.olympicnationalparks.com/things-to-do/boat-tours-of-lake-quinault/

360-288-2900. Take a summer morning tour, or an afternoon or sunset lake tour. See otters, bald eagles, and osprey fishing, and learn about the lake and rainforest area, wildlife, tribes, and history. Boat leaves and returns to Lake Quinault Lodge.

Hardcore Hiking Opportunities

North Fork Trail

Trail wanders along the North Fork of the Quinault River into the back country. From the trailhead you can pack in for as long as the supplies last. Wilderness passes required for all overnight backpacking trips. These are available either in the Port Angeles Information Center, or in the Olympic National Forest and Park Information Station on the south shore of Lake Quinault.

Graves Creek Trailhead

Two trails lead into the high backcountry, one through Enchanted Valley to Anderson Pass and beyond, and another to Wynoochee Pass or Sundown Pass and into Olympic National Forest.

Colonel Bob Trailhead

Tough hike with seven miles of altitude gain. Colonel Bob Peak rises to 4,492 feet (1369 m) and directly overlooks the Quinault Valley on the south side of the Quinault River.

Lodging on Lake Quinault's North Shore

Lake Quinault Vacation Homes, Amanda Park, WA 98526

360-580-4908.

Email: 638northshore@gmail.com.

http://lakequinaultvacationhomes.com/

Several very nice and scenic vacation homes on the shore of Lake Quinault. Pets subject to approval.

Lochaerie Resort, 638 N. Shore Rd., Amanda Park, WA 98526

360-288-2215. http://www.lochaerie.com/

Private and historical cabins on Lake Quinault, open year round since 1926. Fireplace, kitchen, private bath, linens, firewood bundle per day.

Lodging on Lake Quinault's South Shore

Rain Forest Resort Village, 516 S. Shore Rd., Quinault, WA 98575

360-288-2535; Reservations: 1-800-255-6936.

http://www.rainforestresort.com/index.htm

Hours: 9a-9p every day. Basic rooms to fireplace suites, all on the shore of Lake Quinault. The "Largest Spruce Tree in the World" grows here.

Lake Quinault Lodge, 345 S. Shore Rd., Quinault, WA 98575

360-288-2900. http://www.olympicnationalparks.com/lodging/lake-quinault-lodge/

Part of the Olympic National Park. A variety of accommodations are available, from rooms in the historic main lodge, to "Lake Quinault's finest," roomy fireplace suites. Full service restaurant on site – Roosevelt Dining Room (see below).

Campgrounds

Olympic National Park-administered campgrounds: Subject to Park entry fee. Open year round. First-come, first-served; see website for full details: https://www.nps.gov/olym/planyourvisit/camping.htm

https://www.nps.gov/olym/planyourvisit/campgroundstatus.htm

- **Graves Creek Campground** at end of Graves Creek Road. Thirty sites.
- **North Fork Campground** North Shore Road beyond loop. Nine sites.

Lake Quinault RV and Campgrounds, managed by the Olympic National Forest

http://www.olympicnationalparks.com/rv-camping/lake-quinault-rv-campground/

360-288-2900; 800-562-6672 (toll free). Recreation pass required, or purchase a day-use pass. Choose from these three campgrounds:

- **Willaby Campground**, South Shore Road, west of Lake Quinault Lodge. Open all year. Twenty-one campsites for tents, trailers and up to sixteen-foot RVs. No hook ups.

- **Falls Creek Campground**, South Shore Drive just east of Lake Quinault Lodge and the Quinault Ranger Station at Falls Creek. Open Memorial Day Weekend to Labor Day Weekend. Thirty-one campsites accommodating tents, trailers, and up to sixteen-foot RVs.

- **Gatton Creek Campground**, east of Lake Crescent Lodge at Gatton Creek. Open from early June to Labor Day Weekend. Five walk-in tent sites and paved parking for up to ten self-contained RVs, plus three day-use picnic sites.

Restaurants in Quinault

The Salmon House Restaurant, 516 S. Shore Rd., Quinault, WA 98575

360-288-2535.

http://www.rainforestresort.com/salmon-house-restaurant.htm

Hours: Every day, 4p-9p. Part of the Rain Forest Resort Village. Excellent Northwest cuisine on the grounds of the Rain Forest Resort next to Lake Quinault.

Roosevelt Dining Room in Lake Quinault Lodge, 345 S. Shore Rd., Quinault, WA 98575

360-288-2900.

http://www.olympicnationalparks.com/lodging/dining/lake-quinault-lodge/

Hours: 7:30a-8 or 9p (hours vary somewhat by season). Reservations not required but ARE recommended (call 360-288-2900). Menus are on the website.

> **Next – Segment Q: Wynoochee Lake in Olympic National Forest!**

There are three ways to get there:

1. **From the west via Donkey Creek Road.** Find the junction of Highway 101 and Donkey Creek Road fifteen miles (24.30 km) south of Lake Quinault Lodge and 3.28 miles (5.28 km) north of Humptulips. Donkey Creek angles generally to the northeast, traversing the usual forested hillsides, but also climbs above the surrounding country for stunning views. This is the road I like to take to the lake, but you can also reach Wynoochee Lake via two other roads. See map in Part 4P.

2. **From the south via Wynoochee Valley Road.** From Highway 12 near Montesano, take the Devonshire Road exit. Turn (north) over the highway one block. Turn west (left) on Pioneer Ave and then north (right)

> **NOTE:**
>
> If you go straight when Wynoochee Valley turns left, this will put you on NF-2270, the road to the Maidenhair Falls trailhead.

on Wynoochee Valley Road. Travel approximately thirty-five miles (56 km) on Wynoochee Valley Road, passing through rural farms, forest, and into the Olympic National Forest. Some of the road is paved, other parts are gravel. You'll see signs directing you to the Coho Campground. Follow them another 0.3 mile (0.47km) to a "T" and bear right (north) in order to remain on Wynoochee Valley Road, which will bring you to all the main attractions.

3. **From Shelton in the east**. From downtown Shelton, take West Railroad Avenue headed west, which turns into West Shelton Matlock Road. In Matlock, take Matlock-Brady Road heading south, and then turn west on Boundary Road to Wynoochee Valley Road. Turn north to LakeWynoochee.

4Q) Wynoochee Lake, Humptulips

Wynoochee Lake (pronounced **Why-NOO-chee**) is one of those "best-kept-secret" kinds of places. This is a four-mile-long (6.4 km) dammed lake in the middle of nowhere, meaning the Olympic National Forest. The lake is incredibly scenic, and there are a good number of hiking trails in the vicinity: some easy, some moderate, some hardcore. The US Forest Service has provided a Dam Visitor Center where you can learn about creating hydroelectric power. You can also take a self-guided easy stroll inside a working forest and learn about managing a forest sustainably. All that within old-growth and second-growth forests and incredible views. The elevation is just 900 feet (274 m). Stay at the on-site Coho Campground if you'd like to keep hiking and exploring the area.

A Forest Service Day Pass is required, which costs $5 for a single day for a vehicle and all passengers. This can be purchased online and printed at home for placement in the vehicle:

https://www.fs.usda.gov/detail/olympic/passes-permits/recreation/?cid=fsbdev2_027009

Note that there is no food and no fuel here. Ensure you come stocked with enough of both before setting out.

Coho Campground

The Coho Campground opens in mid-May for tent and RV camping, and closes in early October. Forty-six sites for tents, trailers, RVs; Eight walk-in tent camp units, and three heated, furnished yurts which sleep up to six people. BYOB (bring your own bedding). Get info on fees, passes, and more here: https://www.fs.usda.gov/recarea/olympic/recarea/?recid=47807.

Reservations can be placed online at www.recreation.gov, or by phone: 877-444-6777.

Additionally, the campground provides a day use area with running water, restrooms, cooking pits, and boat ramp.

Wynoochee Dam Visitor Center

Wynoochee Dam Visitor Center is 0.75 mi (1.2 km) from the T intersection. The Wynoochee Dam was built in 1972 for the purpose of water storage and flood control. It is 175 feet (53.34 m) above the riverbed and 1,028 feet (313.33 m) long. The resultant reservoir is 4.4 miles (7 km) long with thirteen miles (21 km) of shoreline. For more info or to take a free group tour, call Tacoma Power: 253-502-8759.

Wynoochee Lake Working Forest Interpretive Trail

This is a short half-mile (0.8 km) loop starting and ending at Loop B in the Coho Campground. Learn more about how the Washington State working forests are managed with sustainability in mind.

Wynoochee Lake Shore Trail

The trailhead for this sixteen-mile (26 km)—twelve miles or 19.3 km if you can safely ford the river—loop around Wynoochee Lake is located very near the dam; you'll see signs as you near the lake. The trail itself more or less parallels the lake, an easy walk if a long one crossing several creeks. If you take the trail beyond the end of the lake to the bridge over the Wynoochee River, this will extend your hike to sixteen miles, and will also bring you within view of Maidenhair Falls.

Forest Service PDF map: https://www.fs.usda.gov/Internet/FSE_DOCUMENTS/stelprdb5379765.pdf.

Maidenhair Falls

Maidenhair Falls is a couple miles (3.2 km) away from Wynoochee Lake along the west branch of the Wynoochee River. The very cool thing is that you don't have to hike the entire Lake Shore Trail to get there. You can drive along the east shore of Wynoochee Lake on NF-2312 to the Maidenhair Falls Trailhead near the bridge over Wynoochee River (beyond the far end of the lake). From the trailhead, the waterfall is a half-mile hike away (0.8 km). The falls and the gorge it drops into are wonderfully scenic locations.

There are more destinations near Wynoochee Lake than these! If you're game for more adventure in this neck of the woods, for example, Satsop Lakes, or Spoon Creek Falls (and there are still more adventures than these), see this link to "Points of Interest Descriptions:"

https://www.fs.usda.gov/Internet/FSE_MEDIA/stelprdb5376271.jpg

Humptulips

The tiny bump in the road called Humptulips, population 255 (as of the 2010 census), is 18.6 miles (30 km) south of Quinault, WA, and 25.6 miles (41 km) north of Aberdeen, WA on Highway 101, and only 3.25 miles (5.2 km) south of the junction of Highway 101 with Donkey Creek Road.

Don't blink! There is gas and a grocery and tackle shop—all at the **Humptulips Grocery** located at the intersection of Highway 101 and Kirkpatrick Road. Two outhouses sit near the parking area, in case you are in need at the time you're passing through.

Humptulips Grocery, 1935 Kirkpatrick Rd., Hoquiam, WA 98550

360-987-2335. https://www.facebook.com/HumptulipsGroceryStore/

Country store offering gasoline, fishing tackle, snacks and other convenience items. Pick up some water, snacks, or even a quart of oil or windshield wiper fluid for the car. There are no other amenities in Humptulips. The next services are twenty-two miles south in **Hoquiam.**

Highway 101 looking northbound. That's all there is at Humptulips! If you'd like to head to Ocean Shores, follow the signs here and head west to ocean beaches via Kirkpatrick Road.

How the heck did they come up with the name Humptulips??

Jokes about the town's name notwithstanding, the band of Chehalis Indians who lived here along the river perhaps thousands of years ago were the source of the name. In their tongue, "*humptulips*" meant "hard to pole," that is, maneuvering their dugout canoes up and down the river was difficult because the river was choked by deadfalls and drift logs.

"The Hump," as the river is affectionately called by locals today, is prime spawning grounds, offering excellent salmon and steelhead fishing. Not surprisingly, given the beauty of the region, the fishing, and the nearby attractions of the Olympic National Park, approximately 500,000 people travel this stretch of Highway 101 every year, either coming or going. I bet the Humptulips Grocery makes a killing every summer.

> **Next – Segment R: Grays Harbor!**

Aberdeen, Hoquiam, Ocean Shores and Westport:

Getting there from the east: Aberdeen is situated at the tip of Grays Harbor on Highway 101. It is 11.2 miles (18 km) west of Montesano, WA, and thirty miles (48 km) west of McCleary WA.

Getting there from the north: Aberdeen is forty miles (60 km) south of Quinault, WA, and 25.6 miles (41 km) north of Aberdeen, WA.

4R) Grays Harbor: Aberdeen, Hoquiam, Ocean Shores, Westport

At the point at which the Chehalis River meets the Pacific Ocean, it first empties into Grays Harbor, a large herniation of water inland between two spits of land that protect the harbor from the pounding waves of the Pacific Ocean. The name "Grays Harbor" has nothing to do with the color of stormy weather. It was originally called Bullfinch Harbor. Then the first Europeans in the area, Captain Robert Gray and his sailors aboard the *Columbia* officially discovered the area in 1792. Bullfinch Harbor was subsequently renamed for Captain Gray.

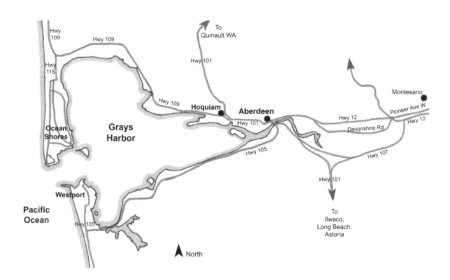

Because the population centers of Aberdeen and Hoquiam literally run together into one, though they are governed separately, they are considered Twin Cities. Still working towns, Aberdeen and Hoquiam now additionally focus on tourism, welcoming visitors to enjoy their waters and forests. And even more focused on tourism are the towns of Ocean Shores and Westport, located as they are at the mouth of Grays Harbor and the edge of the Pacific Ocean.

Together with the county seat of Montesano, these communities serve as a southern gateway to Pacific Coast beaches, the Olympic Peninsula, and the Olympic National Park.

Short History of the Grays Harbor Region

Grays Harbor and surrounding areas are the ancestral home of the Quinault, Humptulips, Wynoochee and Chehalis tribes, which thrived on the abundance of rich forests and ocean.

After the discovery of Grays Harbor, loggers and fishermen began to drift in, the first arriving in 1857. The latter half of the 1800s marked a slow but steady influx of hardy individuals. At the same time, Isaac Stevens, the Washington State Governor and Indian Agent, was waging a sometimes-brutal campaign to limit the tribes to various reservations. The Quinault Indians secured a large tract of land along the Quinault River in 1856, but the Chehalis and Humptulips Indians refused any negotiations with Stevens, and also refused to move off land that had always been theirs.

The flow of settlers into Washington State began in earnest during the later-1800s. The main industry at the time was logging. The population of Hoquiam and Aberdeen hovered in the 400 range until 1889, when it sharply soared to 1,500 due to work and railroad rumors.

The first logging mill was built in 1894 and eventually the dense forests supported an additional 36 lumber mills. During the lumber heyday of the 1920s, Grays Harbor became the first port in the world to ship out an incredible one billion board feet of lumber by water.

As in other areas of the Olympic Peninsula, the logging industry waxed, and then waned due both to the Depression and then to environmental regulations. The number of mills dwindled to nine. With the waning of the logging industry, tourism is playing a greater economic role in the area.

Things to do in Aberdeen

Aberdeen Museum of History, 111 E. 3rd St., Aberdeen, WA 98520

360-533-1976. museum@aberdeen-museum.org.

www.aberdeen-museum.org

Hours: Tue-Sat 10a-5p; Sun 12p-4p; Mon closed. Housed in the historic Aberdeen Armory Building, this charming museum contains exhibits of local history and events. Do your own research at their research facility, leaf through rare books, historical photographs and more. Also, ask about the Kurt Cobain Walking Tour. The museum is free, although donations are accepted and appreciated.

Wishka River Distillery, 2210 Port Industrial Rd., Suite A, Aberdeen, WA 98520

360-612-4756. http://www.wishkahriver.com/

Hours: Tue-Sat 12p-5:30p. Sample or purchase a variety of handcrafted distillery delights, vodka, gin or whiskey. The distillery also offers tours by appointment: tours@wishkariver.com.

Grays Harbor Historical Seaport, non-profit organization that operates the Lady Washington,

800-200-5239. ghhsa_admin@historicalseaport.org; http://www.historicalseaport.org/

The Lady Washington is a full-scale reproduction of the tall ship that was the first American vessel to visit the West Coast. Aberdeen is its home port; however, it visits ports up and down the West Coast. Check the website for the current location of the Lady Washington as it may or may not be in town.

Kurt Cobain Landing, at the Young Street Bridge at the end of E. 2nd St., Aberdeen, WA 98520. Aberdeen, hometown of Kurt Cobain, has set aside a tiny memorial park near the Young Street Bridge over the Wishka River. A large guitar sculpture and plaques on the premises commemorate Kurt Cobain. If Nirvana is your thing, then "come as you are" and pay your respects. Just note that there is no dedicated parking; find a side street on which to leave the car (Stanton Street, 2nd Street), and walk to the park.

Explore the Chehalis River Basin

The Chehalis River snakes in multiple slithering tributaries across a surge plain that is up to two miles (3.2 km) wide at the widest area. None of that is actually visible from the ground; however, at Preacher's Slough Road, you will find the trailhead for two easy walking trails:

- Preacher's Slough Trail is 3.6 miles long (5.8 km one way), and parallels Blue Slough Road from Blue Slough to Preacher's Slough Road.

- Riverside Fishing Trail is 0.6 miles long (0.96 km one way) and is ADA-accessible. This is an easy walking trail along the banks of the main branch of the Chehalis River.

Consider this attraction on an as-needed basis – it is an opportunity for a rain forest stroll along a wide river, and a picnic lunch if you bring one. **Getting there:** From Highway 101 South in Aberdeen, cross the Chehalis River and take Blue Slough Road to Highway 107. Take Highway 107 to Preacher's Slough Road, and turn north (left). Find the parking area and trailhead for both trails here. (There is also an access point for Preacher's Slough Trail at its far end if you prefer. Look for signs for a Blue Slough boat ramp and small gravel parking area.)

Things to do in Hoquiam

Grays Harbor Farmer's Market and Craft Fair, 1956 Riverside Avenue, Hoquiam, WA 98550

360-538-9747. **Hours:** Every day 9a-5p. Fifty-one vendors of produce and artisanal goods in a single enclosed building, and one of only two Farmer's Markets on the West Coast open year round. Produce is high quality, organic, sourced locally if possible.

Tour Historic Hoquiam spots:

- **Historic Olympic Stadium, 101 28th St., Hoquiam, WA 98550.**

  http://cityofhoquiam.com/attraction/historic-olympic-staduim/

- **Polson Museum National Historic Site, 1611 Riverside Avenue, Hoquiam, WA 98550**

  360-553-5862; http://www.polsonmuseum.org/

  Hours: Wed-Sat 11a-4p, Sun 12p-4p. Families $10, Adults $4, Students $2, Under Twelve $1. Named for one of the wealthiest lumber families in the history of Washington.

- **7th Street Theatre, 313 7th St., Hoquiam, WA 98550**

  360-537-7400; http://www.7thstreettheatre.com/

  This unique and historic 1928 "atmospheric-style" theatre offers classic movies, and professional and amateur performances.

Things to Do in Ocean Shores and along Highway 109

Ocean Shores Visitor Information Center, 120 West Chance a La Mer NW, Ocean Shores, WA 98569.

360-289-9586. http://www.tourismoceanshores.com/

Hours: Mon-Fri 10a-4p, Sat 10a-3p, Sun 10a-2p

Coastal Interpretive Center, 1033 Catala Avenue SE, Ocean Shores, WA 98569

360-289-4617. http://www.interpretivecenter.org/

Hours: Sat-Sun 10a-4p, Mon 10a-2p, though hours can vary so check their website.

Wonderful exhibits of wildlife, rocks, shells, shipwreck stories with photos, lectures, and a nature trail winding through coastal forest and wetland. If you're a history buff, they'll also provide you with the history of Ocean Shores and the area. This is a great family stop. Tours are available with docents or self-guided. Donations accepted.

Coastal Interpretive Center

North Jetty, E. Ocean Shores Blvd. SW, Ocean Shores, WA 98569

At the very southernmost tip of the northern peninsula sits this stellar ocean viewing spot. Park your car at the North Jetty Public Parking lot, and then enjoy a stroll on the beach and out onto the North Jetty. Imagine storm-watching from here! (As always, be alert on the jetty—rogue waves can crash over rocks unexpectedly.)

Damon Point Trail (Protection Island), Ocean Shores, WA 98569

Access via Discovery Avenue SE at the tip of Point Brown in Ocean Shores. Fishing, wildlife, birding, beachcombing, walking.

Ocean Shores Kites. Two Locations:

- 172 West Chance A La Mer Blvd, Ocean Shores, WA 98569 (in the Shores Mall).

- 759 Point Brown Avenue, Ocean Shores, WA 98569 (at the boardwalk shops).

360-289-4103. http://www.oceanshoreskites.com/

Multiple vendors—you'll get the perfect kite. Also beach toys, parts and repair, and lessons on kite-flying.

Shop at Sharky's, 695 Ocean Shores Blvd NW, Ocean Shores, WA 98569

360-289-4462. https://sharkysos.com/. **Hours:** Every day 10a-7p. Clothes, hats, toys, books. If you're into sharks, you'll find a LOT to love in this souvenir shop.

State Parks for Day Use and Camping
Ocean City State Park, 148 SR 115, Hoquiam, WA 98550

360-289-3553. http://parks.state.wa.us/554/Ocean-City

Beachfront recreation, clamming, birding, year-round camping. Requires a Discover Pass.

Griffiths-Priday Ocean State Park, Benner Rd., Copalis Beach, WA 98535

360-902-8844. http://parks.state.wa.us/516/Griffith-Priday-Ocean

This is a BIG state park. Explore and go birding on the "Copalis River Spit," a huge sand bar on the ocean side of Copalis River as it empties into the Pacific. **Getting there:** From Highway 109 heading north, turn left (west) on Benner Road and go 1 block. The parking lot is on the right side of the road. Requires a Discover Pass.

Moclips

Museum of the North Beach, 4658 WA-109, Moclips, WA 98562

360-276-4441. http://www.moclips.org/. https://www.facebook.com/pages/Museum-of-the-North-Beach/126071047464043

Hours: Sat-Sun 11a-4p. Closed Mon-Fri. Local history and displays.

What else is there to do in and near Ocean Shores? Check these local websites:

- http://www.dooceanshores.com/
- http://www.tourismoceanshores.com/pageid/2/default.aspx

Things to do in Westport

Westport Light State Park, 1595 Ocean Avenue, Westport, WA 98595

Westhaven State Park, 2700 Jetty Haul Rd., Westport, WA 98595

360-268-9717. http://parks.state.wa.us/284/Westport-Light

Hours: Summer 8a-10p; Winter 8a-6p. Open year round for day use. Check website for winter camping schedule. For a great beachcombing jaunt, take the three mile (4.8 km) round trip Westport Light Trail along the ocean to the Westport Light State Park and Grays Harbor Lighthouse. This ADA-accessible trail can be reached from either the north point at Westhaven State Park, or south at Westport Light State Park. **Discover Pass** required (Part 3F).

Parking is available at both locations:

- **Westhaven at the north**: at the west end of Jetty Haul Road. Westhaven is also called South Jetty Park.
- **Westport Light at the south**: on the west end of W. Ocean Avenue.

Grays Harbor Lighthouse, 1020 W. Ocean Avenue, Westport, WA 98595. 360-268-0078. http://www.lighthousefriends.com/light.asp?ID=117

http://www.westportmaritimemuseum.com/lighthouse-history/

Hours: Feb 1-May 31, Fri-Sat 12p-4p; Jun 1-Aug 31, Thur-Mon 10a-4p; Sep 1-Nov 30: Sat-Sun 12n-4p. Closed Thanksgiving, Dec, Jan, and during adverse weather. $1.00 discount with proof of visit to Westport Maritime Museum. At 107 feet tall, this mid-1800s lighthouse is the tallest in Washington State. Hike to the top for amazing views.

Westport Maritime Museum, 2201 Westhaven Drive, Westport, WA 98595

360-268-0078. http://www.westportmaritimemuseum.com/

Hours: Apr 1-Sep 30, 10a-4p; Oct 1-Mar 31, 12p-4p; Closed Tue, Wed, Christmas.

Overlooking the marina at Westhaven Cove, this maritime and natural history museum houses exhibits depicting the life and history of the area, including the Whale House. It's currently the home of the Destruction Island lighthouse lens that guided sailors safely on their way. Tours are available for

Westport Maritime Museum

five or more persons. It is a good idea to call ahead for current hours, rates, and to arrange tours or events. Rates discounted with proof of purchase of visit to Westport Lighthouse.

Westport Viewing Tower, at the corner of Westhaven Drive and Cove Avenue, very near Neddie Rose Drive at the tip of the Westport Peninsula. The tower is in the shape of a lighthouse. Climb three flights to the top platform for stellar views of Westport and Grays Harbor area and beyond on clear days.

More Strolling Opportunities:

While at the tip of Westport, stroll along Westhaven Drive around Westhaven Cove and Marina. Be sure to hike all the way out Neddie Rose Drive for some beautiful ocean views and great beachcombing.

Westport Viewing Tower

Or, check out the **Boardwalk:** a short wooden structure at the end of Neddie Rose Drive next to the Harbor Resort. The boardwalk offer views of Grays Harbor and boats entering and exiting the Westport Marina. There is a telescope contraption there as well, to magnify your views.

More State Parks for Day-Use and Camping

Westport Light State Park isn't the only act in town. For the price of a Discover Pass you can check out two other nearby state parks, hike through coastal forest and several miles of Pacific Beaches, and go fishing, clamming, beachcombing, bicycling, and more. Each of these state parks offers a **Nature Trail** for education and enjoyment. Plus, use one of these as your base for forays into Westport or surrounding regions.

- **Twin Harbors State Park, 3120 WA-105, Westport, WA 98595**

  360-268-9717.

  http://parks.state.wa.us/431/Twin-Harbors-State-Park

- **Grayland Beach State Park, 3120 WA-105, Grayland, WA 98547**

  360-267-4301.

  http://parks.state.wa.us/426/Grayland-Beach-State-Park

Which additional Westport activities might catch your attention?

- **Westport Aquarium, 321 Harbor Avenue, Westport, WA 98595;**

  360-268-7070. http://westportaquarium.weebly.com/

  Interpretive exhibits, hands-on tanks, and displays of fish from local Pacific waters.

- **Birding:** Huge numbers of birds live here or stop by along their migratory routes from winter homes to arctic nesting areas.

- **Agate Hunting:** On the beach to the south of the South Jetty for roughly a mile can be found agates amongst the other small rocks. The best time to go searching is during low tide.

- **Fishing Charters:** at least 5 charter companies are available to take you out fishing or deep sea fishing. See Part 2H.

- **Crabbing:** Buy or rent pots and bait at various shops in Westport, including Harbor Resort (front desk sells bait, licenses and rental gear for fishing and crabbing).

- **Kite flying:** the consistent afternoon northwest wind makes kite flying a sure thing every afternoon if this is something you enjoy doing with the kids.

- **Go-Karts:** see the info under Breakers Boutique Inn, below.

Restaurants in Hoquiam and Aberdeen

Al's Humdinger, 104 Lincoln St., Hoquiam, WA 98550

360-533-2754. Open for lunch and dinner, Reasonable prices. No indoor seating.

Great burgers, hot dogs, fish-n-chips and more.

Taqueria Franco, 501 Simpson Avenue, Hoquiam, WA 98550

360-532-0609.

https://www.facebook.com/pages/Taqueria-Franco/1472500 372997572

Hours: Mon-Sat 10a-8p; Sun 10a-4p. Open for lunch and dinner. Traditional Mexican food.

8th Street Ale House, 207 8th St., Hoquiam, WA 98550

360-612-3455. http://www.8thstreetalehouse.com/; https://www.facebook.com/8th-St-Ale-House-245090343337/.

Hours: Sun-Thurs 11a-11p, Fri-Sat 11a-1a. Casual local pub serving salads, burgers, pizza, steaks, seafood, pasta, wine, beer, spirits.

7th Street Deli & Sweet Shoppe, 317 7th St., Hoquiam, WA 98550

360-533-7112. Next to the 7th Street Theatre, this "olde time" sandwich and sweet shop is the longest continuously operated soda shop in western WA. Call for hours.

Billy's Bar and Grill, 322 E. Heron St., Aberdeen, WA 98520

360-533-7144. http://billysaberdeen.com/index.html

Hours: Mon-Sat 7a-11p; Sun 7a-9p. Very "local" American cuisine, except for the yak burgers, of all things.

Rediviva, 118 E. Wishkah St., Aberdeen, WA 98520

360-637-9259; http://redivivarestaurant.com/

Hours: Tue-Thur 4p-11p; Fri-Sat 4p-1a

From Farm to Fork Restaurant, 1 S. Arbor Rd., Aberdeen, WA 98520

360-648-2224. info@westportwinery.com. https://www.westportwinery.com/

Hours: Every day 8a-7p. Worth the drive half-way to Westport on Highway 105.

Anne Marie's Café, 110 S. I St., Aberdeen, WA 98520

360-538-0141. **Hours:** 7a-2:30p. https://www.facebook.com/Anne-Maries-Cafe-652194304867494/. Another very local cafe, serving breakfast and lunch, homemade-on-premises bakery items. Their 2:30 pm close time is seen as unfortunate.

La Unica Bakery, 307 S. Park St., Aberdeen, WA 98520

360-533-9902. https://www.facebook.com/pages/La-Unica-Bakery/149406928418110

Hours: Tue-Fri 8a-9p; Sat 8a-8p; Sun 8a-7p; closed Mon. Latin American Restaurant serving excellent tacos and burritos, plus sweet bakery items, donuts, churros, etc.

Restaurants in Ocean Shores and along Highway 109

Galway Bay Irish Pub, 880 Point Brown Avenue NE, Ocean Shores, WA 98569

360-289-2300. http://www.galwaybayirishpub.com/

Hours: Sun-Thurs 11a-10p, Fri-Sat 11a-closing. Irish pub on western Washington shores, the largest, they say, in the Pacific Northwest. Really delicious traditional Irish fare.

Bennett's Fish Shack, 131 E. Chance a La Mer NE, Ocean Shores, WA 98569

360-289-2847. http://www.bennettsdining.com/

Sun-Thur 10:30a-9p, Fri-Sat 10:30a-10p. Chowders, sandwiches, fish & chips, burgers, steaks, chicken, seafood, pasta. Voted best fish & chips on the Twin Harbors.

Los IV Hermanos Mexican Restaurant, 824 Point Brown Avenue NE, Ocean Shores, WA 98569

360-289-0481.

Hours: Mon-Thur 11a-8:30p; Fri-Sat 11a-9:30p; Sun 10a-8:30p. Good place for fresh, homemade Mexican food with great service.

Mike's Seafood, 830 Point Brown Avenue NE, Ocean Shores, WA 98569

360-289-0532. http://www.oceanshoresseafood.com/

Steak, seafood, oysters, sushi. They call themselves unassuming; the food is artfully done.

Our Place Restaurant, 676 Ocean Shores Blvd. NW, Ocean Shores, WA 98569

360-940-7314. Facebook: https://www.facebook.com/ourplaceos/

Hours: Wed-Mon 7a-2p. Closed Tuesdays. Serving breakfast and brunch. Weekly specials.

Westport Restaurants

Westport Winery & Garden Resort, 1 S. Arbor Rd., Aberdeen, WA 98520

See listing under Hoquiam and Aberdeen Restaurants.

Cranberry Road Winery and Bog Water Brewing, 2858 S. Forest Rd., Westport, WA 98595

360-268-7082. http://www.cranberryroad.net/

Enjoy handcrafted wine, beer and food made from locally grown bounty. Cranberry wines made from locally grown cranberries.

Blue Buoy Restaurant, 2323 Westhaven Drive, Westport, WA 98595
360-268-7065.

Facebook: https://www.facebook.com/bluebuoyrestaurant/

Hours: Mon-Fri 8a-1p; Sat-Sun 8a-2:30p. Great local place for breakfast and lunch.

Omelettes, chowders.

Tinderbox Coffee Roasters, 101 N. Montesano St., Westport, WA 98595. 360-612-0555. http://tinderboxroasters.com/

Beans roasted on site. Great stop for great coffee. "Best coffee ever" - that's my review. We bought beans to go and beans for gifts.

Tinderbox Coffee Roasters

Lodging in Aberdeen and Hoquiam

Bed and Breakfast

A Harbor View Inn, 111 W. 11th St., Aberdeen, WA 98520

360-533-7996; 360-533-0433. http://www.aharborview.com/

Cozy B&B in an historic home with a Victorian flavor. Great breakfast served in the sunroom. Water views.

Motels

Econo Lodge Inn and Suites, 910 Simpson Avenue, Hoquiam, WA 98550

360-532-8161. https://www.choicehotels.com/washington/hoquiam/econo-lodge-hotels/wa213?source=gyxt.

Best Western, 701 E. Heron, Aberdeen, WA 98520

866-902-7218; Traditional Best Western Inn, recently renovated, pool.

https://www.bestwestern.com/content/best-western/en_US/booking-path/hotel-details.48177.html?propertyCode=48177&iata=00171970&sob=TRIPHWS&cm_mmc=BL-_-TRIP-_-TRIPHWS-_-GENERAL.

Lodging in Ocean Shores

The Collins Inn & Seaside Cottages, 318 Marina Court SE, Ocean Shores, WA 98569

800-491-9631. http://www.collinsinn.com/

Beautiful inn, full breakfast, private baths, wi-fi, bicycles, Direct beach access. No kids.

Caroline Inn, 1341 Ocean Shores Blvd. SW, Ocean Shores, WA 98569

360-310-7502. http://www.thecarolineinn.com/

Lovely one-bedroom suites, full kitchen, ocean views, walkable beach, electric fireplace, jacuzzi, wi fi, on two levels with bedroom and bath upstairs, half bath downstairs.

MorningGlory Hotel, Resort and Suites, 685 Ocean Shores Blvd NW, Ocean Shores, WA 98569

360-289-4900. http://morninggloryhotel.com/

Family owned. Hot breakfast included.

The Judith Ann Inn, 855 Ocean Shores Blvd. NW, Ocean Shores, WA 98569

360-289-0222. http://www.judithanninn.com/

Quinault Sweet Grass Hotel, 845 Ocean Shores Blvd. NW, Ocean Shores, WA 98569

866-671-7700. http://www.quinaultsweetgrass.com/

On the beach, free shuttle to sister casino and gaming center: http://www.quinaultbeachresort.com/casino/

Grey Gull, 651 Ocean Shores Blvd. NW, Ocean Shores, WA 98569

844-344-3133. http://www.thegreygull.com/the-grey-gull

Standard suites, studios, 1 bedroom condos, on the beach, outdoor pool, wi-fi.

Snuggler's Cove Resort, 343 Marine View Drive SE, Ocean Shores, WA 98569

360-590-2709. http://www.snugglerscoveresort.com/

Cabin rentals within a couple minutes of the harbor and Protection Island.

Polynesian Resort, 615 Ocean Shores Blvd. NW, Ocean Shores, WA 98569

360-289-3361. http://www.booking.com/hotel/us/the-polynesian-resort.en-gb.html?aid=1181684&label=DXB3.

Quality Inn, 773 Ocean Shores Blvd. NW, Ocean Shores, WA 98569

855-849-1513. https://www.choicehotels.com/washington/ocean-shores/quality-inn-hotels/wa111?source=pmftripblaw&pmf=tripbl.

Camping, RV Parks

Ocean City State Park: Located just south of Highway 109 on Highway 115.

http://parks.state.wa.us/554/Ocean-City

Day-use or camping. Requires a Discover Pass.

Screamin' Eagle Campground, 17 2nd Avenue, Ocean City, WA 98569

855-627-4673. http://secampground.com/

Horses welcome! Located just a block off the beach, on the beach access road.

Lodging in Westport

Breakers Boutique Inn, 971 N. Montesano St., Westport, WA 98595

360-268-0848. http://breakersboutiqueinn.com/

Charming inn, affordable, very casual with nice patio. Single rooms, Jacuzzi suites, kitchen suites, family group wing; microwaves, coffee pot, refrigerators in all rooms. Interestingly: The inn comes with a **Go Kart track**, billed as *"Westport's most enjoyable non-beach activity."*

Harbor Resort, 871 Neddie Rose Drive, Westport, WA 98595

360-268-0169. http://www.harborresort.com/

Modest accommodations, but surrounded on three sides by marina or Grays Harbor.

The Westport Inn, 2501 Nyhus St. N., Westport, WA 98595

360-268-0111. http://www.westportwamotel.com/

Homey and affordable quarters; rooftop deck with ocean views; just a block or two from beach, marina, and downtown amenities.

Westport Marina Cottages, 481 E. Neddie Rose Drive, Westport, WA 98595

360-268-7680. http://www.marinacottages.com/

Full kitchen, marina or bay views, front porch, electric fireplaces, outdoor fire pits. The cottages are a bit close, but there are no shared walls. Within walking distance to all the charms of Westport: restaurants, museum, viewing tower, lighthouse.

Next - Segment S: Montesano, Elma, McCleary!

Getting there from the east: McCleary is 17.5 miles (28 km) west of Shelton, and 21.7 (34.9 km) miles west of Olympia, WA.

Getting there from the west: Montesano is eleven miles (18 km) east of Aberdeen on Highway 101.

4S) Montesano, Elma, McCleary

From Aberdeen to the west of Montesano you *could* head east by taking Highway 12, and then Highway 8 all the way to Highway 101 just northwest of Olympia, WA. It would certainly save a bit of time. But what's the fun of that, when you can cruise through a series of backwater towns nearly forgotten by time?

Spurn Highway 12: Travel from Montesano to McCleary along Main Street

If there's no need for speed, then experience the flavor of old-town Pacific Northwest Americana. Hop OFF the madly rushing highway (and by "highway," I mean four lanes total, two in each direction), and hop ONTO "Main Street:" the original main road that directly connects Montesano, Brady, Satsop, Elma, and McCleary like so many pearls on a rustic rural necklace.

This wonderful transit lasts for just nineteen or so miles (30.6 km) past the charming old buildings of yesteryear's downtowns. You won't get lost, because the two-lane main boulevard parallels the busy highway. At the same time, you'll drive past all the central gas stations, restaurants, motels, RV parks, and campgrounds in the various villages, providing additional choices should you have the flexibility or desire to change up your plans. (Keep in mind that lodging options fill up very fast in the summer and advance reservations are ideal.)

From Aberdeen: As you're heading east on Highway 101 in downtown Aberdeen, follow the signs leading to Highway 12 east. Travel 9.5 miles and take the Devonshire Road exit. Turn left (north), and then turn right (east) on Pioneer Avenue West.

Montesano's main drag, **Pioneer Avenue West**, goes through a few name changes as it proceeds east through various villages and then ends in McCleary as West Simpson Avenue, also called Highway 108.

Don't let that official-sounding name fool you—it's still a two-lane road.

Heading west from either Shelton or Olympia in the east, you can just as easily jump onto this stretch of Main Street in McCleary via Highway 8 or Highway 108, and take it all the way to Montesano.

Montesano, Washington

Montesano, population 3,976 (2010 census) and the seat of Grays Harbor County government, is a small town halfway between Olympia and the ocean beaches of Grays Harbor County. It sits cradled in the notch formed by Wynoochee River to the west and the heavy-flowing Chehalis River to its south and east. Temperatures average in the mid-70s (23 C) in summer to mid-30s (2 C) in winter, with rainfall averages of 87 inches (221 cm) per year.

When Montesano was first platted in 1838, farming was a major enterprise. Before long, the lush forests attracted loggers, and its proximity to Grays Harbor and the ocean drew the ships and sailors to haul the fallen timber. In 1883, Montesano was incorporated as a city and in 1886, it was voted in as the county seat of Grays Harbor County.

One of the original settlers in the area, the prominent and very religious Mrs. Lorinda Scammon, wanted to name the town Mount Zion. An alternate suggestion was made of Montesano, meaning Mountain of Health, which satisfied all parties, so Montesano, now pronounced **Mont-eh-SAY-no**, was adopted as the town's official name.

One of Montesano's attractions is the impressive circa 1911 county courthouse. The interior is wrapped in murals depicting the area's history. Should you stop, be sure to notice the dent in the door where the sheriff shot at an escaping felon. This prompts the town motto: *"Come on vacation and leave on probation."*

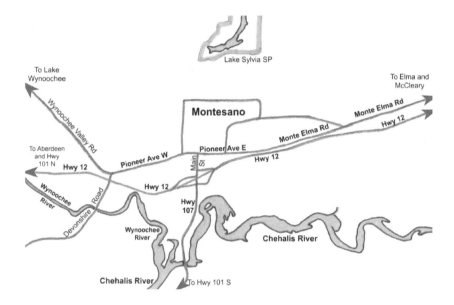

Today, Montesano is a friendly town surrounded by the beauty of the Pacific Northwest.

Things to do in Montesano

Wynoochee Lake: At the west end of Montesano, Wynoochee Valley Road heads thirty-five miles north to Wynoochee Lake. If you've never been there and have the time, it is a worthy destination with lots to see and do. See Part 4Q.

Lake Sylvia State Park, 1812 N. Lake Sylvia Rd., Montesano, WA 98563

360-249-3621. http://parks.state.wa.us/534/Lake-Sylvia

233-acre camping park with 15,000 feet of freshwater shoreline. Includes an old logging camp with fascinating displays. Excellent for an outing and the fishing is good. Five miles of hiking trails, of which fully one-half mile is ADA accessible. Playground equipment, boat ramp – non-motorized boats and kayaks permitted. **Discover Pass** required (Part 3F).

Restaurants in Montesano

Crow's Nest Drive Inn, 441 S. Main St., Montesano, WA 98563

360-249-5505. http://crowsnestdrivein.com/

Hours: Labor Day to Memorial Day (winter hours): Sun-Thurs 9a-8p; Fri 9a-9p; Sat 8a-8p. Memorial Day to Labor Day (summer hours): Sun-Fri 9a-9p; Sat 8a-9p.

Gepetto's Italian Restaurant & Sports Bar, 126 E. Pioneer Avenue, Montesano, WA 98563

360-249-4445. http://www.gepettos4food.com/

Hours: Mon-Fri 8a-8p; Sat-Sun 9a-10p (closing time is flexible). In downtown Montesano, this sports bar doubles as an *attraction* in its own right. Build yourself a custom pizza or enjoy other excellent Italian cuisine while watching sports on flat screen TVs, enjoying live entertainment, or duking it out at pool table or air hockey tables.

All Wrapped Up, 110 E. Pioneer St., Montesano, WA 98563

360-249-6694.

https://www.facebook.com/All-Wrapped-Up-68049828834/

Hours: 6:30a-5p. Breakfast, coffee, bakery items.

Organics 101 Market, 316 S. Main St., Montesano, WA 98563

360-249-8371. http://www.organics101market.com/

Hours: 9:30a-7:30p. Juice bar, coffee, sandwiches, fresh seasonal organic produce. Pick up goodies for a wonderful picnic.

Lodging in Montesano

Guesthouse Inn & Suites/Red Lion Hotels, 100 Brumfield Avenue, Montesano, WA 98563

360-249-4424. https://www.redlion.com/montesano?chebs=tasp-betterin3s-sale-WAMONT

Newly renovated in the heart of town. Free wi-fi and breakfast. Laundry facilities available. See website for special deals/packages. Pet friendly with $15 per pet fee, per night. Rates from $79.

Friends Landing and Camping, 300 Katon Rd., Montesano, WA 98563

360-482-1600. Reservations: 360-249-5117 (7am-9pm). http://www. friendslanding.org/

Hours: Every day 7a-9p. Recreation, boating, hiking, camping opportunities on Lake Quigg and the Chehalis River, southwest of Montesano. **Getting there:** From Highway 12, take the Devonshire Road exit and head south. Turn left (south) on Katon Road. Katon runs right into Friends Landing.

From Montesano to Elma

In the east side of Montesano, **Pioneer Avenue East turns into Monte Elma Road**. Monte Elma Road continues to parallel Highway 12, cutting its path through the one-stoplight village of **Brady**. After Brady is a second little town, **Satsop**, all four square blocks of it, and maybe a little more. Two towers of the Satsop Nuclear Power Plant are there. Construction began in 1977 and stopped in 1983 after a budget shortfall and bond default. The nuclear plant never did function.

Elma

Monte Elma Road pulls into Elma and changes its name to **West Main Street**. Elma is a little village sitting at the point where Highway 12 turns into Highway 8. Downtown Elma (*pictured*) centers on Main and Third Street. Here is where you'll find restaurants, banks, stores, etc. West Main changes to **East Main Street** beyond Third Street.

Elma is cute-cute-cute! And nostalgic. It embodies the essence of old Americana. The Elma Info Center, for example, is located in an old red-and-white Mobil gas station still displaying its old Pegasus logo, a flying red horse. Across the street is an old two-story building dated 1917.

Downtown Elma; Elma "info" station

There's fuel, fast food, a grocery and deli in Elma. There's even a couple restaurants and a motel. This is a fine pit stop on your way either east or west.

Main Street, Elma

Elma Restaurants

El Ranchon Mexican Restaurant, 324 W. Main St., Elma, WA 98541

360-482-5722. (No website, but they are reviewed on Yelp). Call for hours. The real deal when it comes to authentic Mexican cuisine.

Rusty Tractor Family Restaurant, 602 E. Young St., Elma, WA 98541

360-482-3100. **Hours:** Mon-Thurs 6a-8:30p; Fri-Sat 6a-9p; Sun 6a-8p.

https://www.facebook.com/Rusty-Tractor-Family-Restaurant-550337944976407/.

Unique place, American cuisine, good menu.

Top Wok Chinese Restaurant, 302 W. Waldrop St., Elma, WA 98541

360-482-1483.

https://www.facebook.com/pages/Top-Wok/184974474866716

Hours: Tue-Thur 11a-8:30p; Fri-Sat 11a-9p; Sun 11a-8:30p. Closed Mon.

Elma Lodging

Elma Hotel – StayBeyond Inn & Suites, 800 E. Main St., Elma, WA 98541

360-482-6868.

http://www.elmahotelwa.com/. Newly refreshed motel.

Travel Inn Resort (K/M Resorts), 801 E. Main St., Elma, WA 98541

360-482-3877; 1-800-392-5722.

https://kmresorts.com/travel-inn-resort/

RV campground, 134 sites, huge array of amenities.

As you leave Elma and pass Fairgrounds Road, East Main Street becomes **Elma McCleary Road**. Keep on going. It might feel like you're lost in the sticks, but you're still tracking alongside the highway, now SR 8. (SR 8 East will take you directly into the Olympia suburbs and end at Highway 101.) As Elma McCleary Road approaches the town of McCleary, it will bend to the right (east) and turn into West Simpson Avenue. In another heartbeat, West Simpson Avenue also becomes **Highway 108** taking you into downtown McCleary.

McCleary

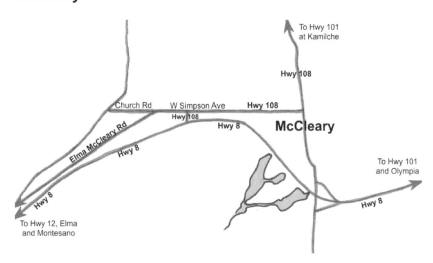

The town of McCleary is the end point of your trek along yesteryear's Main Streets. The population of McCleary was estimated at 1,620 in 2013, which is somewhat reduced from the official 2010 census number of 1,653. The town is named after Henry McCleary, who built two sawmills and set up a door manufacturing company. All of this was eventually sold to the Simpson Logging Company. The Simpson Door Company still turns out high quality wood doors.

McCleary's other claim to fame is its Bear Festival. The problem in the mid-1950s that set the scene for the festival was too many hungry bears in the backcountry in early spring. These foraged by stripping the bark off trees, resulting in lots of dead trees. This is a big problem when timber is your livelihood. Someone wisecracked that local bears, when properly cooked, must certainly be the world's most delicious. They needed no further convincing to set up the first "Bear Festival," the goal being to reduce and manage the local bear population. Fifteen bears went into the stewpot at the first festival. The fifty-seventh iteration occurred in 2016, during which they used a smidgeon of properly inspected bear meat along with lots of beef to make their signature "Bear Stew." If you're passing through McCleary during the second weekend in July, stop in for the festivities! See Part 2C.

West Simpson Avenue (Highway 108) will take you past several restaurants, a Subway (fast food), a market, and a gas station. If food is in order, try the aptly named Rain Country Restaurant.

Rain Country Restaurant, 124 W. Simpson Avenue, McCleary, WA 98557

360-495-3600. http://www.raincountryrestaurantwa.com/

Hours: Mon-Sat 7a-8p; Sun 8a-7p. Family owned and operated, offers a wide variety of American cuisine, including apple pie, and free wi-fi while you're there.

McCleary is also where you get to make some choices as to how to continue your journey.

1. Would you like to visit **Olympia**? If so, see Part 4T. The downtown heart of Olympia makes for a fascinating visit, filled as it is with many attractions relating to government, nature, parks, and artesian wells.

2. Do you want to make a beeline for Highway 101 and head straight for **Shelton and the Hood Canal**? See Part 4U.

**Next – Segment T: Olympia,
Capital of Washington State!**

Getting there from the north: Olympia is twenty-two miles (35.4 km) south of Shelton on Highway 101.

Getting there from the west: Olympia is 21.7 miles (35 km) east of McCleary: Take Highway 8 east to Highway 101 east, which will bring you directly to Olympia.

4T) Olympia, Capital of Washington State

Olympia, WA, population 50,302 (2015 est.), is not technically on the Olympic Peninsula. But it is the state capital; it is on Highway 101, and there are some really cool, natural, and historic attractions in this very modern city.

Olympia, Washington History

Olympia is located sixty miles southwest of Seattle. The original inhabitants of the areas surrounding what is now Olympia were Lushootseed-speaking peoples: the Nisqually, Chehalis, Puyallup, Suquamish, Squaxin and Duwamish. They lived, hunted and fished in the areas surrounding the shores of the lower Puget Sound, from (approximately) Kamilche through Olympia and along the Sound to Seattle.

The area received its first European visit in 1792, when Peter Puget charted the waters for the Vancouver Expedition. Soon after, streams of immigrants traveling west along the Oregon Trail began flowing into the lower Puget Sound area surrounding Olympia. The town itself began to take shape in 1850. Settlers chose the name "Olympia," a nod to the beautiful Olympic Mountains dominating the northwestern skyline.

Map of Olympia

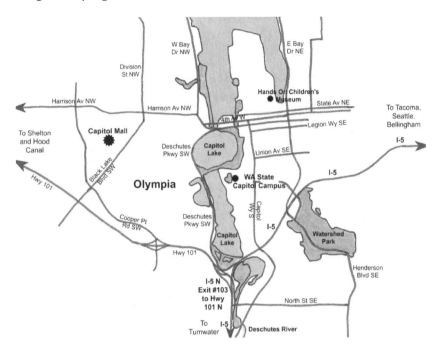

Isaac Stevens, territorial governor and Indian Agent, arrived in Olympia in 1854, and appointed the town as the territorial capital. Olympia had a population of 100 souls at the time. When it was officially incorporated as a city in 1859, the population numbered 1,000.

Over the next fifty years and continuing, Olympia matured into a respectable capital. Washington State was admitted to the Union on November 11, 1889. Swampy land in the downtown area was filled in and the area developed. Capitol Lake was created by damming the Deschutes River at Budd Inlet.

Today the state government sits on a rise overlooking Capitol Lake. The Washington State Capitol Campus comprises a number of government buildings designed in classic architectural style. Public visits are welcome.

Olympia's Artesian Springs

At one time, many natural artesian springs could be found throughout the city limits of Olympia. Fresh pure spring water easily supplied the needs of Olympia's swelling population. A 1940s survey revealed ninety-six living and active artesian wells and springs within the downtown area alone. The wells also provided water for steam trains, fountains and places of business. The Olympia Brewery, doing business from 1896 to 2003, was fed by twenty-six artesian springs, prompting their slogan, "*It's the Water*."

View of Capitol Lake and Budd Inlet from the vantage point of the Washington State Capitol Campus, looking toward Puget Sound and the Olympic Mountain Range.

As urbanization overtook Olympia and more and more wells were capped or paved over in the name of progress, efforts began in the early 1990s to preserve as many remaining wells as possible. They have been only marginally successful. Dozens are still paved over. Others flow inside private buildings and the waters are simply channeled into the sewer system. However, several still survive in the public domain and are maintained by the city.

- **Artesian Commons Park** (415 Fourth Avenue East). It's not grassy, but it might be worth a visit to you. Bring some containers – the water is free and tastes amazing.

- Fourth and Jefferson (421 Fourth Street)

- Corner of Olympia and Washington Streets

- Bigelow Neighborhood Park

- Watershed Park

Parks in Olympia

Olympia has set aside a remarkable 900-plus acres (3.6 sq. km) dedicated to numerous parks, both forested and waterside. These are available to the public. Here are five of the special ones. Visit any of these on an *as-needed* basis.

Heritage Park, 330 5th Avenue SW, Olympia, WA 98501

This grassy, well-landscaped park with twenty-four acres curving around the east side of Capitol Lake marks the end of the Oregon Trail. Since it sits at the foot of the Washington State Capitol Campus, visitors can take a switchback foot path from the park up to the government buildings. The path is part of Heritage Park Trail, which includes a walking/jogging path encircling the north end of Capitol Lake. You are likely to see a variety of waterfowl and otters, along with stellar views of the Capitol Dome to the south, and the Olympic Mountains to the northwest.

Percival Landing, 217 Thurston Avenue NW, Olympia, WA 98501

This small waterfront park on the east side of Budd Bay is located about two blocks north of Heritage Park. Your kids will love the playground equipment and access to a bit of the shoreline. This offers great views of the Olympic Mountains, the marina, the bay, and public art displays.

Watershed Park, 2500 Henderson Blvd. SE, Olympia, WA 98501

The original artesian well for city water is now a 153-acre park with some of the best hiking trails in the city winding through wetlands and rain forest. Some sections of the park are steep with steps and boardwalks over wetlands. Though all access points provide some barrier-free access to view sites, the easiest pedestrian access is from Henderson Blvd.

Parking: 2500 Henderson Boulevard SE. Pedestrian access is also possible from Eastside Street.

Tumwater Falls Park, 110 Deschutes Parkway SW, Tumwater, WA 98501

360-943-2550.

http://www.olytumfoundation.org/tumwater-falls-park/

Hours: Every day 8a-7p. As the Deschutes River nears the end of its journey, it must squeeze through a gorge and drop over several waterfalls. This is a beautiful park to visit, complete with a fish hatchery, restaurant, fountain, walking trails, and Pacific Northwest-naturalized landscape. **Getting there:** Address is at the corner of Deschutes Way SW and C Street SW. From Deschutes Parkway SW, continue south to C Street SW and turn left (east) on C Street SW. From northbound I-5 exit 103, go straight on Deschutes Way SW and turn right (east) on C Street SW.

Priest Point Park, 2600 E. Bay Drive NE, Olympia, WA 98506

A very large park with shoreline along Budd Bay. Much of it is wooded, with hiking trails, ball courts, playground and the Samarkand Rose Garden. Open during daylight hours, and offers several restrooms. City-owned, no passes required.

Things to Do in Olympia

Hands-On Children's Museum 414 Jefferson St. NE, Olympia, WA 98501

360-956-0818. http://www.hocm.org/

Hours: Tues-Sat 10a-5p; Sun-Mon 11a-5p. **Admission:** See website for current entrance fees. Gold Star Military, Museum Members and babies 0-23 months are free. Hands-on learning experience and lots of fun in art and science for kids, parents and teachers.

Washington State Capitol Campus, 416 Syd Snider Avenue SW, Olympia, WA 98504

Visitor Info: 360-902-8880; http://www.des.wa.gov/; **Access WA:** http://access.wa.gov/. **Hours:** Mon-Fri 7a-5:30p; Sat-Sun and holidays 11a-4p; closed the holidays of Thanksgiving and the day after, Christmas and New Year's.

The historic and beautiful Washington State Capitol Campus is high on the list of Olympia destinations. It is home to several historic buildings: the 1928 Legislative Building, 1909 Governor's Mansion, and the 1912 Washington State Supreme Court Temple of Justice. Additionally, works of art and memorials are scattered around the grounds.

Links to specific information regarding Washington State Capitol Campus visits:

- **Legislative Building Tours are available**: tours@des.wa.gov; for the Governor's Mansion: http://wagovmansion.org/index.php/tours/. Free; 45-60 minutes in length.

- **Things to See**: http://www.des.wa.gov/services/facilities-leasing/capitol-campus/tours/things-see-capitol-campus

- **Memorials and Artworks**: http://www.des.wa.gov/services/facilities-leasing/capitol-campus/memorials-and-artwork

- **Parking Information, locations and fees**: http://www.des.wa.gov/services/travel-cars-parking/parking/parking-visitors

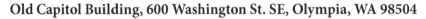

Old Capitol Building, 600 Washington St. SE, Olympia, WA 98504

"The Castle," as the Old Capitol Building is known to locals, was under construction from

1890–1892 as the Thurston County Courthouse and later became the Capitol Building of the State of Washington. Eventually, the state outgrew the space. Its current role is office space for the Superintendent of Public Instruction. Its architecture is remarkable. It looks medieval. Ten of its twelve original towers were destroyed by earthquake; after massive repairs, two remain. If you are into history and architecture, you may enjoy a walk around this building.

Nisqually National Wildlife Refuge, 100 Brown Farm Rd. NE, Olympia, WA 98516

360-753-9467. https://www.fws.gov/refuge/Billy_Frank_Jr_Nisqually/visit/plan_your_visit.html

Hours: Visitor center is open Wed-Sun 9a-4p, closed major holidays. Trails are open seven days a week, sunrise to sunset. Boating, birding, hiking, educational visitor's center, interpretive walks. No pets allowed.

Olympic Flight Museum, 7637-A Old Highway 99 SE, Tumwater, WA 98501

360-705-3925. http://www.olympicflightmuseum.com/visitors.php

Hours: 11a-5p as follows: Jan-Apr open Wed-Sun, Tues by appointment; May-Sept open Mon-Sun; Oct-Dec open Tues-Sun. Closed Thanksgiving and Christmas. **Admission:** See website for current entrance fees. Children 6 & under Free; AAA Member discount. Located in the Olympic Regional Airport. This museum exhibits all kinds of aircraft and memorabilia. See website for current events, air shows and interactive programs.

Restaurants in Olympia

Fifth Avenue Sandwich Shop, 117 5th Avenue SE, Olympia, WA 98501

360-705-3393. http://5thavesandwich.com/. **Hours:** Mon-Fri 10a-4p; Sat 11a-4p.

Really good sandwiches, hot and cold; soups, salads, and beautiful pies. Get it to-go if needed.

Anthony's Hearthfire Grill, 1675 Marine Dr. NE, Olympia, WA 98501

360-705-3473. https://www.anthonys.com/

Hours: Sun-Thu 11:30a-9:30p; Fri-Sat 11:30a-10:30p

Dine at the tip of the marina. Fresh, seasonal, sustainable. Great seafood and atmosphere.

Gardner's Restaurant, 111 Thurston Avenue NW, Olympia, WA 98501

360-786-8466. http://gardnersrestaurant.com/

Hours: Tue-Sat 5p-8:15p. Pasta, seafood, steaks, soup, salad, desserts. Signature cocktails, wine. Near Percival Landing Park and the downtown waterfront. Reservations recommended.

Old School Pizzeria, 108 Franklin St. NE, Olympia, WA 98501

360-786-9640. http://www.oldschool-pizzeria.com/

Hours: Mon-Thu 11a-10p; Fri-Sat: 11a-11p; Sun 11a-11p. Great classic pizza options and New York-style pies. Pleasant atmosphere.

The Gyro Spot, 317 Fourth Avenue E, Olympia, WA 98501

360-352-5251. http://thegyrospot.com/menu/

Hours: Sun-Thu 11a-9p; Fri-Sat 11a-2:30a. Greek and Middle-Eastern cuisine.

Batdorf & Bronson Coffee Roasters, Two locations:

- 516 Capitol Way S., Olympia, WA 98501; 360-786-6717.
  Hours: Mon-Fri 6:30a-6p; Sat-Sun 7a-6p.

- 200 Market St. NE, Olympia, WA 98501; 360-753-4057.
  Hours: Wed-Sun 9a-4p; Mon-Tues closed.

https://www.batdorfcoffee.com/. Coffee beans roasted to order; great coffee and bakery items. Spacious and comfortable seating will coax you to linger by the fireplace.

Budd Bay Café, 525 Columbia St. NW, Olympia, WA 98501

360-357-6963. http://www.buddbaycafe.com/.

Hours: Mon-Thu 6:30a-8:30p; Fri-Sat 6:30a-9p; Sun 9:30a-8:30p

Dockside Bistro and Wine Bar, 501 Columbia St. NW #B, Olympia, WA 98501

360-956-1928. https://www.docksidebistro.com/

Hours: Lunch served Tue-Sat 11a-3p. Dinner served Tue-Sun 5p-9p. Closed Mondays.

Tugboat Annie's, 2100 W. Bay Drive NW, Olympia, WA 98502

360-943-1850. https://tugboatannies.com/

Hours: Mon-Thur 11a-8:30p; Fri 11a-10p; Sat 9a-10p; Sun 9a-8:30p.

Restaurant, bar, kayaks for rent. (Kayak rentals not available in the winter.)

Waterstreet Café, 610 Water St. SW, Olympia 98501. 360-709-9090. http://www.waterstreetcafeandbar.com/

Hours: Sun-Thur 10:30a-9p; Fri-Sat 10:30a-10p. Ultra-fresh food, excellent dining experience, world-class wines, and great microbrews. Borders Heritage Park and Capitol Lake.

Meconi's Italian Subs, 1018 Capitol Way S. #101, Olympia, WA 98501

360-534-0240. http://www.meconissubs.com/

Hours: Mon-Fri 10a-8p; Sat 10a-7pm; Sun closed. Near the Capitol complex; hot and cold subs; offers gluten-free breads. Add soup or salad.

RJ's Gourmet Grill, 318 Fourth Avenue E, Olympia, WA 98501

360-350-0612. http://www.rjsgourmetgrill.com/

Hours: Mon-Sat 11a-9p; Sun closed. Really good food. Burgers are great. Excellent Indian plates. Gluten-free choices.

Narai Asian Cuisine, 320 Fourth Avenue E, Olympia, WA 98501

360-754-1332. http://www.naraiasiancuisine.com/

Hours: Tue-Wed 11a-9p; Thu-Fri 11a-10p; Sat 12p-10p; Sun 12p-9p. Closed Monday. "Authentic taste of Thailand." Consistently good and offering choices that suit those with food intolerances.

Lodging in Olympia

Listed are but a few of the possible lodging options in Olympia.

Ramada Inn, 4520 Martin Way E, Olympia, WA 98516

Direct: 360-459-8866.   https://www.wyndhamhotels.com/ramada/ olympia-washington/ramada-olympia-wa/overview?cid=fe:ra: 20160930:tabl:pp:rampaci:30856&tel=18009465338

Hampton Inn and Suites, 4301 Martin Way E, Olympia, WA 98516

Direct: 360-459-5000.   http://hamptoninn3.hilton.com/en/hotels/ washington/hampton-inn-and-suites-olympia-lacey-LACOLHX/ index.html?WT.mc_id=zLADA0WW1HX2OLX3DA4HWB5TAB L6LACOLHX

Double Tree by Hilton Hotel Olympia, 415 Capitol Way N, Olympia, WA 98501

360-570-0555. http://doubletree3.hilton.com/en/hotels/washington/ doubletree-by-hilton-hotel-olympia-OLMCWDT/index.html.

Quality Inn, 1211 Quince St. SE, Olympia, WA 98501

360-943-4710.   https://www.choicehotels.com/washington/olympia/ quality-inn-hotels/wa130

Bed and Breakfast:

The Inn at Mallard Cove 5025 Meridian Rd. NE, Olympia, WA 98516

360-491-9795 or 800-320-3590.

http://www.theinnatmallardcove.com/

A charming Tudor style bed and breakfast inn located on fourteen private, forested acres at the edge of Puget Sound. Three romantic guest rooms with private baths, jetted tubs, water or forest views, fireplaces, all cozy and beautifully decorated with three-course gourmet breakfast.

Swantown Inn and Spa, 1431 11th St. SE, Olympia, WA 98501

360-753-9123. http://www.swantowninn.com/

Historic Queen Anne/Eastlake Victorian home located in a quiet area in the heart of Olympia. Garden views and views of the Capitol. On-site day spa, massage, three-course breakfast. Private baths, king beds, luxury bathrobes and towels; free wi-fi.

> **Next - Segment U: Shelton!**

Getting there from the north: Shelton is on Highway 101, located 15.4 miles (24.8 km) south of Hoodsport along the Hood Canal. Take Highway 101 south.

Getting there from the west: Shelton is 17.5 miles east of McCleary, WA. Take Highway 108 east, then Highway 101 north, then Highway 3 north into downtown Shelton.

Getting there from the south: Shelton is twenty-two miles north of Olympia, WA. Take Highway 101 north, then Highway 3 north into downtown Shelton.

4U) Shelton

Shelton sits at the far southern end of the Puget Sound at the elbow of Oakland Bay, a little northwest of Olympia. Harstine Island lurks just offshore, accessible via bridge.

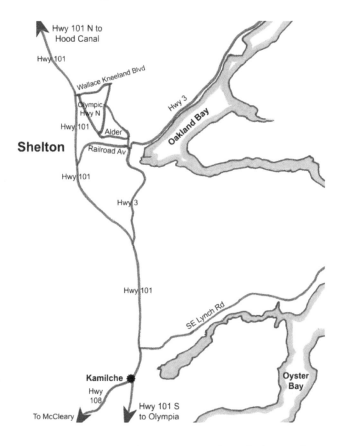

The town was incorporated in 1890, founded on logging, farming, dairy ranching and shellfish, particularly oysters. All of these enterprises are still pursued in and around the area. Today, this relatively small town of about 10,000 residents calls itself the "Christmas Tree Capital."

Like many other areas in the Pacific Northwest, Shelton can be quite damp. It receives about sixty-five inches of rain per year, but also like other PNW areas, most of that precipitation falls in autumn, winter, and springtime. You can expect summer temperatures in the 70s F (22C), however don't be surprised if the mercury hits 100 degrees F (37.7C) or more, though I highly doubt it would stay THAT hot for your entire vacation.

Shelton is mostly a working town. It is host to the Shelton Port on Puget Sound, the Sanderson Field airport, the Washington Corrections Center, and a training post for Washington State Troopers. There isn't a lot of "touristy" stuff to do, and Highway 101 detours around the town. But, I enjoy Shelton's downtown area. Perhaps you will too.

Shelton Tourist Information can be found in the caboose of a city-block-long train display located in front of the Shelton Post Office, on West Railroad Avenue between North 2nd Street and North 4th Street.

Quick Tips: Shelton is the last stop in a decent population center until Aberdeen in the west or Sequim or Port Townsend in the north. If you happen to need supplies, coffee or other essentials, take the Wallace Kneeland Boulevard exit north of Shelton and go east a stone's throw to find a Walmart Supercenter, gas stations, several coffee shops and restaurants.

Kamilche, Washington

At the east end of the short-lived Highway 108, seven miles south of Shelton, is the whistle stop known as Kamilche. The area is part of greater Shelton, except for Kamilche, which pertains to the Squaxin Island tribe, "People of the Water." Are you in need of a pit stop, some vittles, or a good night's rest at this point in your travels? Is gaming your thing? Then a stop might be just the ticket.

Squaxin Indian Gaming and Attractions

Squaxin Island Reservation: http://squaxinisland.org/

Little Creek Casino Resort, 91 W. SR-108, Shelton, WA 98584

800-667-7711. https://www.little-creek.com/. Located at the junction of Highway 108 and Highway 101, Little Creek Casino Resort offers plenty of gaming, plus all the amenities: *"relaxed lodging, dining, and entertainment, plus a spa and golf course."*

Salish Cliffs Golf Club

360-462-3673. http://www.salish-cliffs.com/.

Part of the Little Creek Casino & Resort, Salish Cliffs Golf Club is a twelve-minute walk from the casino. Beautifully situated amongst evergreen trees, this highly rated golf course offers lodging/golf packages, PGA-professional golf instructors and on-site spa.

Kamilche Trading Post, 61 SR-108, Shelton, WA 98584

360-426-5254. http://kamilchetradingpost.com/

A "full tribal convenience store" where you can get Shell fuel (including diesel) and deli food, coffee, and soda/water (and lots more) to go.

In the same complex are several restaurants affiliated with the casino or the golf course: **Creekside Buffet, Island Grille, Salish Cliffs Grille.** (See tribal website.) Want a good food-ordering tip? Order seafood, because, "people of the water." If you aren't a fan of seafood, then prime rib.

Things to do in or near Shelton

Taylor Shellfish Farms, 130 SE Lynch Rd., Shelton, WA 98584 360-426-6178. https://www.taylorshellfishfarms.com/

Hours: Every day 10a-6p. Ask about tours, classes, and "shellfish seeds."

Absolutely-fresh-from-the-water shellfish, geoduck, clams, mussels, and oysters, along with chowders and merchandise such as branded t-shirts and caps. Call to inquire about taking a tour of the plant.

Walter Dacon Wines, 50 SE Skookum Inlet Rd., Shelton, WA 98584

360-426-5913; 866-939-4637.

Email: winemaker@walterdaconwines.com

http://www.walterdaconwines.com/. **Hours:** Wed-Sun 12n-6p (closed Mon-Tue).

Getting there: SE Lynch Road to SE Skookum Inlet Road, turn right (south) to address.

Rhone and Mediterranean-style wines crafted from Eastern Washington grapes. Wine tasting. Purchase wines and gifts.

Mason County Historical Society Museum, at Fifth and Railroad Avenue, Shelton, WA 98584

360-426-1020. http://www.masoncountyhistoricalsociety.org/

Hours: Tue-Fri 11a-5p, Sat 11a-4p. Nice collection of historical documents, photos and more, depicting early Shelton life.

Jarrell Cove State Park, 391 E. Wingert Rd., Shelton, WA 98584

360-426-9226. http://parks.state.wa.us/523/Jarrell-Cove

Peaceful park along the water at Jarrell Cove on the north end of Harstine Island. This park is way off the beaten path; most folks arrive by boat. Waterside camping available, picnicking, hiking, small marina. A **Discover Pass** is required (Part 3F), and also camping fees. **Getting there:** Take Highway 3 North out of downtown Shelton for 11.9 miles (19 km), turn right (SE) onto East Pickering Road, and go to Graham Point. Take East Harstine Bridge Road over the bridge and then go left (north) on East North Island Drive to East Wingert Road. East Wingert bears to the left. Address is on left, almost to the end of East Wingert Road. If you get to East Old Meadow Road, you've gone too far.

Harstine Island State Park, E. Yates Rd., Shelton, WA 98584

360-426-9226. Another pretty park, quiet and sheltered. Steep hike down to the beach, where you can picnic and go beachcombing or clamming. Time your visit for low tide or there may be minimal beach left at the bottom of the trail. Day-use, outdoor bathrooms, no pets. **Discover Pass** is required, or pay $10 to enter. **Getting there:** Following the directions above, cross the Harstine Bridge and turn left on East North Island Drive. Turn right (south) on East Harstine Island Drive and go almost a mile (1.6 km) to East Yates Road. Travel less than a mile (1.49 km) on East Yates, and look for the right turn into the park.

Potlatch State Park, 2120 N. Highway 101, Shelton, WA 98584.

360-877-5361; 360-796-4415. http://parks.state.wa.us/569/Potlatch

Campsite Accommodations: 888-226-7688. **Discover Pass** required. **Hours:** 8a-dusk for day use. **Getting there:** Highway 101 transits right through Potlatch State Park, which is at the southern end of the Hood Canal about 19 minutes (12 miles or 19.3 km) north of Shelton. It's a great spot for a quick stop or a short hike while taking in the panoramic view. Nice bathroom facilities; camping is possible in season. Check the website for open and close dates.

Restaurants in Shelton

Smoking Mo's BBQ, 203 W. Railroad Avenue, Shelton, WA 98584

360-462-0163. http://www.smokingmos.com/

Hours: Fri-Sat 11a-9p, Sun-Thur 11a-8p. Classic BBQ, pulled pork, craft beer, moonshine.

Sisters Restaurant, 116 W. Railroad Avenue, Suite 100, Shelton, WA 98584

360-462-3287; sistersrest@hotmail.com. https://www.facebook.com/ Sisters-Restaurant-170214836521576/. **Hours:** Mon-Thur 6a-7:30p; Fri 6a-8p; Sat-Sun 7a-7:30p. American cuisine. The locals come here a LOT.

Doug's Place, 118 S. Third St., Shelton, WA 98584

360-426-3811. http://dougsplacesandwiches.weebly.com/

Hours: Mon-Sat 11a-4p. Sandwiches and side dishes—everything is made from scratch in-house.

Happy Garden Chinese Restaurant, 124 N. First St., Shelton, WA 98584

360-426-4411. http://www.happygardenchineseshelton.com/

Hours: Tue-Sun 11a-9p; closed Mon.

Ritz Drive-In, 325 S. First St., Shelton, WA 98584

360-427-9294.

https://facebook.com/The-Ritz-Burgers-169164936447767/

This burger joint makes the list of burger joints that will "make your taste buds explode." http://www.onlyinyourstate.com/washington/more-wa-burgers/

Coffee Creek Espresso, 1781 W. Shelton Matlock Rd., Shelton, WA 98584

360-427-0686. **Hours:** Mon-Fri 6a-5:30p; Sat 7a-5:30p; Sun 7a-5p. Great coffee shack.

Lodging in Shelton

Make reservations early! Even in winter the very few rooms are full or nearly full.

Super 8 Shelton, 2943 Northview Circle, Shelton, WA 98584

360-426-1654.

https://www.wyndhamhotels.com/super-8/shelton-washington/super-8-shelton/overview?cid=fe:se:20160930:tabl:pp:senat:03908&tel=18005361211

Shelton Inn, 628 W. Railroad Avenue, Shelton, WA 98584

360-426-4468. www.sheltoninn.com

Budget motel with adjoining restaurant (Blondies). Decent little place; my stay here was great.

Bed and Breakfast

A Lighthouse on Hammersley Bed &Breakfast, 292 E. Libby Rd., Shelton, WA 98584

360-427-1107. Email: lh.onhammersley@gmail.com

http://www.lighthouseonham.com/index.htm

Lovely, top-rated bed and breakfast situated on Hammersley Inlet.

Next - Segment V: Hood Canal!

Getting there from the south: The Hood Canal is 10 miles (16 km) north of Shelton in the south. Highway 101 follows the western shore of Hood Canal from the Skokomish Indian Reservation near Shelton in the south, nearly the full length of the Hood Canal, to north Brinnon in the south.

Getting there from the north: The Hood Canal is 8.5 miles (14 km) to the south of Quilcene in the north.

Your view of the Olympic Mountains on Highway 101 heading north from Shelton.

4V) Hood Canal

From Shelton north nearly to Quilcene, the Hood Canal dominates the road and the landscape. The 70-mile-long Hood Canal is technically a fjord, one of only two in the lower 48 states.

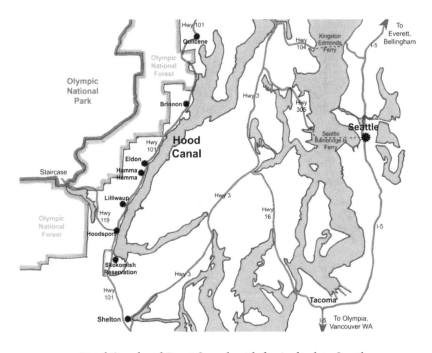

Hood Canal and Puget Sound, with ferries back to Seattle

This stretch of Highway 101 is as delightful as it is scenic. Here is where Highway 101 weaves together forest, quaint towns, ideal fishing spots and state parks. Names like Potlatch, Lilliwaup and Hamma Hamma add to the aura of native mysteries with waterfronts and vine-draped, fairy tale dreams.

The Hood Canal feels very remote, despite the presence of Highway 101 and a distance of only an hour and a half from Seattle. It contains several wonderful staging spots from which to go camping, biking and hiking along the trails that wind throughout the area and up into the Olympic National Park. Kayaking, boating, scuba-diving, fishing and other outdoor sports are abundantly available.

The Hood Canal's fish-hook shape should be a hint as to what is one of the most popular activities in these waters: fishing. Oysters, mussels, clams, crab and salmon can all be harvested seasonally. For more information about open seasons, see the WA State Department of Fishing and Wildlife:

http://wdfw.wa.gov/fishing/shellfish/crab/19/.

The Hood Canal on Facebook:

https://www.facebook.com/ExploreHoodCanal/

The Hood Canal online: www.ExploreHoodCanal.com

Let's travel Highway 101 northward along the Hood Canal, village by village.

Skokomish Indian Reservation

Things to Do

Lucky Dog Casino, 19330 US-101, Skokomish, WA 98584

360-877-5656. https://www.myluckydogcasino.com/index.cfm

Hours: Mon-Thur 9a-1a; Fri-Sat 9a-2a; Sun 9a-midnight. Feeling lucky? If gaming is your thing, here's your chance to do a little gambling.

The Twin Totems Convenience Store (360-427-9099) is right next to the Lucky Dog Casino, in case you need fuel or convenience items.

Food in Skokomish

Northfork Grill in the Lucky Dog Casino, 19330 US-101, Skokomish, WA 98584

360-877-5656. https://www.myluckydogcasino.com/northfork/index. cfm?MenuID=7

Hours: Mon-Thur 9a-12a; Fri-Sat 9a-2a; Sun 9a-1a.

Lodging in Skokomish

Well actually, the following lodging choices are in **Union**, which is immediately east of Skokomish but close enough to count. I've included these two upscale resorts, because the Hood Canal needs a few more upscale choices.

Robin Hood Village Resort, 6780 State Route 106, Union, WA 98592

369-898-2163. www.robinhoodvillageresort.com/

Historic resort built in 1934. A collection of unique and charming cottages, some on the water, some with hot tubs, some with full kitchens and some with kitchenettes. Restaurant and pub on site, and walking distance to additional restaurants.

Alderbrook Resort and Spa, 10 E. Alderbrook Avenue, Union, WA 98592

360-898-2200. www.alderbrookresort.com/

Alderbrook Resort is a "woodsy, upscale spa hotel" with excellent views of the Olympic Mountains. Open since 1913, it is probably the most historic and iconic of resorts on the Hood Canal. It boasts elegantly appointed hotel rooms, one- and two-bedroom cottages and classic Pacific Northwest grounds. Restaurant on site; dining offers a creative menu featuring local produce, seafood, cheese and wine.

Potlatch

With a creek named *No-Name* nearby, you'll not be surprised that Potlatch is little more than a hiccup in the highway. Nevertheless, it offers a lovely State Park on the water, a hamburger joint, and very pleasant lodging.

Potlatch State Park, 21020 US-101, Shelton, WA 98584.360-877-5361. http://parks.state.wa.us/569/Potlatch

Hours: Day Use: 6a-6p. 5,700 feet of beach, with campsites, picnic areas, and mooring buoys. **Discover Pass** required (Part 3F). This is an *as-needed* attraction.

Potlatch State Park

Food in Potlatch:

Kelsey's All Natural, 21391 US-101, Shelton, WA 98584

360-877-5696. **Hours:** Every day: 10a-9p. Just north of Potlatch. Serves lunch and dinner; Pancakes, variety of burgers, hot dogs, fish and chips, fries, ice cream, shakes, scones.

Lodging in Potlatch:

Waterfront Resort, 21660 US-101, Skokomish, WA 98584

360-877-9422. http://www.wfresort.com/

Just 0.6 miles (1 km) north of Potlatch State Park: Rooms and RV sites overlooking the Hood Canal, plus a clubhouse and beach.

Hoodsport

Just north of Potlatch is Hoodsport, the hub of tourism on the Hood Canal. Quaint buildings line Highway 101 and accent the blue water.

Highway 119 (Lake Cushman Road) intersects Highway 101 at downtown Hoodsport. A 4.5-mile (7.24 km) drive into the hills will bring you to **Lake Cushman** and into the eastern part of the Olympic National Park. Lake Cushman provides additional boating, water sport opportunities, and camping.

Hoodsport History

Hoodsport was first settled by Captain G.K. Robbins, who hauled lumber along the Hood Canal, and who also started the Hama Hama Oyster Company, now run by his descendants. At that time Hoodsport depended mostly on farming and logging. Today the area's greatest assets include bounty from the sea such as oysters and clams, and the many outdoor activities enhanced by the sheer beauty of the surrounding forests, lakes, and rivers.

Visitor Information Center, 150 N. Lake Cushman Rd., Hoodsport, WA 98548

360-877-2021. Call for hours. Located a few blocks from the intersection of Highway 101 and Lake Cushman Road. Obtain detailed info about the area and the options for recreation, food and lodging.

Things to do in Hoodsport

Shop Till You Drop in Hoodsport: Well, okay, there aren't enough shops in Hoodsport to drain your energy completely, but there are probably enough shops to please you.

Lots of opportunity to shop for souvenirs in Hoodsport, WA

Hoodsport Winery, 23501 Highway 101, Hoodsport, WA 98548

360-877-9894; (800) 580-9894. http://www.hoodsport.com/

Hours: Every day 10a-6p. The Hoodsport Winery, established in 1978 and located at the south end of town, is a scenic spot for wine tasting. Purchase award-winning wines, coffee, chocolate raspberry wine truffles, jams and more.

The Hardware Distillery, 24210 US-101, Hoodsport, WA 98548

206-300-0877. http://www.thehardwaredistillery.com/

Summer Hours (beginning Memorial Day weekend)**:** Every day 10a-6p.

Winter Hours: Thurs, Fri, Sun: 12p-5p. A distillery tour includes free tasting and "entertaining and fresh" history and commentary.

At Lake Cushman

Hood Canal Adventures, 7211 N. Lake Cushman Rd., Hoodsport, WA 98548

360-898-2628. http://hoodcanaladventures.com/lake-cushman/

Kayak and paddleboat rentals, plus canoe and kayak tours, and more.

Skokomish Park at Lake Cushman, 7211 N. Lake Cushman Rd., Hoodsport, WA 98548

360-877-5760; info@skokomishpark.com.

http://www.skokomishpark.com/.

The Lake Cushman Road entrance to Skokomish Park at Lake Cushman is well-marked. Enjoy large camping and RV sites, ample boat launch ($10/launch), and large day-use area ($10/day). Included are nine miles of hiking trails.

Lake Cushman is rich in recreation and views.

Lake Cushman Resort, 4621 N. Lake Cushman Rd., Hoodsport, WA 98548

360-877-9630. http://www.lakecushman.com/index.html

Drive about five miles east on State Route 119 to Lake Cushman for fresh water boating and fishing. While you're at it, enjoy hiking, camping and swimming. Casual and family oriented, the Lake Cushman Resort is open seasonally during the summer. See website for more information.

Staircase Campground and Ranger Station in Olympic National Park

Getting there: Take Highway 119 (Cushman Lake Road) past Cushman Lake to road's end, then continue on NF-24 to Staircase Campground and Ranger Station. NF-24 is closed from November to May. At Staircase find multiple trailheads; for example, the Staircase Rapids Trail, 1.9 nearly level miles (3 km) round trip amidst beautiful scenery along the north fork of the Skokomish River. Or, if you're a little more ambitious, you can amplify the hike to a not-as-level 4.0 miles (6.4 km) roundtrip. The following links provide more detail.

- Staircase brochure:

  https://www.nps.gov/olym/planyourvisit/upload/Staircase.pdf

  http://www.wta.org/go-hiking/hikes/staircase

- Olympic National Park description and links:

  https://www.nps.gov/olym/planyourvisit/visiting-staircase.htm

- Campground details:

  https://www.nps.gov/olym/planyourvisit/camping.htm

Restaurants at Hoodsport

Hoodsport Coffee Company, 24240 US-101, Hoodsport, WA 98548
360-877-6732. http://www.hoodsportcoffee.com/

Hours: Every day 6a-5p. Grab a coffee at the Hoodsport Coffee Company, of course, but also soups, breakfast and lunch sandwiches, baked goods, and scoops of Olympic Mountain Ice Cream. Oh, and information. Some people call this "Hoodsport Information Central."

Burger Stand, 24311 US-101, Hoodsport, WA 98548
360-877-6122.

https://www.facebook.com/pages/Burger-Stand/156034444436779

Model T Pub & Eatery, 24281 US-101, Hoodsport, WA 98548
360-877-9883. https://www.facebook.com/ModelTpubneat
Hours: Sun-Thu 11a-11p; Fri-Sat 11a-12a.

El Puerto de Angeles, 24080 US-101, Hoodsport, WA 98548 360-877-5921; 360-432-1085. http://elpuertodeangeles.com/
Hours: Every day 11a-9:30p. Mexican fast food right on/over the water.

The Tides Family Restaurant, 27061 US-101, Hoodsport, WA 98548 360-877-8921. https://www.facebook.com/The-Tides-272207179712/

Hours: Winter; Fri-Sun 8a-2:45p; Summer; Mon-Thur 7a-3p; Fri-Sun 7a-8p.

Lodging in Hoodsport

Glen Ayr Resort, 25381 N. Highway 101, Hoodsport, WA 98548

360-877-9522. www.glenayr.com/

Situated on the water, this resort offers motel lodging/suites and RV sites, a deep water dock w/moorage for ten vessels, fishing, crabbing, diving, hot tub, guest laundry area, clubhouse, picnic areas.

Lake Cushman Resort, 4621 N. Lake Cushman Rd., Hoodsport, WA 98548

Phone: 360-877-9630; from Canada: 1-800-588-9630. http://www.lakecushman.com/

Open from mid-April to the end of October. Day use, plus cabins, plus RV sites and tent camping.

Lilliwaup

The small town of Lilliwaup is basically a country store and a post office; everything from Lilliwaup to Brinnon has a Lilliwaup address.

The village was almost famous in the 1920s, with reports of movie stars "almost" buying homes there. Nowadays, it provides access to Hood Canal fishing and, of course, oysters. But more than anything, it's got a cool name and quaint, old-west buildings tucked away into the

Eagle Creek Saloon

folds of the bay, and you can mail your postcards with a **"Lilliwaup"** postmark.

Food at Lilliwaup

The Eagle Creek Saloon, 31281 US-101, Lilliwaup, WA 98555

360-877-6729.

https://www.facebook.com/Eagle-Creek-Saloon-215078549451/

Hours: 12p-9p. Located at Eagle Creek and Highway 101 in Lilliwaup in the middle of nowhere, but south of Hamma Hamma. You can't miss it: there is a giant cheeseburger the size of your car propped up over the door. **Hint:** Prime rib on Fridays.

Hamma Hamma

You'll find nothing of touristic value at Hamma Hamma. You have to drive farther north, closer to Eldon to come to the jewel of the Hood Canal: the **Hama Hama Oyster Saloon and Shop**. They've been around since 1922, have a great family story and an unbeatable location.

Hama Hama Oyster Saloon, 35846 US-101, Lilliwaup, WA 98555
360-877-5811. http://www.hamahamaoysters.com/

Oyster Saloon Hours: 12n-5:30p. Stop here if you're hankering for raw or ultra-fresh seafood such as oysters, clams, or salmon. Both oysters and salmon chowder are delish!

Mitch at the Oyster Saloon asked me, "Have you ever eaten oysters?" Getting an answer in the negative, he assured me, "The first one is on us."

How, er, generous? I was game to try the raw oyster he handed me. Seriously, with a squeeze of lemon, raw oyster is quite tasty, as far as oysters go. I liked it (I like sushi, too), but for lunch I opted for variety: a half-dozen grilled oysters. Really delicious!

Grilled oysters from the Hama Hama Oyster Bar

The Hama Hama Seafood Company Store has the same contact info as the Oyster Saloon.

Store Hours: Every day 9a-5:30p. Both store and saloon are *"located a shell's-throw from the tide flats."* Make a fresh seafood purchase, watch the guys shuck the oysters and take a self-guided tour of the farm. The farm also hosts special events throughout the year – check the website for more info.

Eldon

Eldon is nothing more than a name on a map, except for the modern gas station and mini-mart that serves a long stretch of near-empty road. Remember this should you find yourself running low on fuel, water, or snacks.

Eldon Store, 36870 US-101, Lilliwaup, WA 98555

360-877-5374. **Hours:** Every day, 7a-6p. Gas, oil, decent little mini-mart. Get your permits here for shellfish digging and seaweed harvesting.

Brinnon

Brinnon, population 900, sits right on the water near the northwestern end of the Hood Canal. It is a long narrow town with miles of water frontage along the Hood Canal. Brinnon provides gorgeous, wide-open water views. See http://www.brinnoninfo.com/. (The website appears to be neglected, but might still give you some decent information about the area.)

Things to Do in Brinnon

Duckabush Tidal Flats - Take a bucket and shovel to this wide open public tide flats and beach, because it's great for clam and oyster digging. **Getting there:** Heading north on Highway 101 and about twenty miles north of Hoodsport in Brinnon (but still four miles (6.4 km) south of "downtown" Brinnon), find public parking between mile 311 and 310. Look for GREEN "Public Parking" signs posted on Highway 101 directing you to public parking on the left (west) side of the highway just before the Duckabush River bridge. Duck into the forested parking lot on the west side of the highway, and then look for trail signs to the beach. This Fish and Wildlife web page gives more info, plus a link for buying your shellfishing license online: http://wdfw.wa.gov/fishing/shellfish/beaches/270286/

Duckabush Estuary

Whitney Gardens and Nursery, 306264 US-101, Brinnon, WA 98320

360-796-4411. http://www.whitneygardens.com/

Hours: Every day 9a-6p. Whitney Gardens explodes with color during the rhododendron and azalea bloom. Best time to visit is springtime, of course. Peruse their on-site gift shop any time of the year.

Dosewallips State Park, 306996 US-101, Brinnon, WA 98320

360-796-4415. Reservations: 888-226-7688.

http://parks.state.wa.us/412/Dosewallips-State-Park.

Year-round camping park; **Discover Pass** required (Part 3F). Dosewallips SP offers over a mile of saltwater canal frontage as well as freshwater river frontage. It is a beautiful place for camping, hiking and water activities. Stroll the forested trails within the park, or wander out onto the tide flats. Make reservations online or by phone up to nine months in advance.

Restaurants in Brinnon

Geoduck Restaurant and Lounge, 307103 US-101, Brinnon, WA 98320

360-796-4430. https://www.facebook.com/thegeoduck/

Hours: 11a-midnight. Yes, this is a lounge (read bar), but it is also billed as a family restaurant because they CAN accommodate families away from the bar. Food and service are both good.

Lodging in Brinnon

Elk Meadows Farm B&B, 3485 Dosewallips Rd., Brinnon, WA 98320

360-796-4886; elk@dishmail.net;

https://elkmeadowswa.com/lodging/

Five suites, a cabin and tent cabin camping all nestled along the Dosewallips River. Great farm-stay experience. Delicious breakfasts created from local ingredients.

Pleasant Harbor, 308913 US-101, Brinnon, WA 98320

360-796-4611. http://www.pleasantharbormarina.com/index.html

This pretty harbor, tucked away in a little cove, provides "the best year-round moorage on the Hood Canal," a galley and pub, various activities, and B&B lodging (two- night minimum).

Seal Rock Campground, 295142 US-101, Brinnon, WA 98320

https://www.fs.usda.gov/recarea/olympic/recarea/?recid=47917

Located two miles (3.2 km) north of Brinnon on Highway 101. Beautiful and popular forested campground on Hood Canal with beach access; okay to harvest oysters. First-come, first-served tent/RV sites, though no hook-ups. Potable water, toilets, garbage service. Recreation pass required, can be purchased online at the above website. Open from early-May to late-October.

Highway 101 North from Brinnon to Discovery Bay

North of Brinnon, Highway 101 takes a jaunt inland (westward) away from the Hood Canal as it heads toward Quilcene. But not to worry, there still remains another opportunity for amazing views of both the Hood Canal and the Olympic Mountains from the nearby peak of Mount Walker in the Olympic National Forest.

Mount Walker Peak – North and South Viewpoints

Getting there: The road to the top of Mount Walker—Mount Walker Viewpoint Road (Forest Service Road 2730)—intersects Highway 101 a quarter-mile (0.40 km) after a big BROWN sign announcing: "Mt Walker View Point 1/4 Mile." Take Mount Walker Viewpoint Road to the north (right—the only way possible), and follow it for four miles (6.44 km) all the way to the top of Mt. Walker. You'll find parking, vault toilets, but no water.

View of the northern reaches of the Hood Canal from the South Viewpoint atop Mt. Walker. On this day, the clouds hovered literally just overhead.

The views are spectacular; be sure to catch the view from both the north and the south viewpoints for top-o'-the-world vistas of the Hood Canal and the mountains beyond, even Mount Rainier on clear days. This is definitely a worthy stop.

Mount Walker Viewpoint Trail

If it's hiking you want, it's hiking you can certainly have! After all, what are mountains for, if not to climb? Mount Walker gifts you with 4.5 miles (7.24 km) roundtrip of strenuous hiking. The reward at the top is the crazy-awesome view.

The trailhead for a hike to the top of Mount Walker is just 0.4 miles (644 m) along Mount Walker Viewpoint Road from Highway 101. Park and hike to the top (uphill all the way: 2,000+ feet of elevation gain). Two miles (3.22 km) will bring you to the North Lookout point. Add another 0.5 miles (0.8 km) level walk to the South Viewpoint. The trail is open year round; the road is open generally spring through fall, weather permitting.

Waterfall near Falls View Campground

https://www.fs.usda.gov/recarea/olympic/recarea/?recid=47829

Falls View Campground may be closed for repairs, but if so, you can still park in the picnic area parking lot and take the Falls View Loop Trail, a short and easy 0.1 mile (0.16 km) stroll to picnic tables and an overlook of a very nice waterfall dropping into a canyon. You can also hike down into the canyon on the 0.6 mile (1 km) Falls View Canyon Trail.

Quilcene

After Mount Walker heading north, there is nothing but a lot of big trees, until you arrive in Quilcene, population 596 (2010 census). The name "Quilcene" is an anglicized version of the Twana Indian name, "Kwilsid" *(the "d" is pronounced like an "n," don't ask me why!)*, possibly meaning "salt water people." Quilcene's history is littered with broken aspirations and efforts abandoned.

But some fortunes may be turning. Quilcene oysters are internationally known among restaurateurs, according to Wikipedia. **Coast Seafoods Company** operates a hatchery on Hood Canal's Quilcene Bay near the Herb Beck Marina (*pictured*) that sustainably grows, feeds, harvests and ships fresh and frozen clams, oysters and mussels.

Quilcene Points of Interest

Quilcene National Fish Hatchery, 281 Fish Hatchery Rd., Quilcene, WA 98376

360-765-3334. https://www.fws.gov/quilcenenfh/

Getting there: Located just south of Quilcene. From Highway 101, turn west on Fish Hatchery Road. The hatchery is about 0.25 mile (0.40 km) on the left. Since 1911, this hatchery has been working with many partners to raise salmon and monitor local salmon programs. Visitors welcome. Call for more information.

Hood Canal Ranger Station and Visitor Center, 295142 Highway 101 S, Quilcene, WA 98376

360-765-2200.

https://www.fs.usda.gov/recarea/olympic/recarea/?recid=47691

Summer Hours: Memorial Day-Labor Day: Daily, including holidays 8a-4:30p.

Winter Hours: Mon-Fri 8a-4:30p. Interpretive sales area open on weekends and holidays 9a-3p; closed Thanksgiving, Christmas Day and New Year's Day. Stop here for area information on Olympic National Forest, Hood Canal, and other local points of interest.

Quilcene Historical Museum, 151 E. Columbia St., PO Box 574, Quilcene, WA 98376

360-765-4848. https://quilcenemuseum.org/

Summer Hours: Fri-Mon 1p-5p, Apr-Oct. The Quilcene Museum preserves the unique history of the Quilcene area. **Getting there:** When Highway 101 veers to the left as it leaves Quilcene heading north, go straight on Center Road (toward Chimacum) one block to East Columbia Street.

Wildwood Antiques and Collectibles, 293211 Highway 101, Quilcene, WA 98376

360-765-0425.

https://www.facebook.com/Wildwood-Antiques-Collectibles-166195456740448/.

Hours: 10a-6p, closed Mondays. Located on Highway 101 toward the north end of Quilcene. Funky exterior, great browsing inside.

Restaurants in Quilcene

Olympic Timberhouse Restaurant, 295534 Highway 101, Quilcene, WA 98376

360-765-0129. https://olympictimberhouse.com/menu/

Hours: Wed-Sun 11a-8p, closed Mon-Tues.

Steaks, seafood, prime rib, soups, salads served in Pacific Northwest-style dining room, outdoor dining surrounded by lush landscaping. Gift shop.

Gear Head Deli, 294963 Highway 101, Quilcene, WA 98376

360-301-3244;

https://www.facebook.com/Gear-Head-Deli-408362732661414/

Hours: 9a-3p. "Farm to fork," deli sandwiches, burgers, soups, salads all made fresh to order with seasonal ingredients.

101 Brewery & Twana Roadhouse, 294793 Highway 101, Quilcene, WA 98376

360-765-6485; https://101brewery.com/

Hours: Mon-Sat 7a-8p; Sun 8a-8p. Pizza, salad, burgers, seafood, pie, handcrafted beer.

Lodging in Quilcene

Mount Walker Inn, 61 Maple Grove Rd., Quilcene, WA 98376

360-765-3410. http://visit.mountwalkerinn.com/

Quilcene has only one hotel; this is it. Charmingly rustic, simple but clean rooms.

Next – Segment W: Home Again

4W) Home Again

Between Quilcene and Discovery Bay where *Beautiful Olympic Peninsula Travel Guide* began, there is virtually nothing left except twelve vacant wooded miles (19.3 km) along Highway 101 back to Discovery Bay and the junction of Highways 104 and 101.

If you traveled the full Highway 101 Loop, whether as a road trip or as part of your own custom-planned vacation, you will have traveled 330 miles (531 km), not counting the miles to and from various other destination points on the Peninsula.

*St. Paul's Church in **Port Gamble**, modeled after the Congregational Church of East Machias, Maine*

I hope you had a fabulous time!

And now, if you're ready, what route would you like to take as you leave the Olympic Peninsula to return to Seattle or to your home?

You have a couple options:

1. **Continue northbound on Highway 101** and take Highway 20, leaving the Olympic Peninsula via Port Townsend and the ferry to Coupeville on Whidbey Island.

On Whidbey Island, turn south (right) off the ferry and follow Highway 20 to Highway 525. Turn right (south) and follow Highway 525 to the Clinton-Mukilteo ferry to the mainland. In Mukilteo continue straight on Highway 525 to meet up with the main interstate highways such as I-5. Or:

2. **Turn right (eastbound) on Highway 104.** This will give you two more choices once you cross the Hood Canal Bridge:

    a. Turn left (northeast) after the Hood Canal Bridge, continuing to follow Highway 104 eastbound to Kingston. Catch the Kingston ferry to Edmonds. This route passes through **Port Gamble**, a delightful old village built in the style of New England. Port Gamble is a tourist stop in its own right, with gas, food, lodging, and souvenirs if you like. It wouldn't be a bad idea to allow yourself an hour or two here. In Edmonds, follow Highway 104 east to I-5.

    b. Or: Turn right (south) after the Hood Canal Bridge. Take Highway 3 and Highway 305, following the signs to Bainbridge Island/Seattle ferry. If you have time, plan to drive through downtown Poulsbo and stop a bit! The Norwegian architecture is beautiful, and so are the offerings from restaurants and international bakeries.

PART 5

Tools as you Travel

5A) Road Conditions

WA Department of Transportation

http://www.wsdot.wa.gov/

This is the main website for checking road conditions, weather forecasts, local construction issues, travel alerts and traffic snarls in all Washington state counties.

- Washington State Traffic and Cameras:
  http://www.wsdot.com/Traffic/
- Statewide Traffic Alerts:
  http://www.wsdot.com/traffic/trafficalerts/default.aspx
- WA State Ferries:
  http://www.wsdot.com/ferries/schedule/
- WA State Troopers: see Law Enforcement below.

Call 511: State highway traffic and weather information is available by dialing "511" from most phones. More info: http://www.wsdot.wa.gov/traffic/511/

Olympic National Park Road info

https://www.nps.gov/olym/planyourvisit/current-road-conditions.htm

Phone: (360) 565-3131.

See Mileage Charts: Part 5G.

5B) Motion Sickness Aids

I hear that Dramamine, ginger, and Sea Bands (acupressure) can all reduce or eliminate motion sickness. I can personally vouch for ginger capsules, which will help prevent nausea without making you drowsy. Stocking up on one or more of these options might rescue your day. My recommendations are here: http://www.beautifulpacificnorthwest.com/black-ball-ferry.html.

5C) Law Enforcement/Emergency Services

Always Dial 911 in emergency situations

Other Washington State law enforcement and highway services numbers—hopefully you won't actually need these numbers:

WA State Patrol (Troopers):

WA State Combined Transportation Center, Tacoma: 253-538-3240

http://www.wsp.wa.gov/information/directory.htm

Travel & Road Conditions: http://www.wsdot.com/traffic/

County Sheriff Offices:

- **Thurston** County Non-emergency - 360-754-3800; http://www.co.thurston.wa.us/contact.htm
- **Mason** County Non-emergency - 360-426-4441; http://so.co.mason.wa.us/

- □ South Mason County - 360-427-9670
- □ North Mason County - 360-277-5080
- □ West Mason County - 360-482-5269
- **Grays Harbor** County Non-emergency - 360-249-3711, 360-532-3284, 800-562-8714;

  http://www.co.grays-harbor.wa.us/departments/sheriff/index.php
- **Jefferson** County Non-emergency - 360-385-3831;

  http://www.jeffersonsheriff.org/
- **Clallam** County Non-emergency - 360-417-2459;

  http://www.clallam.net/sheriff/

City Police Departments:

The following phone numbers are for non-emergency issues:

- Aberdeen - 360-533-8765;

  http://aberdeenwa.gov/police-department/apd-homepage/
- Forks - 360-374-2223;

  http://forkswashington.org/police-corrections/
- Hoquiam - 360-532-0892;

  http://cityofhoquiam.com/our-departments/hoquiam-police-department/
- Lake Quinault - Quinault Tribal Police in Taholah -

  276-8215; http://www.road-police.com/police/Washington/Taholah/property_16384/police.html
- Neah Bay - Makah Tribal Police - 360-645-2701;

  http://www.road-police.com/police/Washington/Neah_Bay/property_16382/police.html

- Olympia - 360-704-2740; http://m.olympiawa.gov/city-services/police-department
- Port Angeles - 360-457-0411; http://wa-portangeles.civicplus.com/
- Port Townsend - 360-385-2322; http://www.cityofpt.us/police/
- Sequim - 360-683-7227; http://www.sequimwa.gov/index.aspx?NID=111
- Shelton - 360-426-4441; 360-432-5145; http://www.ci.shelton.wa.us/departments/police_department/index.php
- Westport - 360-268-9197; http://www.ci.westport.wa.us/police.html

5D) Weather Forecasts

http://www.wrh.noaa.gov/sew/ - Seattle office of the National Weather Service. See the forecast for Seattle, WA, and select many other destinations on the Olympic Peninsula for a more precise forecast. (See local rainfall averages charts, Part 5I.)

Quick links to weather forecasts for areas within the Olympic National Park:

https://www.nps.gov/olym/planyourvisit/weather.htm - Choose the area you are interested in, then click through to the National Weather Service report for that area.

Daily Precipitation Map for Olympic Peninsula and Puget Sound:
http://olympex.atmos.washington.edu/

Apple Device Weather Apps:

- **MyRadar NOAA Weather Radar, Forecasts & Storms**, by Aviation Data Systems, Inc – Free. Rated 5* (7,870 reviews): https://appsto.re/us/2Saot.i

- **The Weather Channel App** – Free. Rated 4.5* (19,792 reviews) – best local forecast, radar map, and storm tracking by The Weather Channel Interactive: https://appsto.re/us/y1GTv.i

Android Weather Apps:

- **NOAA Weather app for Android** – Free. Rated 4.5* (59,138 reviews):

  https://play.google.com/store/apps/details?id=com.nstudio.weatherhere.free&hl=en

- **Weather Underground App for Android** – Free. Rated 4.5* (265,389 reviews):

  https://play.google.com/store/apps/details?id=com.wunderground.android.weather&hl=en

5E) Tides, Tide Charts, Tide Apps

Some coastal areas are only accessible during low tide. The ocean is unrelenting and really doesn't care if you are unaware of its tides. Additionally, tide pools are only enjoyable at low tide. Tide charts are available in hard copy at visitor centers and coastal ranger stations. Or, check an online or smart-app tide chart. Always have one on hand, or online, and know how to read them. If you have any questions ask at a Visitor Center or Ranger Station.

We also highly recommend you acquire a topographical map which shows coastal details such as headlands. This will tell you what areas are passable at any given tide level. More information on hiking the coast: https://www.nps.gov/olym/planyourvisit/wilderness-coast. htm

Olympic National Park Topographical Map: http://amzn.to/2lq5Vh6

Tide Charts Online:

The most accurate and current tide prediction charts are found at the NOAA website, which offers this disclaimer: "*These data are based upon the latest information available as of the date of your request, and may differ from the published tide tables.*" https://tidesandcurrents. noaa.gov/tide_predictions.html?gid=1415#listing – Click on the location of your choice.

Olympic National Park: https://www.nps.gov/olym/planyourvisit/ tides-and-your-safety.htm This link is specific for tides at ONP beaches at La Push/Quillayute River, with a note for adjusting the times for the Ozette and Shi Shi beaches.

Free Tide Chart Apps for Apple and Android smart phones:

Search the iTunes store or Google Play for one or more of these apps:

- **Tides Near Me-Free**, by Randy MEECH (5 star by 908 reviewers) – gives local tides and the option to see tide tables in the area of your choice.

  Android:
  https://play.google.com/store/apps/details?hl=en&id= me.tidesnear.free
  iPhone:
  https://itunes.apple.com/us/app/tides-near-me-free/ id585223877?mt=8

- **Tide Charts Near Me – Free**, by 7th Gear (5 star by 303 reviewers) – gives tides nearest to your GPS location, along with weather and astronomic info. I love the presentation of tides in graph form. Click a red "pin" to add and access tide info in a different location.

Android:
https://play.google.com/store/apps/details?id=com.
SeventhGear.tides&hl=en

iPhone:
https://itunes.apple.com/us/app/tide-charts-near-me-free/id957143504?mt=8

- **Saltwater Tides**, by Tide High and Low, Inc. (3 star by 5 reviewers) – no frills. You input region, area, zone, site, and date of your choice, and the app will provide the tide chart, along with sun and moon rising and setting.

  Android:
  https://play.google.com/store/apps/details?id=com.
  saltwatertides.mobileapp&hl=en

  iPhone:
  https://itunes.apple.com/us/app/saltwater-tides/id9100
  10496?mt=8

There are a dozen more apps providing the same and much more info for US$0.99 to $30+ (including navigational aids), and even more that add fishing information to the mix.

Where will the road take you?

5F) Highway Mileage Charts

Two separate highway mileage charts follow.

- Miles and transit times
- Kilometers and transit times

Highway Mileage Chart in Miles

Miles	Aberdeen	Forks	Hoh	Hoodsport	Kalaloch	Lake Crescent	Neah Bay	Quinault	Port Angeles	Port Townsend	Sequim	Shelton	Sol Duc
Sol Duc	149 3h	40 55m	71 1h42m	124 2h45m	74 1h35m	21.3 38m	64.2 1h34m	107 2h12m	41.2 1h 5m	88 2h7m	57.6 1.5h	139 3h9m	◇
Shelton	46 1h	148 3h	153 3h9m	15.4 24m	114 2h13m	119 2.5h	169 3h47m	84.6 1h45m	98.6 2h6m	77.3 1h45m	82.8 1h45m	◇	139 3h9m
Sequim	128 2h35m	73 1.5h	104 2h19m	67.3 1h22m	107 2h12m	37.2 51m	87.1 2h5m	140 2h49m	16.8 24m	31.1 43m	◇	82.8 1h45m	57.6 1.5h
Port Townsend	122 2.5h	103 2h11m	134 3h	62 1h21m	137 2h51m	67.4 1.5h	117 2h44m	161 3h21m	47 1h	◇	31.1 43m	77.3 1h45m	88 2h7m
Port Angeles	144 3h	56.3 1h9m	87.5 2h	83.3 1h 3m	91 1h49m	20.6 30m	70.4 1h43m	124 2.5h	◇	47 1h	16.8 24m	98.6 2h6m	41.2 1h 5m
Quinault	44 54m	67.3 1h18m	72.3 1.5h	99 2h	33 37m	104 2h2m	116 2.5h	◇	124 2.5h	161 3h21m	140 2h49m	84.6 1h45m	107 2h12m
Neah Bay	156 3h13m	49 1h10m	80.1 2h	153 3.5h	83.3 1h50m	61.1 1h24m	◇	116 2.5h	70.4 1h43m	117 2h44m	87.1 2h5m	169 3h47m	64.2 1h34m
Lake Crescent	144 2h47m	36.7 44m	67.8 1.5h	104 2h10m	70.9 1h24m	◇	61.1 1h24m	104 2h2m	20.6 30m	67.4 1.5h	37.2 51m	119 2.5h	21.3 38m
Kalaloch	73 1h23m	34.3 41m	39.3 56m	128 2.5h	◇	70.9 1h24m	83.3 1h50m	33 37m	91 1h49m	137 2h51m	107 2h12m	114 2h13m	74 1h35m
Hoodsport	43.5 1h13m	139 2h49m	168 3h3m	◇	128 2.5h	104 2h10m	153 3.5h	99 2h	83.3 1h 3m	62 1h21m	67.3 1h22m	15.4 24m	124 2h45m
Hoh	112 2h18m	31 48m	◇	168 3h3m	39.3 56m	67.8 1.5h	80.1 2h	72.3 1.5h	87.5 2h	134 3h	104 2h19m	153 3h9m	71 1h42m
Forks	107 2 h	◇	31 48m	139 2h49m	34.3 41m	36.7 44m	49 1h10m	67.3 1h18m	56.3 1h9m	103 2h11m	73 1.5h	148 3h	40 55m
Aberdeen	◇	107 2 h	112 2h18m	43.5 1h13m	73 1h23m	144 2h47m	156 3h13m	44 54m	144 3h	122 2.5h	128 2h35m	46 1h	149 3h
Olympia	50 1h	152 2h49m	157 3h4m	36.7 42m	118 2h8m	140 2h51m	201 4h	88.5 1h40m	120 2h24m	106 2h	104 2h4m	22 28m	160 3.5h
Seattle	109 1h51m	138 3h41m	216 4h	96.1 1h40m	177 3h6m	102 3h	152 4h15m	148 2h38m	82 2.5h	56 2h11m	66.1 2h11m	81.6 1.5h	123 3.5h
Victoria, BC	168 5h	81 3h16m	112 4h4m	108 3h49m	115 4h	45.3 2h36m	95.1 3h50m	148 4.5h	25.1 2h9m	71.7 3h10m	41.5 2.5h	123 4h12m	65.6 3h10m

Highway Mileage Chart in Miles

Km	Aberdeen	Forks	Hoh	Hoodsport	Kalaloch	Lake Crescent	Neah Bay	Quinault	Port Angeles	Port Townsend	Sequim	Shelton	Sol Duc
Aberdeen	◊	173 / 2h	180 / 2h18m	70 / 1h13m	117 / 1h23m	232 / 2h47m	251 / 3h13m	71 / 54m	232 / 3h	196 / 2.5h	206 / 2h35m	74 / 1h	240 / 3h
Forks	173 / 2h	◊	50 / 48m	224 / 2h49m	55 / 41m	59 / 44m	79 / 1h10m	108 / 1h18m	91 / 1h9m	166 / 2h11m	117 / 1.5h	238 / 3h	64 / 55m
Hoh	180 / 2h18m	50 / 48m	◊	270 / 3h3m	63 / 56m	109 / 1.5h	129 / 2h	116 / 1.5h	141 / 2h	216 / 3h	167 / 2h19m	246 / 3h9m	114 / 1h42m
Hoodsport	70 / 1h13m	224 / 2h49m	270 / 3h3m	◊	206 / 2.5h	167 / 2h10m	246 / 3.5h	159 / 2h	134 / 1h3m	100 / 1h21m	108 / 1h22m	25 / 24m	200 / 2h45m
Kalaloch	117 / 1h23m	55 / 41m	63 / 56m	206 / 2.5h	◊	114 / 1h24m	134 / 1h50m	53 / 37m	146 / 1h49m	220 / 2h51m	172 / 2h12m	183 / 2h13m	119 / 1h35m
Lake Crescent	232 / 2h47m	59 / 44m	109 / 1.5h	167 / 2h10m	114 / 1h24m	◊	98 / 1h24m	167 / 2h2m	33 / 30m	108 / 1.5h	60 / 51m	192 / 2.5h	34 / 38m
Neah Bay	251 / 3h13m	79 / 1h10m	129 / 2h	246 / 3.5h	134 / 1h50m	98 / 1h24m	◊	187 / 2.5h	113 / 1h43m	188 / 2h44m	140 / 2h5m	272 / 3h47m	103 / 1h34m
Quinault	71 / 54m	108 / 1h18m	116 / 1.5h	159 / 2h	53 / 37m	167 / 2h2m	187 / 2.5h	◊	200 / 2.5h	159 / 3h21m	225 / 2h49m	136 / 1h45m	172 / 2h12m
Port Angeles	232 / 3h	91 / 1h9m	141 / 2h	134 / 1h3m	146 / 1h49m	33 / 30m	113 / 1h43m	200 / 2.5h	◊	76 / 1h	27 / 24m	159 / 2h6m	66 / 1h5m
Port Townsend	196 / 2.5h	166 / 2h11m	216 / 3h	100 / 1h21m	220 / 2h51m	108 / 1.5h	188 / 2h44m	159 / 3h21m	76 / 1h	◊	50 / 43m	124 / 1h45m	142 / 2h7m
Sequim	206 / 2h35m	117 / 1.5h	167 / 2h19m	108 / 1h22m	172 / 2h12m	60 / 51m	140 / 2h5m	225 / 2h49m	27 / 24m	50 / 43m	◊	133 / 1h45m	93 / 1.5h
Shelton	74 / 1h	238 / 3h	246 / 3h9m	25 / 24m	183 / 2h13m	192 / 2.5h	272 / 3h47m	136 / 1h45m	159 / 2h6m	124 / 1h45m	133 / 1h45m	◊	224 / 3h9m
Sol Duc	240 / 3h	64 / 55m	114 / 1h42m	200 / 2h45m	119 / 1h35m	34 / 38m	103 / 1h34m	172 / 2h12m	66 / 1h5m	142 / 2h7m	93 / 1.5h	224 / 3h9m	◊
Olympia	80 / 1h	245 / 2h49m	253 / 3h4m	59 / 42m	190 / 2h8m	225 / 2h51m	323 / 4h	142 / 1h40m	193 / 2h24m	171 / 2h	167 / 2h4m	35 / 28m	257 / 3.5h
Seattle	175 / 1h51m	222 / 3h41m	348 / 4h	155 / 1h40m	285 / 3h6m	164 / 3h	245 / 4h15m	238 / 2h38m	132 / 2.5h	90 / 2h11m	106 / 2h11m	131 / 1.5h	198 / 3.5h
Victoria, BC	270 / 5h	130 / 3h16m	180 / 4h4m	174 / 3h49m	185 / 4h	73 / 2h36m	153 / 3h50m	238 / 4.5h	40 / 2h9m	115 / 3h10m	67 / 2.5h	198 / 4h12m	106 / 3h10m

5G) Rainfall Averages on the Olympic Peninsula in Inches

Inches:	Sequim	Port Angeles	Neah Bay	Forks	La Push	Hoh Rain Forest	Amanda Park	Hoquiam	Shelton	Quilcene
Per Year	16	26	100	120	102	128	116	116	66	54
Jan	2.05	3.86	14.61	18.27	13.65	24.86	17.83	17.83	9.92	7.41
Feb	1.18	2.8	10.35	12.72	12.35	11.70	12.34	12.32	8.5	7.36
Mar	1.3	2.13	10.83	13.54	10.98	14.45	12.38	12.36	6.85	5.94
Apr	1.06	1.3	7.85	9.21	7.44	10.27	8.59	8.58	4.49	3.82
May	1.26	1.06	5.11	5.79	5.51	5.80	5.41	5.39	2.64	2.83
Jun	0.98	0.87	3.50	3.90	3.5	3.72	3.99	3.98	1.81	2.13
Jul	0.55	0.59	1.98	2.48	2.34	2.23	2.14	2.13	0.98	1.3
Aug	0.59	0.75	2.49	2.60	2.67	3.14	2.23	2.56	1.22	1.22
Sep	0.79	1.06	3.82	4.02	4.15	6.37	4.02	4.02	2.48	1.61
Oct	1.46	2.44	10.49	11.81	9.81	10.12	11.28	11.3	5.28	4.13
Nov	2.68	4.41	15.52	18.62	14.82	20.88	18.60	18.58	10.55	7.99
Dec	2.17	4.41	12.99	16.77	14.5	14.27	16.48	16.5	10.98	8.66

5H) Rainfall Averages on the Olympic Peninsula in Centimeters

Cm:	Sequim	Port Angeles	Neah Bay	Forks	La Push	Hoh Rain Forest	Amanda Park	Hoquiam	Shelton	Quilcene
Per Year	41	65	253	304	259	325	295	295	170	138
Jan	5.2	9.8	37.1	46.4	34.7	63.1	45.3	45.3	25.2	18.8
Feb	3	7.1	26.3	32.3	31.4	29.7	31.34	31.3	21.6	18.7
Mar	3.3	5.4	27.5	34.4	27.9	36.7	31.44	31.4	17.4	15.1
Apr	2.7	3.3	19.9	23.4	18.9	26.1	21.8	21.8	11.4	9.7
May	3.2	2.7	13	14.7	14	14.7	13.74	13.7	6.7	7.2
Jun	2.49	2.2	8.9	9.9	8.9	9.5	10.13	10	4.6	5.4
Jul	1.4	1.5	5.0	6.3	5.9	5.7	5.44	5.4	2.5	3.3
Aug	1.5	1.9	6.3	6.6	6.8	8	5.66	6.5	3.1	3.1
Sep	2	2.7	9.7	10.2	10.5	16.2	10.21	10.2	6.3	4.1
Oct	3.7	6.2	26.6	30	25	25.7	28.7	28.7	13.4	10.5
Nov	6.8	11.2	39.4	47.3	37.6	53	47.24	47.2	26.8	20.3
Dec	5.5	11.2	33	42.6	36.9	36.3	42	41.9	27.9	22

PART 6

Index

CPSIA information can be obtained
at www.ICGtesting.com
Printed in the USA
LVHW07s2051210218
567417LV00026B/340/P